THE STANCE OF PLATO

THE STANCE OF PLATO

ALBERT COOK

LITTLEFIELD ADAMS BOOKS

LITTLEFIELD ADAMS BOOKS

Published in the United States of America
by Rowman & Littlefield Publishers, Inc.
4720 Boston Way, Lanham, Maryland 20706

3 Henrietta Street
London WC2E 8LU, England

British Cataloging in Publication Information Available

Library of Congress Cataloging-in-Publication Data

Cook, Albert Spaulding.
The stance of Plato / by Albert Cook.
p.   cm.
Includes bibliographical references and index.
1. Plato. I. Title.
B395.C65   1996   184—dc20   96–434   CIP

ISBN 0–8226–3048–6 (cloth : alk. paper)
ISBN 0–8226–3049–4 (pbk. : alk. paper)

Printed in the United States of America

⊖™ The paper used in this publication meets the minimum requirements of
American National Standard for Information Sciences—Permanence of
Paper for Printed Library Materials, ANSI Z39.48–1984.

To A. K. O'Donoghue
across the continents and years

Contents

Preface

This book, like virtually all my previous ones, is not conceived on a linear model, but rather as a series of probes along particular angles of Plato's discourse, with the intention of having them converge in something approaching an overall view. Thus while I do not offer an interlocking and sequenced argument, or a separately formulable thesis, it is my hope that the conception of Plato's activity offered here will be understood as a coherent one, and that it will, more generally, advance the question of the interdependence of literature and philosophy. Questions about this interdependence are so broad and deep, however, that they may be presumed to persist beyond any given presentation. To solve the interdependence of literature and philosophy in the work of Plato would entail solving such questions generally, and this possibility may be foreclosed by something like a Gödelian constraint. The very question remains open whether there are two domains here—literature and philosophy—or just one, with markedly various approaches that may sometimes fuse, as in the work of Plato and some others. And whether literature and philosophy are separable or associable activities, in whole or in part, they would be subject to at least one such constraint, and possibly to at least two. Under such conditions we still may confidently, though cautiously, proceed.

Acknowledgments

I began this book in spring 1982 while I was a fellow at Clare Hall, Cambridge, and I would like to thank that college for providing an environment in which to work. I am grateful as well to the Fondation Hardt in Geneva, where a crucial period of study and writing during the spring of 1987 brought me to the point of giving the book something like an outline of its present form; once again, a brief stay in August 1994 facilitated some late amplifications. The process there was abetted by André Hurst when he invited me to lecture on Plato at the University of Geneva, where I gave the *"Ion"* portion of my chapter on poetry. I also found useful the opportunities to present a part of the "particles" chapter to the section on philosophical language of the Modern Language Association in December 1988, and a shorter form of my tenth chapter to the International Society for Philosophy and Literature in May 1991. I am grateful to the journals that published earlier versions of my chapters on Socrates, on particles, and on the *Phaedrus: Arethusa, The American Journal of Philology,* and *Quaderni Urbinati di Cultura Classica.* The Wayne University Press published versions of two of these chapters in my book *Soundings* (1991).

For the past several years I have participated in the ancient philosophy discussion group at Brown, where sharp questioning and collegial dialogue have invigorated my thinking on these questions; I would like to thank the group and its many members, especially its organizer Martha Nussbaum, Dolores Velkley, Martin Andic, David Konstan, Marina Barabas, Victor Caston, Anthony Price, Giles Milhaven, Justin Broackes, Malcolm Hyman, and Margaret Graver. I would also like to thank the editors of journals for helpful comments: Diskin Clay, John Peradotto, and Herb Golder, as well as an anonymous reader for another press. John Sullivan, Gary Handwerk, Thomas MacCary, James Bunn, and Jeffrey Barnouw generously read and commented on the manuscript. I remain indebted to my resourceful and capable research assistant, Dr. Blossom S. Kirschenbaum. I am grateful to Timothy Seid for his skilled and expeditious help with computer preparation of the final text. My wife, as always, is responsible for the sustaining atmosphere and loving encouragement in which alone such work can be carried out.

Chapter 1

Prolegomena to the Interpretation of Plato

1.

Plato is at once the Webern and the Beethoven of philosophy, an essentialist who is at the same time powerfully polyphonic. If we may stay with this metaphor, one which he himself uses ("Philosophy is the greatest music," *Phaedo* 61a), then it is difficult to account for his harmonics while at the same time explaining the meaning of his music. Just to assess his dominant mode of philosophical investigation we must somehow bring together the elements of logical exposition, hermeneutic explanation, and radical questioning. And we must integrate with this already complex philosophical ground in his work the melodic lines of irony and the seemingly divergent tutti of his myths. In trying to account for the unified utterance of a whole dialogue of Plato, and still more of the body of his writings, we have to try to be anthropologists, literary critics, and responsible philosophers all at once, at the risk of putting asunder what it was his unique achievement to put in perilous equipoise together.

Not only in such matters as his attitudes toward poetry and love, but at the heart of his ontology, Plato, to begin with, will sometimes present divergent doctrines. As Julius Stenzel says, the assertion in the *Sophist* that "non-being" exists is "in direct conflict with *Republic* 478b and *Theaetetus* 189a-b, where Non-Being was declared to be not only unknowable, but inconceivable, because nothingness cannot be conceived."[1] Again, "the *Sophist* distinguishes between philosopher and statesman, the *Republic* identifies them." Generally, an awareness of the integrally philosophical, the propositional, character of the interplay, irony, and various suspensions, in a whole dialogue, should hold the reader back from propounding without qualification doctrines for the whole of Plato's work that come up just in a given part.[2]

Yet the truth value Plato would have assigned to the whole utterance that constitutes a Platonic dialogue cannot be ascertained just by adjudicating the etymology of *aletheia*.[3] Heidegger, who proposes a philosophy based not on enchainment of argument but on a hermeneutic "laying bare" (*Unverborgenheit*) of the human situation, reads the word, and the work of Plato, as corresponding to his enterprise. Yet there is much in Plato's discourse that will sustain reading *aletheia* as just a fair synonym for English *truth* (or German *Wahrheit*), without lining him up exclusively with any of the modern theories of truth. The intricacy of Plato's thought with respect to enchained propositions, and his responsibility to some canons of logic, has been ascertained through attentive deduction in the tradition of modern interpretation running, say, from Paul Natorp to Gregory Vlastos. Yet just in his propositional presentation, Plato does not always resolve his questions or even settle them in contradictory fashion; he often, and characteristically, leaves them open. In doing so he can easily be assimilated to a third modern tradition, that of the later Wittgenstein, in which philosophy is conceived as a technique for bringing thought beyond the point where it might get bogged down in pseudoquestions and preliminary questions, to a brink of questioning.[4] Aristotle (*Physics,* Book 1. 184) seeks knowledge through increasing clarity; but in Plato there remains what Hermann Gundert calls "this twofold experience of clarification and the enigmatic."[5]

Plato can be accounted pretty much the originator of hermeneutic philosophy. He is a strong developer of philosophy based on propositions and the philosophy of radical questioning. Except for Heraclitus, most of his predecessors, from the evidence we have, occupied themselves exclusively with expounding and amplifying—and it would seem only rarely even refining—a comprehensive cosmological or social system.

But these three approaches, reconcilable as they may be, themselves only complicate the contradiction inherent in an adequate modern approach to Plato. The approach to questioning that he mounted had the effect of endowing Western philosophy steadfastly with its topics and methods. Yet questions arising through these topics often do not admit of Plato's solutions, however tentative. Even where strong doctrines do emerge and develop into clarity, about such central questions as justice, virtue, happiness, and love, they carry with them the nuances of their embedding in the dialogue form, and also the emphasis of their embodiment in an ideal figure, Socrates.

The Eleatics, Parmenides and Zeno, did enchain propositions. Zeno, too, was a radical questioner. Yet though Plato, in his dialogues, accords respectful attention particularly to the Eleatics, and though when he sets up *aporiai* in the *Parmenides* he acts like an Eleatic, Plato is of course much more than a post-Eleatic.

Furthermore, except in late works like *The Laws*, the dramatic method of the dialogues, and the myths they often contain, are not just a clever presentational strategy and a method of graphic illustration. The drama and the myth are inextricably interwoven with the hermeneutic function, the arguments, and the questioning of a given dialogue.[6]

Writers who center their consideration of Plato on the enchainment of propositions or on his hermeneutics are not unaware of his dramatic method, and they do not ignore the myths. But they effectually bracket them by subsuming drama under "irony" and by simply translating the myths into doctrines, if they treat them at all. In so doing they effectually deny their force, and for Plato their indissoluble connection, with propositions and questions. This attends just to the dialogues, leaving aside the letters and the unwritten teachings.

Without at all wishing to displace other methods of approach to Plato, in this book I shall concentrate on aspects of how his handling of a literary orientation bears on his conclusions. This approach is in itself becoming a much-shared one at this time, and it is my hope largely to extend or supplement, rather than to duplicate or contravert, the many others taking approaches similar to mine.[7]

As Stanley Rosen says, "If we reduce the dramatic structure of the dialogues to the status of an external contingency, we arbitrarily ignore their most obvious and pervasive feature." Rosen sets up two oppositions, one between the dialogue form and the "abstract" ratiocinative dialectic excerpted from the dialogues by Robinson and Vlastos (among others).[8] The second opposition obtains between the dialogues and the letters, "In his *Epistles* Plato explicitly renounces the writings and other public accounts of views that have been attributed to him" [citations to *Letters* 2. 314b7; 7. 341c1 ff].

To begin with, Stenzel has shown that " *doxa* and *diairesis* are two logical operations in indissoluble union; each method depends on the assistance of the other." *Doxa* often roughly comprises the hermeneutic function (*doxa, Sophist* 237e, etc.). *Diairesis*, the reasoning division into categories (a main locus in the *Phaedrus*, 266b), is a function of testing logical propositions, but it stops short at myth, which is also aimed to get beyond *doxa*. Further, a central topic of the *Phaedrus*, the meaning of *eros*, is bound up with the gods, and with myth.

In his radical recasting of literary expression into the dialogue form, and in his centering it on the elenchic process of considering the questions he permanently formed for philosophical discourse, Plato still has not left the conditions governing the social function of writing in the society of his time. The myths in his work cannot be fully disengaged from the religion, nor can either be disengaged from the philosophical *elenchos*. In facing Plato, to put it in a starkly schematic way, we are like anthropologists facing someone who is totally indigenous in a culture with many primitive features but who is at the same time one of the most powerful thinkers in the history of the world. Where Plato most rarely contradicts himself is in areas connected with the society in which he was rooted: religion including the afterlife and the social roles of sophist, doctor, craftsman, pilot, tyrant, and the like.[9] Even the *"pensée sauvage"* delineated by Lévi-Strauss consists of moderately ordinary inductive, deductive, and constructive techniques, and Plato's handling of religion is too deeply rooted in tradition, his handling of myth too manipulative, to be subsumable under the categories and transformational logic of Lévi-Strauss, which might have been thought to provide the means of realigning myth and religion in Plato's work to the ratiocinative processes as the center of his dialogues.[10] A genius of Plato's order presents—we may say, continues to present—endlessly riddling problems, especially as the dialogues we have are only part, if a large and essential part, of his total philosophical activity.[11]

Plato reflects, and contains within himself, the elements of large shifts in Greek society. The predominance of the oral in Homer carries with it, on Havelock's showing, a whole set of assumptions about the closed order of this early society.[12] Carrying out the extension of possibilities by the written word, Plato intentionally breaks the hold of this order. Yet the hold is still upon him; the *Phaedrus* concludes by opting for the superiority of the oral over the written; the dialogue, as the written presentation of an oral method, permutes the two. Communication in the Academy would have been oral, and the *Seventh Letter* affirms the importance of such transmission. Further, the structure of the Academy carries traces of affinity with the organization of the Pythagorean circle, a little society with a closed order that it has chosen for itself.[13]

Emphasis on the military also reveals a closed order, as Homer well exemplifies. In the Third Book of the *Republic* Plato, as he constructs his conjectural society from scratch, makes the point that it will need a military component; he then invents the guardians, who will lead the society but also ensure that its order is closed. Strangely to us, Plato at points attributes "freedom," *eleutheria*, to this society, giving it attributes that were a key feature of the Greek city-states as they developed away from a closed order.[14] Many other places in the dialogues dwell on the military aspect of virtue. Though in the *Protagoras* (349d) courage is singled out as a virtue "very different from the others" and as not implying the other virtues, it is still an important topic for discussion. Courage is one of the two traits used to characterize the "lovers of wisdom" (*philomatheis*) in the *Phaedo* (83e), who are "orderly" (*kosmioi*) and "brave" (*andreioi*). Phaedrus in the first speech of the *Symposium* enjoins courage while discussing what seems to be the relatively unrelated subject of love, and he raises the possibility, again strange to the modern reader, of an invincible army of lovers (178–79). "Courage" is one of Socrates' personal virtues, and his conduct as a soldier is attested to by Alcibiades in the *Symposium* and by Laches in the *Laches*. This dialogue concerns itself with the component of courage in virtue generally, incidentally touching on the musical element in education which for a Greek went along with its military training as part of the same package. Indeed, in the *Protagoras* it is asserted that the war *techne* is part of the political *techne* (322b5).

This military emphasis, which goes back to the second millennium and before, is being attenuated in Greek society, and Plato's dialogues reflect the large change. Their concerns are already on the way to becoming those of the world of Epicurus, whom Plato anticipates as well as precedes (though he revulses from the hedonistic life of southern Italy and Sicily on his first visit there, *Seventh Letter*, 326). The dialogues were written almost contemporaneously with the new "softness" of the sculpture of Praxiteles (active 370–320 B.C.E.) and are already in the process of working away from the fifth century world of Plato's youth, in which the dominant sculpture of Polyclitus (mentioned at *Protagoras* 311c, 328c) exhibited a severity consonant with the military sternness that Plato both retains—in his admiration of Sparta, for example—and deeply modifies.

Mythos characterizes this earlier world and *logos* the later. Plato demonstrates the inseparability of the two precisely by always effectually keeping them recognizably distinct, both in the construction of his dialogues and in the deployment of different ontological layers and kinds of certitude and conclusion in them. However this may be, the dialogues have a special character in the light of his unwritten teaching, whatever it could have been; it was probably somewhat doctrinaire, more certain than we certainly can ask the dialogues to be. They again return us to the richness of the Greek context, and in that way too Plato is an *amicus* who sometimes defers and always dimensionalizes *veritas*.

Plato's rootedness in the older society shows not only in his defense of religion but also in the deference he depicts for the unjustly condemned Socrates, who has determined not to avail himself of the opportunity to escape, he says in the *Crito*, because even unjust decisions of the city must be obeyed. At this point, as in other ways, Plato fuses a deeply conventional posture with a startlingly radical definition of the posture of the just man.[15] In the *Seventh Letter* Plato compares obedience to the state to obedience owed a father and a mother (331c-d).

Nevertheless, the social circumstances of the dialogues themselves encapsulate the loosening of a closed order. The leisure (*scholé*) that is fundamental to Socrates' role as a gadfly, a leisure he often stresses, would sort ill with the closed order of the sort of society for which the Homeric poems are an early model. The typical dialogue begins as a random encounter, albeit one linked with collective social activities such as a religious festival (*Republic*), a celebration over a victory in the dramatic contests (*Symposium*), or a simple encounter in a gymnasium (*Euthydemus, Lysis*). The scene may also remain undesignated (*Meno*), so randomized is the encounter. Or it may be a private walk, albeit also after a festival, as in the *Phaedrus*.

In the dialogues the discourse is presented as beginning with a random inquiry, unconditioned by social purposes either traditional, like those in an educational setting, or innovative, like the formal lessons of a Sophist or the formal discussions in a philosopher's circle— or in the Platonic Academy, which is automatically bracketed as a later development by the presence of a living Socrates inside the dialogues.

The notions of Socrates himself vary more than the procedures do. These procedures are clearly being recommended, and the recommendation strikes home. They will get institutionalized into the Academy, where, once the opinions, the *doxai*, are frozen, they gradually free the notions from the initiating dialogue: In the Academy the presentational strategies would have been reached that were so vastly elaborated in the practise of Aristotle. Still, Aristotle's categories in the *Rhetoric*, in so far as there he persistently adduces final and postrhetorical questions, are still putting (dialogic) rhetoric into relationship with philosophical notions. His types of rhetoric could be used, in fact, partly to situate the Platonic dialogues, where dialogue and propositional rhetoric and philosophy are mixed in the quick of oral interchange. The dialogue gives an image of maintaining them all. For Plato, again, philosophy is defined at this quick. Adding the cross-questioning of *elenchos* to the *logos* makes it more answerable than other verbal discourse. In the sense that both Plato and Aristotle (*Topica* 162a16–17; *De sophisticis elenchis* 171b8) attacked the ends in themselves, as well as the means, of sophism, they were liberating its techniques in order to refine them for their own sake—but also to return them to a purified version of the earlier, collective religious purpose, private and public, of intelligence (*phronesis*).

Further, the very point of the questions about contrast, overlap, force, and justification for the terms *nomos* (law/ custom) and *physis* (nature)[16] indicates a reflective attempt, and even a residual instability, between the terms, a perception of which would oblige, and itself reflect, an opening of society. The mooted and puzzling quotation from Pindar, on the other hand (*Gorgias* 484b), "Nomos is king of all,"[17] may be taken in any sense to glorify a closed society. And in one sense its *nomos* could be taken completely to encapsulate *physis*.

Plato's own relations with Sicily, as they emerge from the letters, indicate the variety of actual combinations that could occur in that fluid society. Under either Dionysius that powerful state combined aspects of the oligarchic, the tyrannic, and the democratic types of government delineated in the *Republic* (Book Eight). Sicily had passed Sparta and Athens in power, but it only partly resembled either; in its organization it most resembled the tyrannies of the sixth century. Its external affairs, perhaps, its long struggle against the Carthaginian Empire, most resembled the struggle of the Greek city-states against Persia at the beginning of the fifth century, though Plato compares Dionysius II unfavorably with the Persian Darius (*Seventh Letter*, 332a-b) and also with Athens at its peak (332b). Dionysius' act of summoning Plato as a political adviser has no exact precedent, though Plato adduces some poetical ones, mostly involving tyrants or some legendary cases (*Second Letter*, 311; supposing it to be genuine); it perhaps looks ahead to the summoning of Aristotle to the Court of Philip of Macedon (also adumbrated in Plato's *Sixth Letter*, a letter written to the Macedonian Hermias, whose niece Aristotle married).

The valuation of philosophy on Dionysius' part, both excessive and unstable, plays a key role in determining Plato's political and personal fortunes in these expeditions, as do Plato's professional relations with other philosophers, especially in southern Italy. Plato thus orchestrated his actions vis-à-vis four communities: a defeated Athens, in which he had aspired to political power in his youth; a rising Sicily; an international community of philosophers represented actively in southern Italy by Archytas and Archedemus; and a traditional base in the Academy. The Academy itself, in turn, drew some of its members from political advisers to distant city-states (as evidenced in the *Sixth Letter*), whatever its organization and preoccupations may have been.[18]

Each of these communities had a different history, a different function, and a different structure from the others. However uncertain and unstable their relations may have been, there was a cosmopolitanism in their very connection that gives Plato's dialogues a much more open situation toward a potential readership than could have been the case for any previous writer, for even an itinerant philosopher like Gorgias or Protagoras. For the central figure in the dialogues, Socrates, his random participation in open dialectic still operates in a far more restricted, far less cosmopolitan, and at the same time far less professional milieu than does the work of the Plato who actually delineates it. In that light the dialogues not only idealize the conditions of Socrates but permit a difference, a distancing, to play over them, a distance that reflects, and also contains, the Socratic irony. That term itself, indeed, as Vlastos has shown us, underwent considerable expansion in Plato's development of it.[19]

Plato, interestingly, couples his "doctrine" (*logos, Seventh Letter* 328a), with "life," implying the philosopher's ideal, though here this is connected to his own actual preoccupations. He denies that Dionysius, if he borrowed from Plato, could have got anything other than orally from him. In connection with that denial, Plato emphasizes that "no writing of mine about these matters exists or ever was" (341c).[20] "These matters" would surely cover at least Plato's oral teaching about practical politics, which in some way, then, he must here be discriminating from the voluminous discussions in the dialogues. Coupled with his earlier insistence on the difficulty of coming to understanding through discipline, it can be presumed that he is referring not to separate doctrines but to a whole *elenchos* in which they would have a place. In other words it is fair to assume he would have tried to play toward Dionysius a version of the role of Socrates.

It is hard to bring into a comprehensive and coherent system Plato's census of the five necessary constituents of philosophy: name; definition or *logos*; image or *eidolon*; knowledge (of the first three), comprising *episteme*, *nous* and *doxa*; and Form (342a-b).[21] The very incommensurability of these terms, if they are compared with each other, and the complexity of each term separately, would substantiate a reading of them as summaries of ongoing philosophical process rather than as a systematic repertoire complete in itself, for all the status of this group of five as one of the fullest, and perforce the latest, of such summaries in Plato's work. Philosophical understanding, he has just said, does not come about as with the acquisition of learning (*mathemata*) but "from much congress over the matter itself and from living together, suddenly, like light kindled from a leaping fire, it comes into the soul and nourishes itself of itself" (341c-d).[22] The process combines the cohesion of the old community and the goal orientation of the new group, of which the Academy is the model: both the Homeric *Gemeinschaft* and the Platonic *Gesellschaft*; both these social structures bring about understanding almost as a by-product of their syncretized process. And an *elenchos* in this connection is further insisted on (344). As Charles Altieri says, "Dialectic begins in the sublation of rhetoric." "In these works Plato must confront the limitations inherent in his own foundational claims—that what counts as a foundation itself depends on prior agreement," and further, "Logos earns its hegemony by the ethos it makes possible."[23]

On a still longer range, Plato shows a recurring tendency, especially in later works, to resume long spans of human time. He subsumes the older model, Homeric society; and the modern, flourishing Athens of his youth; and the newly decentralized Greek world of his maturity, under a conception that coordinates them all into a sequence where the apocalyptic vision of the Orphic writings and the evolutionary demonstrations of the historians have a common ground.[24]

Plato's dialogue form itself is not only a splendidly harmonious freestanding and original literary form, but one which draws on and conflates attributes of many prior traditions. The dialogue, in Jean Laborderie's presentation, includes procedures to be found in Egyptian and Hebrew traditions; in epic, archaic poetry, tragedy, satire, comedy, and mime, as well as the discourse of philosophical poets, rhetors, sophists, and historians—and also the live Socrates.[25] But tradition treats the dialogue form effectually, and I believe correctly, as a generic sport after Plato's practice has ended.[26]

2.

The *Protagoras* may be taken as an example of Plato's dialogic practice, and four procedures can be distinguished in that dialogue. First, Plato derives axioms about the relation of virtue to temperance, justice, holiness (*hosiotes*), courage, and wisdom with the propositional and deductive logic used for standard philosophical proof. Second, he suspends this whole question beyond the "Biconditionality Thesis" delineated by Vlastos,[27] even if we hold short before the suggestion that there are more profound meanings than have been enunciated, Heidegger's "inexpressible" (*Unsägliches*), and also "ambiguity" (*Zweideutigkeit*). Third, the dialogue demonstrates how a model philosophical discussion on any topic should be conducted (as against the set speech of Protagoras, a technique used with variation for the quoted set speech of the absent Lysias in the *Phaedrus*). Fourth, the dialogue integrates several kinds of discourse: the fictionalized setting of conversations among the generational and situational complexities of the interlocutors frames the oppositions between the main participants, the professional Sophist Protagoras versus the philosopher Socrates. All these four procedures are modified by and bear upon the schematized myth of Prometheus and the gnomicized poetic quotations from Simonides and Pittacus—themselves possibly qualified by irony.

Yet with all these complications a clear concern emerges for the conditions under which an ideal of virtue can be ascertained. In its interplay of idea and structure, the *Protagoras*, poses an example of how far the whole utterance of a Platonic dialogue may take us, as distinct from the particular positions enunciated in it. The *Protagoras* makes it clear in advance that considerable interplay and byplay will complicate its doctrines by setting the stage with a wide range of characters—not only Protagoras but Hippias of Elia and Prodicus of Ceos; Callias the wealthy patron of the Sophists and his brother Critias the later politician; Plato's uncle Charmides; Alcibiades and Agathon and Phaedrus and Erixymachus (who all appear in other dialogues); Pau-

sanias (who will also speak in the *Symposium*); the two sons of Pericles; Philippides, the student of Protagoras, and Adeimantus, a participant in the later herm sacrilege with Alcibiades; and a large gathering
of unnamed people (315a-d). At the same time the unifying voice of
Socrates, who tells the dialogue in the first person to an unnamed (and
so unmarked) "companion," makes it clear that the dialogue will
have a main thread.

This main thread is the teachability of virtue, and the ironic reversal has already taken place if it is assumed that Socrates' declared
eagerness at the outset to learn from Protagoras is something of a
parti pris and that, young as he is represented here, his doubt about
the teachability of virtue is already in flagrant contradiction with his
main known position on this question, that knowledge leads to virtue.

It is in answer to the request that he explain how virtue is teachable
that Protagoras first asks whether he and the others would rather have
a *mythos* or a *logos*. He says a myth would be more agreeable (320a-
c). Then he tells the myth of Prometheus, and then he adds a *logos*
declaring that he has covered his ground by integrating his answers in
these supplementary approaches. "I have spoken both a *mythos* and a
logos that virtue is teachable and Athenians think so" (328c3–4).

Still, there is a certain slippage between question and answer.[28]
This will eventually lead to a reversal of roles, with Protagoras asking
the questions (338e and following).

In the meantime it is not clear that the myth of Prometheus,
though it does bear on the question of the teachability of virtue, can
be taken as an answer to that question. The version given here is certainly more schematized than the versions in Hesiod and in Aeschylus,[29] and it is also more schematized than many other myths in Plato.
The puzzle about the Sophist as against sculptor, poet, and doctor, applies also to Socrates himself, at least by implication (311d). And it
creates by analogy a question never directly refuted, except that Socrates acts beyond it and so disproves it. The question is raised at the
approach of the Sophist (314d) and before Socrates sees him.[30]

In the *Protagoras*, Socrates says to Protagoras just before the
Prometheus fable, "I bend and I think you say something because I
consider that you have become experienced in many things and have
learned many things and have yourself found them out" (320b).[31]

This cannot be a simple irony, in which Protagoras is actually exposed for exhibiting the opposite of these qualities. Protagoras' boasting is contrasted with the *eiron* from an early point (317). Yet here, as well as in the *Meno* and elsewhere, a respectful picture of Protagoras is given. And of course it is not simple praise, because Protagoras shows himself to be inadequate to the argument, for a failure to inquire, and for too great a reliance on his experience. Similarly, his accounts and answers do not offer just error, but a mixture of error, commonplace, superficial truth, and captiousness—a mixture that he will not sort out because he is effectually resting on his laurels and refusing to "find them out," to use the verb that praises him.

Symmetrically, Socrates' stance as an *eiron* is also not simple irony. Socrates is not only knowing while pretending to be ignorant. He is also, in a deeper sense, ignorant both on philosophical principle and on elenchic strategy—which is a form of knowing. The "two turns" to the irony here—the knowing one who is ignorant but knowing enough to be really ignorant—correspond symmetrically to the two turns of the irony in the praise of Protagoras. But instead of a mixture, there is a clean distinction between ignorance used as a lever to "find out," and the commoner kinds of ignorance. The symmetry allows an equality to the confrontation with Protagoras; the difference in the constituents of the ironic terms provides an energy that allows for a demonstration of the possibility of clarity when an actual clarity, as often, is absent—and even though Socrates and Protagoras change positions.

The long sequence of byways partially disguises the fact that Socrates and Protagoras have gradually reversed positions, a state of affairs which the dialogue concludes by remarking on: Protagoras withdraws his assertion that a virtue (courage) could exist without knowledge, and Socrates puts in his own mouth the accusation from an imagined accuser that he has reversed himself (361 b), and so must Protagoras. Their postponement of resolutions to a later discussion, in ending the dialogue, suspends and brackets all the arguments, and indeed all the dramatic interplay that has been gone through, raising the constant, and for Plato penetrating, question, of the status of such discourse—and all the more if their reversal of positions is taken as an ironic qualification of the *antilogike techne*.

Protagoras says that if he had allowed an interlocutor to set his method of speaking—in this case by short questions and answers (*brachylogia*)—he would never have made a name among the Greeks (335a). In asserting this he assumes that making a name is his goal. Socrates has another goal, and Plato embodies that goal in dialogues. The goal involves the *sunousia*, the coming together of persons, which is mentioned throughout here and stated in the *Seventh Letter* to be a necessity of philosophical awareness (341). The *Protagoras* happens to take place in an unusually large *sunousia*, which frames a smaller *sunousia* of Socrates and Protagoras. They can come to a "contest of *logoi*" because they share common questions, even though Protagoras' goal of winning the contest eludes both of them. The dramatized draw between them leaves undiscussed, but demonstrated, what Socrates' goal would be—an indirect goal here, since he cross-examines Protagoras who has the wrong disposition of mind, and is also too old (Plato keeps emphasizing Protagoras' age) to be a pupil. The discrepancy between them engages many of the others as intermediaries, but only momentarily (336–37).

In all this, Plato retains the tensile posing and management of contradiction attained by Heraclitus. But instead of reducing his statement to the bare bones, as Heraclitus had done,[32] he orchestrates its elements on a vast scale. The *Laches* early sets into opposition speaking one's mind (*parrhesiazo*) and holding back, deferring, and managing (*stochazomai*).

Protagoras' best statement, "man is the measure of all things"— on which Plato rings many changes —does not come up in this dialogue but in others (*Theaetetus* 152a; *Cratylus* 385e; *Statesman* 269). Yet whatever this maxim can mean, it may be taken for its common association to Protagoras as a measure of this dialogue and of the nature of dialogue as the *Protagoras* exemplifies it.

In Plato the degree of fictionality surrounding the persons interposes a middle construct between the definite historical person mentioned and Man. This procedure is reminiscent of the hierarchy in the doctrine of ideas; it gives dimension both ways to the key figure of the Third Man in that doctrine, in addition to the logical puzzle of endless regress embedded in it.

Gorgias in the *Gorgias* is firmly identified as a political figure, without the philosophical purchase of Protagoras or the direct and specific forensic purchase of the Isocrates presented in the *Phaedrus*. And that is the portrait of him given in the *Gorgias:* he governs the focus of the topic to the relation between power and virtue, the single subject of that long dialogue. It is a difficult subject not because it is hard to understand but because, then as now, the human will is resistant to its conclusions. And also it is a new problem in society. Such choices as those imagined in such dialogues would be inconceivable in Homeric society,[33] or in any traditional society, where an evil act would be regarded as a random failing and not as the concerted result of the sort of program that both Polus and Callicles claim would be led to by Gorgias' training, though Gorgias is shown as denying it. Like the Protagoras of that dialogue, Gorgias changes places with Socrates; though in the *Protagoras* it is the philosophical positions that are reversed from beginning to end, with respect to the teachability of virtue. In the *Gorgias*, where the main figure is a rhetorician, it is their rhetorical style that is reversed; the laconic Socrates is now assigned long, expository speeches, while Gorgias agrees eagerly, as a demonstration of rhetorical skill, to the request that Protagoras refuses, that he offer short laconic answers. In any case, after a while he is gracefully bowed out of the picture, with the implication that he is so resistant to philosophical points that he is a poor candidate for *elenchos*. He does not reappear. Instead he is portrayed, so to speak, by being bounded with two contrasting defenders (himself a silent mean between them), the soft, impulsive, overdependent Polus, and the hard, cynical, extremist Callicles. Here (475e) Plato speaks of the "*elenchos* tested against itself."[34] This describes the dialectical procedure, both in general, and at just this point.

In the *Gorgias* (484ff) when Callicles contextualizes the whole abstract discussion and brings in the *nomos-physis* distinction, Socrates offers a counterstatement by denying the doctrine of Anaxagoras, a sort of relativized position that we might easily be induced to think he is taking. He brings up three cases: he has a right opinion but is consistent, he has a wrong opinion but is consistent, he has a wrong opinion and is inconsistent with himself. On all three he imposes his anticontextualism by a second-best case: though in disagreement with the people (*demos*; and so in all three cases inconsistent with their views), it is better to be consistent though wrong than either in agreement (whether they are right or wrong) and inconsistent with himself. This undercuts the contextual argument, which can go to cases—Pericles, Themistocles, Miltiades, and by implication Alcibiades (who is mentioned here in another context).

The eschatology of the end of the *Gorgias* returns the discussion to the final motive for choosing a "good" action. This discussion, as prior to rhetoric, does not return effectively to rhetoric as a subject—just as it brings up eros at the beginning of the Callicles refutation, even making love (*eronte*) the verb governing "philosophia" (481d3).[35] The *Phaedrus* goes farther along all these lines. The *Gorgias* is unremittingly private, in so far as it is preeminently about the deciding man, and unremittingly public, in so far as it is the public action, of Archelaus and others, that counts and is steadily in view, including by implication those whom Gorgias has trained or will train.

3.

Generally, to take Plato's view of discourse, poetic and other, beyond a single dialogue would further complicate, contradict, extend, and qualify this important segment of his thinking. But in many respects he contradicts and qualifies himself, as in his views on poetry. The more important the topic is to him, the more he does so. This irreconcilability is especially the case in his thinking about the Ideas. In fact the *Parmenides* faces that irreconcilability in well-nigh Wittgensteinian fashion—while still being modified by the dramatic condition that this late dialogue is reported from a remote past, the youth of Socrates, and at fourth hand.

Nor can Plato's contradictions and irreconcilabilities merely be chalked up to development, since often as not they occur in dialogues that very possibly were written fairly close together. This would be the case between the *Phaedrus* and the *Symposium*, if the *Phaedrus* did not resist firm placement in a sequence. One would be tempted, indeed, to characterize as reckless the work of the enchainers of propositions in the Natorp-Vlastos tradition who do not confine themselves to a single dialogue in testing one statement against another—were it not for the fact that the enterprise of enchaining propositions, so

astutely carried out by such interpreters, integrally defines one inescapable focus of Plato's discourse, and the one bearing most systematically on modern philosophy. Moreover, the questions Plato
raised are still alive, whereas the dialogue quickly became a moribund
literary form, and the full force of Socratic irony would seem to be
possible only within that form. So that our own concerns distance us
from the form, but in Plato's case thereby also somewhat from the
meanings, of his dialogues.

For one thing, we do not share Plato's credence in the Greek
gods. He gave them some form of credence, however,[36] and even the
myths that do not supplement them or use them as figures partake of
that credence. The myths of the Platonic dialogues do not remain
stable, nor do other features of organization within them. The
Prometheus in the *Protagoras* and the Isles of the Blest in the *Gorgias*
come at different high points of each dialogue. But in the *Republic*
the sequence of the Sun, the Line, the Cave, and then the Myth of Er,
is more complex. Some of the speeches in the *Symposium* offer myths
and others do not. Their coordination puts the myths and the plain
discourses into a sort of equivalence, but at the same time that dialogue's seven accounts of Eros stand in a hierarchy. Dialectic enters
the *Phaedrus* fairly late, and its myths vary in length, in complexity,
and in relation to the topic at hand, without any firm hierarchies beyond Socrates' stated preferences.

Moreover the progression of presentation, and the final bearing,
of the individual dialogues, vary considerably. Leaving aside the early,
elenchic and aporetic ones[37] and the late expositions like the *Timaeus*
and the *Laws*, they do not all conform to the "ladder of certainty"
type, the principle of organization followed by the *Sophist*, the
Statesman, the *Republic*, and differently by the *Symposium*.

An elaborate, enchained exposition, working through to complex
conclusions, is offered by the sequence of the *Theaetetus, Sophist* and
Statesman. In the *Theaetetus* Plato sets up a situation which results in
Socrates' carrying the definitions of knowledge as far as he can, without recourse either to the final doubts of the rescuing cross-genera-
tional memory of the *Meno*. In the *Theaetetus*, actually, memory is
sometimes untrustworthy (191–200), but the dialogue carries through
to definition. Still, the finality of the strenuous definitions here finds a

dramatically qualified terminus in the symbolic situation of the conclusion—that Socrates will now leave his interlocutors to go face his trial. This is a symbol because, unlike the dialogues around his death, it is here a fiction. And in fact the whole dialogue is framed by dire events, since the moment when it is called up from thirty years before, is the moment when the mature Theaetetus has been transported from battle heavily wounded and on the threshold of death.[38] But this systematic approach is continued in discussion with some of the same participants in the address to the question of Forms in the *Sophist* and of proper distinctions in the *Statesman*. Myles Burnyeat, however, points out of "a greater discussion emerging from a lesser one" (172b) that "the issues are both too large and too important to handle argumentatively within the framework of Part I of the *Theaetetus*. They call for a work on the scale of the *Republic* ... and for specifically ethical and psychological explorations."[39] In the *Protagoras* Socrates reverses his position on the central question with his interlocutor, symmetrically; in the *Gorgias* he does the same asymmetrically. There are also the *Apology* and the *Phaedo*, the *Crito* and the *Euthyphro*, which subordinate the doctrines they include to the offering of an exemplum, Socrates, as the great philosopher under mortal duress. There is the *Euthydemus*, which is organized so as to take back at the end what it had seemed to be developing. The principle enlisted here differs both from the intricate evolution of *aporiai* about Forms in the *Parmenides* and the development of modified doubt about how language works in the *Cratylus*. Nor are these types, even in the beginning of a typology that I am sketching, mutually exclusive. The *Phaedrus* in some respects pretends to develop a ladder of certainty that it does not establish, except in some ways, for its main topics, *eros* and rhetoric. And it also strongly illustrates the connection between the personality—as distinct from the capacity—of Socrates and what is said. It also in some respects takes much back at the end by concluding on the faintly ironic praise of Isocrates (278a-279b), who is to outdo Lysias. The connection is left quite open, for example, among the kinds of good madness, and nothing explicit is made of the fact that the other three besides love-madness—the madness of prophecy, of ritual, and of poetry—all involve verbal expression. Full closure is not effectuated for the connection between the best rhetoric and the best love,[40] though in this instance, to be sure, the connection is easily inferred.

The *Phaedrus* also produces *aporiai* without exactly emphasizing them, while at the same time it skillfully dodges a full resolution of the modified doubts it raises.

In addition to its bearing on the questions that it raises and the function of the myths it broaches, a dialogue may vary as to the circumstances under which it takes place, the persistence and depth of doctrinal disagreement it engenders among its participants, the relative semantic loading in the prior careers of the named participants themselves (Gorgias and Aristophanes are "heavier" than Phaedrus), and the number of topics it interconnects. The *Phaedrus* is highly specific as to its physical setting by the Ilissus. The participants mention the temperature, the distance from Athens, the neighboring shrines, and the very species of trees shading them. At one point they even speak of dipping their feet in the water (229a). At the same time the *Phaedrus* restricts itself to two participants, though what could well be an actual speech of a third "heavy" person, Lysias, is quoted verbatim and is protractedly in view. It discusses only two main topics, rhetoric and love, though these prove to entail notions of large import for Plato elsewhere—poetry, the gods, good and evil, *sophrosune*, the Ideas, and the transmigration of souls. And it presents *aporiai* for all these topics. None of these conditions lacks implications for the propositions brought forth in the *Phaedrus*.

On the one hand the appeals to authority, the introduction of myth, the relativizing of positions taken by interlocutors, and the doctrinal twists and turns of the discussion under Socrates' leadership, all tend to qualify the philosophical positions that can be extrapolated from the dialogues. On the other hand, though, Socrates is presented as clearly valuing a clarity and rightness of certain philosophical positions and as deriving these positions from the dialogue. The prevailing modern assumption that Plato held certain positions is powerfully backed up by so little remote and so important an authority as Aristotle, who ascribes such positions to Plato. Further, to hold such positions was the normal procedure for *sophoi* from Thales on. Yet Plato's introduction of the dialogue form would seem to modify such positions, and to have been introduced as a means of modifying them.

Otherwise they would have to rank as obfuscating distractions rather than as the significant mirror they are also (sometimes inconsistently) taken to be. It may be said that the Plato we have, the author of the dialogues, takes the important, overriding position that dialogue is the most desirable form for approaching questions of idea.

Plato's own situation, as one who incorporates religious and literary traditions in order to provide a groundwork for redefining a society which itself is a given, replicates the discrepancy between the relativisms that may be adduced from the fact of the dialogues and their disposition of topics on the one hand, and on the other hand the fixed positions they sometimes arrive at. And we may conjecture a further discrepancy: to state the obvious, Plato is not Socrates, but Socrates (and one rather different from the historical Socrates) is at the center of the dialogues. The Academy, on Aristotle's showing but also by reasonable conjecture, could not have conducted its presentations and discussions wholly after the manner of the Platonic Dialogues. Discourse in that setting must have approached the sorts of defenses and summaries we find in the writings of Aristotle. The Academy must have been more Aristotelian, so to speak, than Socratic, and the discourse in it must have taken its form and temper much more on the model of its immediately succeeding years than on the model of free-form random discussions in the agora.

The exception might well have been mathematics. If a mathematician was Plato's successor as head of the Academy, if Plato's Lecture on the Good contained Pythagorean formulations, and if mathematics is rooted in Plato's thinking in ways we would regard as strange (notably in such complex figurations as those toward the end of the *Republic*), then it could be said that Aristotle's Categories are not only a classifying solution to an overblurring of conceptions in Plato, but a substitute for a spurious overprecision in applying mathematics to other questions. Certainly, looked at in terms of constituents to Plato's discourse rather than to the strains in modern interpretation that draw on them, we must deal with, and explain historically, three indissociable constituents in his work. There is what I will continue to stress, the literary element. Plato did invent the dialogue form, and in doing so he revised the practice of his predecessors. He asked philosophy to revert to something like the suspension and play of possibilities found in tragedy, and therewith to include a version of the root element in tragedy, the myth. Dialogue, then, is a constituent that forces the literary into a place it shares with the second constituent, which professional philosophers take as the main thrust of his discourse, and which dialogue also subserves, the framing and addressing of fundamental questions in philosophical theory. And then there is the third constituent, the most obscure, mathematics.[41] Not being able fully to explain, let alone to justify, the connection among these three constituents, we are thrown back on the attempt to characterize them. But these three approaches, reconcilable as they may be, themselves only complicate the contradiction inherent in an adequate modern approach to Plato. The approach to questioning that he mounted has the effect of endowing Western philosophy steadfastly with its topics and methods. Yet questions arising through these topics do not admit of Plato's solutions, however tentative. And the strength of his method of enunciation through dialogue entails a weakness for the modern philosopher, while to define his utterance we cannot escape the approach through dialogue, with all its anthropologically modified constraints and self-qualifications. Of these the most quickly dealt with, and yet arguably the most fundamental, is the one between oral and written he himself addresses in the *Phaedrus*.

If Plato feels free, as the evidence indicates that he does, to change his doctrines within a single dialogue, or to maintain doctrines we would feel to be contradictory, then he would be all the more free to do so from dialogue to dialogue. There remains, furthermore, the distinct possibility that Plato did not issue his dialogues serially but held on to them throughout his lifetime, perhaps gradually touching up and refining them. The situation of the discrepancy among them, in any case, would prevent our working out the sort of delicately discriminated evolution of his doctrines in any final way, though the broad outlines seem fully to be indicated. But in this regard he differs from Aristotle, who stays firmly with a doctrine as maintained and argued, and whose development, along the lines worked out by such as Jaeger and Owencan be delineated at least by close ratiocination about the factors involved.[42] Along with the always questionable stylometric considerations, in buttressing a "middle" date for the dialogue, however, Owen mainly has recourse to exactly discriminated differences with "later" dialogues, which present doctrines Plato would have "abandoned." But his abandonment of doctrines, I am arguing—his backing and filling, his zigging and zagging—are so persistent that to try to give such discriminations a temporal dimension within Plato's career is really to treat him as though he were Aristotle, the way Aristotle did—who had, to be sure, the whole of Plato before him, written and unwritten, as we do not.

Much of the discourse on Plato since late antiquity to the present has concerned itself, properly but always qualifiably, with the questions of what his opinions and the supporting arguments were on subjects he discusses, when the very diversity of his most emphatic expression shows that he may not have had a fixed opinion, even though the major thrust of the discourse in his dialogues constitutes a search for one, for an *orthe doxa* which has a higher value than "orthodoxy" does in our own thinking, though for him not the highest.

To take a recent example, J. C. B. Gosling's admirable book *Plato* sets out to "tell us what Plato's opinions are on a number of subjects."[43] Gosling proposes a somewhat more sharply focused version of Paul Shorey's *What Plato Said*. But as we begin to read Gosling, we find ourselves at once plunged into the most intricate dialectical backing and filling—quite properly and appositely, but implicitly in qualification of the stated purpose. It does turn out that even within the more restricted area of results from *elenchi*—leaving out myths and the like—what Plato thought on a given topic, like moral good, cannot be disentangled from the particular circumstances into which he has chosen to cast its presentation. This is more remarkable because his immediate predecessors did not do this; they flatly stated, or argued, their conceptions, or else they cast them in a form from which, if we are to find an implied dialogue form, we must go very far behind the surface presentation.[44] It should be steadily insisted that there is a radical difference of modalization between an active Socrates carrying on live discourse and working his way up to the sort of doctrines Xenophon summarizes, and a semifictionalized Socrates who is one of the personae of an imagined dialogue. And this is so quite apart from the question as to whether the living Socrates would have agreed to all the propositions put forth by the fictional Socrates in Plato's dialogues, even if divided into an earlier Socrates and a middle Socrates, the Socrates E and the Socrates M of Vlastos' presentation.[45]

Though the dialogues keep returning to the same topics, and though typically they provide an exact context for their occurrence, they almost always refrain from referring to points made directly and by title in other dialogues. This is the more remarkable in that they do revert again and again to the same topics. The *Timaeus* does refer to the *Republic* and some of its topics. And the Socratic group all refer to aspects of the same context. Both these instances demand interpretation.

Both Plato and Socrates differ from all their predecessors and contemporaries. Socrates, alone wrote nothing, which is anomalous, and is itself a testimony of his at least unconscious devotion to the Socratic method. Moreover, in Socrates' time Protagoras, in what we can infer from what is left of his writings, resembles Plato rather than Socrates. It is really in a late work like the *Parmenides* that Plato comes closest to the questions, and to some degree the procedures, of the pre-Socratics. Plato alone wrote dialogues, the form he had himself discovered. That form bases itself precisely on the Socratic method, and is the "prior" Socratic element in his writings, before any specific doctrines that are ascribed to Socrates.

To make the *elenchos* a basis for writing is a tremendous innovation, one that Aristotle, with the possible exception of lost works, drops in order to return to what has become the regular manner of philosophical presentation. The dialogue form in Plato's hands can be assimilated to tragedy, and to other literary activity. But it is not literary in the restrictive sense, whereas it is philosophical in that sense: as in modern philosophical discourse, the reasoned cross-questioning of ideas is the inherent means of presentation. We would want, therefore, further to ascertain not only the considerable elegances, overtones, and procedural advantages of the dialogue form in Plato's hands, but what those qualities contribute to a philosophic presentation or perception.

The form of the dialogue has the function of preserving the project as a project. This does not mean that the writer places no premium on solutions, and the dialogue can certainly admit of the solutions it sets itself up as seeking. But its form works against accepting the finality of a solution in the light of the overall project, however fully a given solution may be articulated and situated to obtain. It also admits of numbers of social postures just because of the randomness and distance of almost all the encounters recounted. The participants of a dialogue are standing off from social groupings in order to test, but also to admit their bases. Such admissions could certainly include such groups as the Pythagorean, and they could also admit "unwritten doctrines" of a mathematical or Orphic sort as occasional reference points show, like the Persephone of the *Meno* or the Line of the *Republic*. The dialogue often sets itself to aim for the highest generality and will not allow *arete,* for example, to comprise simply a census of virtues. On the other hand the solutions reached stand implicitly this side of the highest generality. The Aristotelian whole (*katholou*) finds no correspondence in Plato, and, as recent commentators have variously shown, the theory of Ideas itself, at such a late stage as the *Parmenides*, may be taken to involve an infinite regress from the more than high generality it propounds. The fourfold consciousness expounded in Book Seven of the *Republic* implicitly leaves room for other notions, and definitions of a different order: this set of categories is just part of the project, a part the dialogue leaves wide open.

The enterprise of understanding Plato is a far longer one, and it stands at far greater remove, than, say, the enterprise of understanding Kant. But the hermeneutic preeminence of Plato is indicated by the richness and well-nigh permanent aptness of the questions he sets, even if it is allowed that he sometimes changes and always modifies his answers. The many and the one, the actual and the ideal, nature and custom, individual and society, knowledge and virtue, the bases of a consistent and informed human activity, the relation of love's imperatives to the rest of life, the organization of authority, the uses of inquiry, the powers and limits of language—these questions, among others, fresh for him in his writing, abide with us still.

Notes

1. D. W. Allen, ed. and tr., Julius Stenzel, *Plato's Method of Dialectic* (Oxford: Clarendon Press, 1940), 53, 76.

2. See, for example, Hans Joachim Krämer, "Die Platonische Akademie und das Problem einer systematischen Interpretation der Philosophie Platons," in Konrad Gaiser, ed., *Das Platonbild* (Hildesheim: Olms, 1969), 198–230.

3. Martin Heidegger, *Sein und Zeit* (Tübingen: Niemeyer, 1963 [1926]), 219 ff; *Platons Lehre von der Wahrheit* (1947) in *Wegmarken* (Frankfurt: Klostermann, 1967), 109–144. Heidegger famously derives the word "*a-letheia*" from "non-forgetfulness." This view is somewhat contested in Paul Friedländer, *Plato: An Introduction* (Princeton: Princeton University Press, 1968), 122–29, though he further qualified his observations (*Platon*, I, Berlin, 1964, 233–36). Marcel Detienne has shown Plato's continuing involvement in the archaic mythical dimensions of *aletheia* in *Les Maîtres de vérité dans la Grèce archaique* (Paris: Maspero, 1967), 114–15.

4. Friedländer (*op. cit.*, 151) graphically characterizes the relation between the composition of a dialogue and its failure to resolve questions: "Just as there are pictures in which the pictorial center remains vacant, and the center of attention is transferred by the arrangement of lines, colors, and light effect to one of the corners, so the dialogue, if seen as a whole, confers essential meaning on that which appeared only as means; and this meaning, in turn, illuminates and deepens even that which, as long as we did not recognize the ironic shift, appears to be its primary purpose." Aristotle's characterization of Socrates is apposite here, "Socrates asked but he did not answer; he confessed (*homologei*) he did not know" (*De sophisticis elenchis*, 183b7, cited by Friedländer, 157).

5. Hermann Gundert, *Der Platonische Dialog* (Heidelberg: Winter, 1968), 5, "diese zweifache Erfahrung von Erhellen und Rätselhaftigkeit."

6. See also Konrad Gaiser, *Platons Ungeschriebene Lehre* (Stuttgart, 1968), and Thomas Slezak, "Dialogform Esoterik, Zur Deutung des platonischen Dialogs Phaidros," *Museum Helveticum* 35 (1978), 18–32; Marie-Dominique Richard, *L'Enseignement orale de Platon* (Paris: Cerf, 1986). All these written dialogues stand under the further shadow of Plato's qualification, in the *Seventh Letter* but also in the *Phaedrus* (276a), that oral communication is in some ways superior to written.

7. Among those who pay attention to the form of Plato's presentation are such divergent figures as Hans-Georg Gadamer, Martha Nussbaum, Stanley Rosen, and Jacques Derrida, as well as the contributors, and the figures cited, in Charles L. Griswold, Jr.; *Platonic Writings, Platonic Readings* (New York: Routledge, 1988). Still others whom I shall be citing adopt comparable approaches.

8. Stanley Rosen, *Plato's* Symposium (New Haven: Yale University Press, 1968), xiii, xiv.

9. See the list of nine types and further subtypes in the *Phaedrus*, "seeker of wisdom or beauty, follower of the Muses, lover, king, warrior,

statesman, trader, athlete, physician, prophet, priest, poet, artisan, farmer, sophist, tyrant." These are divided into nine reincarnations, according to their affinity each for a specific god (248c-e).

10.   For the limits to Lévi-Strauss's procedures, and their applicability only to a neolithic phase or a neolithic element in social structure, see Albert Cook, "Lévi-Strauss, Myth, and the Neolithic Revolution," *Myth and Language* (Bloomington: Indiana University Press, 1980), 13–56.

11.   See Paul Wilpert, "Eine Elementenlehre im Platonischen Philebos," in Jürgen Wippern, ed., *Das Problem der Ungeschriebenen Lehre Platons* (Darmstadt: Wissenschaftliche Buchhandlung, 1972), 316–28. "The dialogues and the philosophy about first principles, transmitted indirectly, may mutually illuminate each other."

12.   Eric Havelock, *Preface to Plato* (Cambridge: Harvard University Press, 1961).

13.   As Walter Burkert says in *Lore and Science in Ancient Pythagoreanism* (Cambridge: Harvard University Press, 1972), 96, "One might therefore define later Pythagoreanism as Platonism with the Socratic and dialectic element amputated. In fact, Plato remained the principal source for all later Pythagoreans—Plato's myths, and in particular the *Timaeus*."

14.   Kurt F. Raaflaub, *Die Entdeckung der Freiheit* (Munich: Beck, 1985).

15.   Gregory Vlastos, *Socrates, Ironist and Moral Philosopher* (Cambridge: Cambridge University Press, 1991, especially 157–233.

16.   Felix Heinimann, *Nomos und Physis: Herkunft und Bedeutung einer Antithese im griechischen Denken des 5. Jahrhunderts* (Basel: Reinhardt, 1945); W. K. C. Guthrie, *A History of Greek Philosophy* (Cambridge: Cambridge University Press, 1969), III, 55–135, especially the discussion about ambiguities in the "unwritten law," whose *nomos* carries some implications of *physis* (117–31).

17.   This is also noted in the *Eighth Letter* (354b), if it is genuine. I am following a strong modern tradition in accepting the authenticity of some letters, and notably the *Seventh*.

18.   On the uncertainty about the activities of the Academy and its structure, see Harold Cherniss, *The Riddle of the Early Academy* (New York: Russell & Russell, 1962 [1945]), 60–85.

19.   Gregory Vlastos *Socrates, Ironist and Moral Philosopher*. The first use of the term "irony," (εἰρονεία) is in Aristophanes, where it means "pretense." Socrates himself was a main causal factor in the transition to the more extended modern senses. Quintilian calls Socrates a lifelong ironist. In the *Symposium* (218d) *eironikos* implies talking straight and gives no foothold to the (normal) implications of "deceit." So with εἰρωνευόμενος (216e) and the uses at 217a, 215a, and 215e. Εἰρονεία usually implies

intention to deceive as at *Laws* 901e, *Gorgias* 499d and *Republic* 337a, where it may mean "sham." By the time of Cicero *ironia*=urbanity, as in Quintilian 9, 2, 44. See also Werner Boder, *Die Sokratische Ironie in den platonischen Frühdialogen* (Amsterdam: Grüner, 1973). He cites Anaximenes of Lampsacus, *Wasps* 171, *Birds* 1210–11; and *Laws* 908e2, *Sophist* 267e-f, *Euthydemus* 302b3, and *Cratylus* 348a1. As Egidius Schmalzriedt says in *Platon der Schriftsteller und die Wahrheit* (Munich: Piper, 1969), 24–25. "[There is] no systematically representative unity in Plato's teaching—the genuine is only conceivable in a spontaneous immediacy of living intercourse between the matter [Sache] and the striver—instead of which there is only an ironically delineating depiction of artistically invented converse, with added to it a renunciation of speech and writing as exactly valid means of expression."

20. οὔκουν ἐμόν γε περὶ αὐτῶν ἔστιν σύγγραμμα οὐδὲ μήποτε γένηται.

21. ἐν μὲν ὄνομα, δεύτερον δὲ λόγος, τὸ δὲ τρίτον εἴδωλον, τετάρτον δὲ ἐπιστήμη... καὶ νοῦς ἀληθής τε δόξα περὶ ταῦτ ἐστίν... πέμπτον δ᾽αὐτὸ τιθέναι ὃ δή γνωτόν τε καὶ ἀληθῶς ἔστιν ὄν. These are discussed by Richard Robinson, *Plato's Earlier Dialectic*, 65 ff.; and by W. K. C. Guthrie, *History*, V, 1978, 404–12.

22. As Ortega says, "Socratism or rationalism, however, engenders a double life, in which that which we spontaneouly are—pure reason—comes to replace that which we more truly are—spontaneity," José Ortega y Gasset, "Los Dos Ironias o Socrates y Don Juan," *El Tema de Nuestro Tiempo* (Madrid: Espasa-Calpe, 1938), 54.

23. Charles Altieri, "Plato's Performative Sublime and the Ends of Reading," *Canons and Consequences* (Evanston, Ill.: Northwestern University Press, 1990), 163–188.

24. One account of these partial syntheses is offered in Konrad Gaiser, *Platon und die Geschichte* (Stuttgart: Fromann, 1961). This is expanded in *Platons ungeschriebene Lehre*, 205–92.

25. Jean Laborderie *Le Dialogue platonicien et la maturité* (Paris: Belles Lettres, 1978). For mime, Hermann Reich provides an argument for rich parallels in *Der Mimus* (Berlin: Weideman, 1903). He points out that Aristotle classifies *sokratikoi logoi* in conjunction with mime in one poetic class (34). Duris, Valerius Maximus, Quintilian, Athenaeus, etc., say Plato took the mimes of Sophron as his model (381). In "Das mimische Element bei Plato" (388) he gives the *Euthydemus* as an example (400) and connects mime to Plato's use of myth and parody (404). Helmut Kuhn (*Harvard Studies in Classical Philology*, 1942, 37) reads the *Republic* schematically as a tragedy, a "play of the blessedness of the just and the misery of the unjust."

26. A history of the form is given in R. Hirzel, *Der Dialog, ein*

literarhistoriker Versuch (2 vols.) (Leipzig: S. Hirzel, 1895).

27.   Gregory Vlastos, "The Unity of the Virtues in the *Protagoras,"* *Platonic Studies* (Princeton: Princeton University Press, 1981), 221–65. Vlastos distinguishes among the theses about virtue in this dialogue a "unity" thesis, a "similarity" thesis, and a "biconditionality thesis" which provides a conceptual link between one virtue (wisdom, for example) and another, such as courage. This further occurs along the lines of "Pauline predication" on the pattern "Charity is kind," where to say "Wisdom is courageous" does not actually attribute the virtue courage to an abstract entity like wisdom but implies directly that anyone who instantiates wisdom will also be courageous.

28.   For some slippages of logic in this dialogue, see C. C. W. Taylor, *Protagoras* (Oxford: Clarendon Press, 1976), 71–103.

29.   The outline of an account of the myth is offered in Louis Séchan, *Le Mythe de Prométhée* (Paris: Presses Universitaires de France, 1951).

30.   There is a possible symbol in that a eunuch slams a door in their faces.

31.   κάμπτομαι καὶ οἶμαί τί σε λέγειν διὰ τὸ ἡγεῖσθαί σε πολλῶν μὲν ἔμπειρον γεγονέναι, πολλὰ δὲ μεμαθηκέναι, τὰ δὲ αὐτὸ ἐξηυρηκέναι.

32.   See Albert Cook, "Heraclitus and the Conditions of Utterance," *Myth and Language*, 69–107.

33.   This would be so, I believe, even if a developed set of ethical categories is embedded in the language and situation of the *Iliad,* as forcefully demonstrated by Bernard Williams, *Shame and Necessity* (Berkeley: The University of California Press, 1993). See also Michael Naas, *Turning from Persuasion to Philosophy: Homer's* Iliad (Atlantic Hills, N.J.: Humanities Press, 1995).

34.   ὁ ἔλεγχος παρὰ τὸν ἔλεγχον παραβαλλόμενος. The relation between dialectic and its sterile cousin eristic, and the surprising connection of both with the *anamnesis* and learning techniques discussed in the *Meno*, and even in a rudimentary fashion with the Ideas of the *Republic*, appear in the *Euthydemus*, a figure whom Aristotle (*Sophisticis Elenchis*, 20. 177b12) connects with the origins of these procedures. See Thomas H. Chance, *Plato's* Euthydemus (Berkeley: University of California Press, 1992).

35.   "We are both in love with two things, I with Alcibiades ... and with philosophy," ἐρῶντε δύο, ὄντε δυοῖν ἑκάτερος, ἐγὼ μὲν ᾽Αλκιβιάδου ... καὶ φιλοσοφίας.

36.   Of many possible citations, this from the *Laws* is especially emphatic, as befits this late work, "the god would especially be for us the measure of things, and much more than, as they say, man" (716c), ῞ὁ δὴ θεὸς ἡμῖν πάντων χρημάτων μέτρον ἂν εἴη μάλιστα, καὶ

πολὺ μᾶλλον ἢ πού τις, ὥς φασιν, ἄνθρωπος." This revises, of course, the well-known formula of Protagoras by changing the word "man" to the word "god", and then inserting "man" as a denial.

37. Guthrie (IV, 69) notes the similarity of the impasse and the simple subject of discourse at the end of the *Laches, Charmides, Lysis,* and *Euthyphro.* The impasse, of course, has a different force in the last, because of the situation.

38. There are further qualifications around the *Theaetetus.* Eukleides (142c-143b) long ago as a boy heard Socrates' conversation with Theaetetus, wrote it down, and showed it to Socrates to fill in the gaps and correct it. Then he shows him the book, which leaves out ascriptions of words describing speakers (143c). In thus setting up complicated situations in the more or less remote past, Plato effectually recreates his own relationship to a Socrates who is long dead when he begins to write his dialogues.

39. Myles Burnyeat, *The* Theaetetus *of Plato* (Indianapolis: Hackett, 1990), 33. Eugène Napoléon Tigerstedt, *Interpreting Plato* (Stockholm: Acta Universitaria Stockholmensis 17, 1977).

40. Dialectic here, and especially 265–69, mixes its air of discriminating conclusion with an air of qualification, especially as it weaves in and out of the discourse—and Plato emphasizes the necessity to compose a discourse in a particular order. Diskin Clay in "Socrates' Prayer to Pan," in Glen Bowersock *et al,* eds., *Arktouros* (Berlin, 1979), 345–53 is able to relate the prayer to Pan, Socrates' last full statement, intricately to other themes in the dialogue.

41. At the beginning of Book Seven of the *Republic,* the three elements converge: myths, mathematics, and abstract categories.

42. For Plato—puzzlingly in view of the traditional sense of a late date for the dialogue— Owen argues that the *Timaeus,* for example is not "late," but roughly contemporaneous with the *Republic,* as indeed the extraordinary situation of the reference to continuity with the *Republic* at the very beginning of the *Timaeus* may be taken to indicate. See G. E. L. Owen, "The Place of the *Timaeus* in Plato's Dialogues," *Logic, Science, and Dialectic* (Ithaca: Cornell University Press, 1986), 65–84.

43. J.C.B. Gosling, *Plato* (London: Routledge & Kegan Paul, 1973); Paul Shorey, *What Plato Said* (Chicago: University of Chicago Press, 1933).

44. Alexander Mourelatos *The Route of Parmenides* (New Haven: Yale University Press, 1973). See also my chapter on Heraclitus in *Myth and Language,* as cited above.

45. Gregory Vlastos, *Socrates: Ironist and Moral Philosopher,* 45–81.

Chapter 2

Equanimity and Danger: Distribution of Questions and Style of Confrontation in the Four Dialogues around Socrates' Trial

1.

In the four dialogues around his trial Socrates is not only a leader of discussion. He is also an exemplum, and a historical exemplum. Uniquely these dialogues center on his capital exposure, a circumstance that should be taken as orienting and in a sense subordinating all these discussions, and also as orienting each of them toward the others.[1] Consequently, an interaction is set up between positions canvassed or taken and the person of the central figure. The duress under which Socrates reviews ideas makes him something other than a disinterested inquirer.

This situation, common to the four dialogues around his trial, groups them together, nor would the prevailing careful assessment of plausibilities about dating much dissociate them one from another—

nor can the topics themselves be used in any firm way as indicating points in a development. So, for example, the fact that the *Phaedo* does not dwell on politics, which Hackforth mentions, is not just to be taken "developmentally" in a way that allows us to put its individual emphasis down as "earlier" than the *Republic* (for that reason).[2] Nor would the *Phaedo's* nearly total concentration on one pressing question, the immortality of the soul—at an unusual length—derive just from its having been written later. Its associability to the other three is independent of when it may have been written, especially since Plato may be conceived as holding onto all the dialogues, and even of adding touches to them, throughout his lifetime.

For all four dialogues, though Socrates speaks in the *Apology* (31e) of having avoided politics during his life, the situation in view is a highly political one and cannot be divorced from other manifestations of Plato's historical consciousness, either the more short-range one of the types of government and their causal sequence in the *Republic*, or the more long-range ones in the *Timaeus* and the *Critias*, which overlap in topic with the arguments about the soul and the Pythagoreanism of the *Phaedo*. In this dialogue, one can say that Plato is most political when he is least political. A beginning of a long-range view is given with the reference to a legendary religious custom still being observed as the dialogue opens.

It is germane for our purposes, if not for Plato's, that few people would now find Socrates' arguments about the immortality of the soul convincing, not even a believer in the immortality of the soul. So that even the sharp discrimination of what his doctrines are here (and elsewhere)—the prolonged questioning that has preoccupied most modern commentators— must be subordinated, for our purposes, to ascertaining what the thrust of the dialogue is as it has been constructed in context. Our own interest, finally, is historical, not systematic, and the discrimination of particular doctrines serves that historical interest. As it happens, and even in the most elaborate and almost surely the latest of the four, the *Phaedo*, one account of its structure, at least, would make the doctrines a subset of the whole presentation, the siting of Socrates' preoccupations on the threshold of death. The elaborate exordium about Apollo and the ship to and from Delos can be intricately coded not only to anticipate but also to situate those explicit arguments. The same constraint applies to Socrates' preoccupations before the dialogue as they are told in it, where he has been drawing on Aesop, honoring Apollo, following an injunction in a dream, writing poetry and/or music, and at least potentially equating this activity with philosophy—"philosophy is the highest music" (61a). This series of situation-equations and propositions can itself be taken to govern all the other propositions, and notably the philosophical deductions, to which the dialogue rises. The philosophical deductions, however, as the qualifications surrounding these presentations imply, must at the same time be accorded pride of place within the dialogue; they are the highest music. But they are still music, the same in kind though higher in degree, in a way that perhaps goes beyond Pythagoras, for whom the music that was highest, and most mathematical, would still be audible or at least available for composition. And probably for Pythagoras and the Pythagoreans (since music, perhaps often in association with poetry, would be the defining expression), poetry qua poetry would not be in the picture at all, as it is for Plato here, and for Socrates.

There is another poet brought in as an inquirer about the poetry of Socrates and a measure for it, Evenus. He is also a sophistone spoken of in the *Apology* as commanding a large fee (20c), and so his name belongs on the list of thinkers in this dialogue, a list of so many philosophers that one could almost construct a map of the philosophical landscape in 399 B.C.E. by extending their names into the doctrines associated with them and their various masters.[3] This would be all the more the case if these names were supplemented with those of others who held notions germane to the doctrines Socrates goes on to expound. The doctrines of wholeness, of opposites, of mind, of coming to be and passing away, of the permanence of the invisible, of number theory, are topics, if not exactly of the same stripe, that were discussed by Parmenides (65b, 78d, 83b), Empedocles (71c, 96b), Heraclitus (on exchange, 69b; on waking and sleeping 71c, on harmony), Anaximander (109a), Anaxagoras (97c-98d), Philolaus (61d), and perhaps Zeno (96e), as well as by Pythagoras and his followers.

As Socrates says, "My life seems to me not to be sufficient in length for the *logos*," "ὁ βίος μοι δοκεῖ ὁ ἐμός ... τῶι μήκει τοῦ λόγου οὐκ ἐξάρκειν" (108d). This puts the dialectic and the exemplum of the whole life on the same line, incommensurably. Simmias lightly contradicts, "But these things do suffice," "Ἀλλὰ ... καί ταῦτα ἄρκει." The dialogue as a whole offers evidence for both views, which means that the *logos* neither disappears before the life nor can be assigned prominence over it.

2.

Of these four dialogues, the *Phaedo* alone, though conditioned by the external circumstances, does not, for the best of reasons, address them other than incidentally or analogously. Because Socrates faces death, the dialogue recounts his answers to questions about what happens to the soul after death, whereas typically the occasion for a Platonic dialogue is somewhat fortuitous and the topic is presented as coming up freely, somewhat randomly chosen by the discussants. The dialogue immediately preceding in dramatic circumstance, the *Crito*, discusses the ethical question that bears upon an immediate possibility of choice: shall Socrates accept the means to escape offered by his supporters?[4] This situation, in turn, is different from that in the preceding circumstance (though like it in determining what is discussed), the trial in the *Apology*, where Socrates is a defendant and not an inquirer, standing before an audience which has a life-and-death power over him. The first of this series in dramatic time, the *Euthyphro*, also deals with judicial circumstances, but obliquely and ironically; there is a silent irony that Socrates is on the eve of being convicted as he engages in his discussion with Euthyphro, an irony that overrides and conditions all the specific, more usual ironies, of the interchanges that in this case are closest of all four dialogues to the pattern elenchic situation of the early dialogues. Questions about morality with specific reference to the gods are confined to this dialogue of the four (*Euthyphro*, 8). The other three, whatever else they ask, take the gods for granted.

Euthyphro, as a blind unjust accuser within the family, and as an unreflective professional with respect to the gods, is inversely symmetrical to Socrates, and his circularity around "the holy" contrasts with the exemplification of ordinary justice in Socrates' devotion to the gods, not just in the family sphere but publicly, as it is shown especially in the *Apology*, but in the *Crito* and the *Phaedo* as well. It is ominous that, just before Socrates' trial, Euthyphro, a representative if exaggerated custodian of religious values, is so unresponsive to the *elenchos* in his sanctimoniousness. He provides a social base for the attitude of the judges, sealing off the possibility of dialogue by his automatic response.

In the *Euthyphro* Socrates is engaged in conversation with someone who by contrast with Socrates advertises his self-satisfaction. Euthyphro ignores the very large distress engulfing Socrates that Socrates himself allows to pass by, even though the possibility of dire conviction hangs over the dialogue for him and us. Thus does he demonstrate a capacity he once again demonstrates in the *Phaedo*, and more resoundingly, of being able to carry on the *elenchos* in the face of death. The *elenchos*, in this context, proves the selflessness of Socrates' devotion to moulding good citizens, even in so casual and unpromising an encounter as this one with Euthyphro—an encounter which is unpromising because Euthyphro armors himself in a blind devotion to the very gods Socrates will be condemned for supposedly contemning by the very fact of entering an *elenchos*. The living situation, and the best way to teach the connections among knowledge, virtue, the holy, the public life, the private life, and the soul to other citizens, are all embodied in the image of the central figure, in each case properly angled for the question he both bears upon and discusses. Yet this Socrates stands already under the shadow of a future trial that qualifies his utterances.

Euthyphro from the beginning (3b-c) is careful not to get into open debate, but the *elenchos* proceeds relentlessly. As a soothsayer Euthyphro is the opposite of Socrates—more speculative about the gods, and at the same time more conventional. In his attitude toward himself, and also in his posture toward others, he is self-centered and self-protective and self-righteous, perverting family values by his heedlessness to them, indiscriminate in his complicated case.

The comparison between the two is emphasized at the outset by Euthyphro's assumption that Socrates, like himself, has come to the King's Porch not as a defendant but as a plaintiff, and he sees his own prophetic powers as analogous to the *daimonion* of Socrates. Yet they are on opposite sides not only of the court but of an attitude toward the gods. Euthyphro is "piously" bringing a charge of manslaughter by neglect against his own father for leaving a murderer to die bound in a ditch.[5] He sees this rigidity and self-importance as a proper "holiness," where Socrates, confronting constantly both in the charge and in this dialogue what holiness truly means, is called an innovator, a "poet about the gods" (ποιητής θεῶν, 3b). And later (6c) Euthyphro says that poets make up stories about gods, which echoes the charge that Socrates has reported. Where Socrates is accused of corrupting the next generation—which he stresses in the metaphor about young plants in his initial description ("the able farmer will give his attention to the young plants first," 2d)—Euthyphro is actually violating the family pieties about the prior generation. Socrates tries to take the pride of Euthyphro as a handle in getting him to defend Socrates, but the interlocutor misses this cue, as he misses every other, in a way that is ominous for how the Athenians judging Socrates will assess his arguments. They will turn out, just like Euthyphro, to substitute blind censoriousness for true piety. Over the irony, then, that this superhypocrite walks free while Socrates will be condemned, there plays the further irony that his situation is a reverse mirror of Socrates'. Towards the end Socrates continues the identification, though ironically; it is Euthyphro, he says, not Daedalus' descendant Socrates, who has been manipulating the argument like the famous mobile statues of Daedalus, with the result that they have come right round in a circle. This reversion is the more ominous that in this instance the *elenchos* lacks its usual function of sharpening the mind of the interlocutor, which is felt to happen even in dialogues where no progress has been made.

Again uniquely, the speakers stand before two single, specific, public events, Euthyphro's arraignment of his father and Socrates' preparation for his defense. These two trials do not just add qualification to the encounter, as does the festival of Bendis before the discussion of the *Republic*. The two trials center and orient the bearing of the discussion. Euthyphro's casual assumption of priestly solidarity gives him the function of a Job's comforter here. Socrates' cross-questioning about holiness is aimed at giving Euthyphro pause; at inducing him to doubt about the arraignment. But Euthyphro's failure to consider, or even raise, this possibility, hints at a corollary obtuseness in the judges of Socrates, and leaves the theological discussion hanging in the air as it touches on the forms and on the mystery of how holiness cannot be defined as that which is pleasing to the gods. The advanced notion that holiness cannot be conceived of as either prior to the gods' pleasure or posterior to it escapes Euthyphro entirely and is left as an austere, Pyrrhic conclusion for the Socrates who heroically continues producing definitions under these conditions.[6]

Euthyphro says he has never made a prediction that did not come true (3c), but then predicts Socrates will carry his case (3e). Socrates himself in the *Apology* (39e) will make the more accurate prediction, based not on vague good will but on an exact sense of his situation.

As for the questions in the *Euthyphro* about the relation between fear and reverence—these definitions can be brought to bear on the other three dialogues. They would help define a tone of equanimity maintained in the face of danger. They are evaded here by Euthyphro, to whom the *elenchos,* ominously, ends by doing no good. Is the holy just? (11e). This large question cannot get off the ground under these conditions. The real difficulty of the questions about the holy, and the further incapacity of Euthyphro to understand the difficulty (let alone participate in solving it), has a further corollary in the difficulty of defining what its opposite, impiety, might be, in the charge against Socrates. Indeed this question is so elusive that in his defense he wisely refrains from any such rarefied definitions, and instead confines himself to pleading piety along the conventional lines whose contours we can measure from the philosophical superiority of the discussion in the *Euthyphro* to that in the *Apology*.

3.

The *Apology* is not a dialogue; rather, it shows a defendant on a charge that could be (and has turned out to be) mortal, conducting his defense under conditions that empty dialogue of its exploratory force. The pressure of concentrating circumstance in this work is so great as to subvert the possibility of Socrates' constant method. And Meletus easily frustrates his one attempt to get a dialogue going in the court. The *Apology* begins with ominous abruptness by quoting Socrates' answer to charges that are not yet given. In other dialogues the speakers all proceed under the risk of returning to square one of the question or questions asked, and they do so more or less willingly, even Euthyphro. But even if they do return to square one, they are enriched by some momentary clarification, and also by having experienced the possibility of clarification. They have, minimally, been trained for the *elenchos*, and such training is presented as the road for proceeding to "know thyself"—largely a knowledge of starting with the clarification that you so far do not know. The *Apology* has Socrates assert the self-definition of "know thyself" while withdrawing, under pressure, the means of its realization.

In what could well be Socrates' actual recorded words, or an edited version of them,[7] it is assumed that square one is the best that can be hoped for; if Socrates were to be returned to his normal life he would not be intellectually enriched, only spared. Even if his judges had gone so far to accede to his reasonable but contextually absurb proposal that his punishment be to be fed for life at public expense (36d-37a), they for their part would still not have been enlightened. They would simply have performed the just decision which Socrates' acquiescence in it shows is their normative function (though in this instance unjust). Of course he is neither spared nor honored but first voted guilty and then condemned to death. This condition leads back to his being a normative exemplum, since "many other good men have been caught" in the emotional undertow that governs the process of the trial which carries the ironical name of a "justice" (δίκη, 28b). There is, he says, "no danger of the rule breaking in my case" (οὐδὲν δὲ δεινὸν μὴ ἐν ἐμοὶ στῆι). It will "stand." And so Socrates stands fast in the law though caught in the emotional undertow that governs the law, a living *elenchos*.

Still, Socrates does lay bare paradox after paradox in the charge against him. If the charge could be made to hold, effactually, it would still not be true in a deeper sense. This argument holds both with regard to the gods, and with regard to teaching the youth. At the same time he "will construct arguments in my usual way," (ἐν τῶι εἰθότι τρόπωι τούς λόγους ποιῶμαι, 27b), and this permits him easily to extract the admission from his accuser that to believe in divine activities is to believe in divine beings. Not then to be acquitted does reveal that "what will catch me, if it does, is not Meletus or Anytus but the slander and envy of the multitude" (28b). Socrates is right in this counteraccusation. His correct, but fatally incapable, assessment that such slander underlies the accusations has led him from the beginning (18d, where "slander and envy" is first introduced) to build his speech on the circumstance of old and new slander. Many times through the whole of his speech he invokes the noun and verb for slander—based on a verb (διαβάλλω) which emphasizes the displacement of the allegation from its object. This begins the paradox that he is proved right in his assessment by the conviction that declares him wrong; to show the old accusers wrong will not stay the new accusers.

The *Apology* (33c) refers in passing to the entertainment value of conducting an *elenchos* and the possibility of distraction. Entertainment and distraction are just the increments that cannot accrue to the discourse here, though even on the threshold of death they are not wholly absent from the *Phaedo*, with its kindly, pious, celebratory politeness, a tone for very good reasons not to be found so strongly in dialogues of less dire circumstance. In the *Apology* Socrates stands constrained to carry out an *elenchos* combined with a speech, whereas in the *Gorgias*, the *Protagoras*, and elsewhere, as well as in the *Phaedo* (among this group), he presents a dignitary delivering a set speech against which he contrasts an *elenchos*. Protagoras, after delivering a speech in the *Protagoras*, initially refuses the *elenchos* on the grounds that "if I had let my opponent declare the method of my presentation, I would not be famous in Greece" (335a). Now this is just what the court circumstances force Socrates to do. He is constrained to make the speech, which is foreign to his nature and shown in Plato's dialogues as intrinsically constraining for anybody, whatever the person might think.

Belief in the god keeps him from being willing to offer the condition of desisting from philosophy if he is guilty of not believing in god (29d-30). Here Socrates takes the unusual circumstance that is not a pair of philosophical assertions but a pair of legal charges. "There is nothing greater in the city," he says, "than service to the god" (30a). He also combines both parts of the charge and turns them upon each other and around. His last word is of the god he has been condemned for not believing in or innovating about. Throughout he has assumed that the court is governed by emotional prejudice, and there is a tradition of making an emotional appeal to it that he will not avail himself of (35c). He holds up a model of how the court should act by standing on argument rather than emotional appeal. Therefore the very circumstances he invokes in his trial rebuke the judges and bear witness to best judgment.

The Arginusae case, to which he refers, in which he would not co-operate in helping arrest for execution the admirals supposedly implicated in that defeat (32c), is in a sense an earlier version of factors that will stymie the trial.[8]

Socrates addresses not inquirers but judges, and the reply comes not in words but in votes: of guilty, then of death. In the cross-examination of Meletus he acts as a defendant and not just as a philosopher; it is not a voluntary act he is performing here. Still, he invokes the *elenchos,* and on a subject about which he has long been seasoned, how to educate the youth. The replies of Meletus, however, are cruelly curt, almost insulting; and they are far from being truly responsive, to say nothing of their constituting arguments. Refutation, under these constraints, provides neither enlightenment nor exoneration. It irritates and enrages, tipping the jury, presumably, further toward the first conviction (281 to 220), because his next proposals and defenses tip them still further toward the death penalty (360 to 141).

"The unexamined life is not worth living" (38c), and Socrates makes this statement in his initial response to the act of conviction, serenely continuing to examine his own life under this maximum duress, filling out this exemplum in the imagined context, before his sentencing, of how he should live if they let him. Both what he has chosen to say and the conditions under which he says it base his defense on the exemplum of himself.

4.

The *Crito* begins with a reference to the return of the ship of Delos which will signal Socrates' execution, as does the *Phaedo*, and it also opens from an account of a dream, the vision of a woman in white who tells him he will be going to the other world by quoting a line of Homer. This framework picks up the notion expanded at the end of the *Apology* when the desireability of the other world is characterized by the dead man's access to the poets and heroes of the past

(40d-41c). This possibility sets the scene and the tone for Socrates' confrontation, uniquely in this dialogue, of an actual and extremely momentous choice, whether or not to accept the proposal that he escape with the help of the friends who have sent Crito on the errand of finding this out. He casts his refusal in the form of a truncated dialogue, deferred at the end by a long imagined speech put in the mouth of "the laws," who expound a sort of categorical imperative that for them to exist they must be obeyed precisely when they are to a man's disadvantage. In the *Apology* Socrates makes the distinction between uncertain justice and the justice of the judges of the afterworld, "Minos and Rhadamanthus and Aeacus and Triptolemos" (41a). Here the principle of a higher justice is entailed by piety towards the city that has reared him, embodied in its laws. Duty to city is of the same kind as duty to father, but greater (50d). And the term touched on for piety, σέβεσθαι (51b), exactly reverses the charge of impiety, ἀσέβεια, on which he had been condemned.

Here, under radically transformed circumstances, the path of the *Euthyphro* continues to be followed, "the just" once more recombining with "the holy" (51c). Socrates has been hurt by men and not by the laws (54b), and if he were to move to another city he would not be himself because the ground on which he exercises his characteristic activity would be taken from him by his act of inconsistency towards the laws, and towards the principle, often repeated here and elsewhere in his work, that suffering harm is preferable to doing it (53a-54b). As always in these four dialogues, he is an exemplum. What counts is "not living but living well ... beautifully and justly" (48b). This entails dying to be consistent with himself (46). The many do what they happen to do, whether sensible or senseless (44d). If he builds on opinions, he will build on sensible ones (47a), and this emphasis on the opinions of the wise, too, refers the activity of discourse to the personal example, as the personal example is also measured by its activity, of which this dialogue is itself a succinct example, as well as an exploration of a moral question and the record of an actual decision.

5.

The *Apology* ends in a coda over whether there is an afterlife, in an aporia, "To die is one of two things: either the dead man will be as nothing, having no perception of anything; or according to report there will be some change and transfer for the soul of place from here to another place" (40c). "I am to die, you are to live; which of these comes to the best result is unclear to anyone except the god" (42). The principle of Socrates' wisdom as one who knows he does not know is asserted here to the very end; the doubt he asserts under the fresh death sentence proves him to be true to himself.

Obviously the *Phaedo* proclaims a far greater certitude on this question. It contradicts the aporia of the *Apology*; and on the alternative about the afterlife, the preponderant view of Plato himself if we are to judge from the *Republic*, the *Gorgias* and elsewhere, it offers a far more elaborate account and rationale, but one that is situational with respect to the final hope of Socrates. The *Phaedo* is to be integrated into the range of responses in this final phase, if also into the development of his ideas. Yet it should be remembered that the situation is in the text, while the development is conjectural, and based on the questionable assumption of consistent evolution.

Death frames all four of these dialogues, but the *Phaedo* most impendingly. Pitched dramatically at the moment of death, the *Phaedo*, at the same time, is the most speculative philosophically, the longest, and the most intricately reasoned. The *Phaedo* (70d) implies that transmigration may or may not be true. So do other passages in the dialogue, and notably the large shift from the proofs of the first half to the hypotheses of the latter half.

One guide to the complexity of the *Phaedo*, and also to its single-mindedness, and even to its resultant sketchiness on many topics germane to its discussion, is the initial situation. Its frame is set long after the actual event and very far away from it, unlike the other three, which are set at the (itself distant) time in Athens. Phaedo is at a distant place and a later time, looking back as he tells his Pythagorean host about a discussion Socrates had with two other Pythagoreans just before his execution. The initial complexity of this situation matches and projects the arguments about the immortality of the soul, which are in turn implied by, or at least consonant with, the assumptions of the other three dialogues. Those assumptions are preliminary to the dialogue, however, because it moves to the full argument of long-range notions that can be taken in turn as preliminary to them, involving the god mentioned at the very end of the *Apology* and constantly adduced in the *Crito*. The *Phaedo* gives both a range of what a soul can attain through philosophy—the *theion genos*— and what a clear view a soul either freed from the body or uncontaminated by it might attain.

Especially in so complex a dialogue as the *Phaedo*, too great a focus on the clarities of Plato's sometimes close-marshaled reasoning in specific nodal points of ongoing definition—the mode of Vlastos— may result in a stated opposition between rational and irrational elements in Plato (Hackforth, 1981, 101, citing Dodds). Yet as just the phrase θεῖος λόγος (85d4) implies,[9] Plato conceived of the divine not as irrational, Dodds' subject, but as rational. Putting a passing use of this phrase in the mouth of a Pythagorean might be taken to imply that some questions would have to be left begging, however great a claim the speaker might lay to rationality. In speaking of his own aporia, Simmias imagines that it is "difficult or impossible to know clearly" about the topics under discussion. The *elenchos* and other means they employ are like "sailing through life dangerously on a raft, unless one could make one's way through more safely and less dangerously upon a firmer support, some *theios logos*." Here, in the mode of the same metaphor that Socrates uses later on for the "second sailing" of hypothesis, the *theios* is beyond, and inclusive, and endorsing of reasons. Moreover, γνῶθι σεαυτόν has its origins in the oracle of Apollo, though it is also a defining apophthegm for the goal of the *elenchos*. Plato has Socrates propound one repertoire of possibilities for the afterlife in what, seen minimally, are two proof-modes of demonstration and hypothesis.

The opening question exactly frames the interaction between the situation of the condemned Socrates and his topic of discourse, "What did the man say before his death and how did he die?" (57a). The trial is then mentioned, and passed over, not as irrelevant, but as not needing summary. What gave this group the possibility of holding the discussion was first the permission of the rulers; it is stated that they did not forbid Socrates' friends access to him. And, most protractedly, the enabling condition is the delay of the embassy to Delos sent in memory of the "seven pairs" (of youths and maidens) that Theseus saved from sacrifice, "the Athenians say," on the last annual embassy to Crete. Since the embassy is in honor of Apollo, in whose service Socrates has spoken of spending his life (*Apology*, 23c), and whom he will shortly honor by composing poetry, the "unnecessary" story of these circumstances invites an inquiry as to the analogues between the embassy to Delos and the execution of Socrates. The embassy commemorates an execution forestalled by a leader who saved groups of youths and so the state; at the same time the state has decreed the execution of Socrates on the false charges of corrupting the youths (whom he continues to be in the act of "saving") and of failing to honor gods, when it is especially this god, Apollo, whom he continues to honor. A residual sacrifice is commemorated without being carried through, while at the same time an execution is being decreed which, in a modern context, looks like a sort of sacrifice.[10] For Crete Athens substitutes Delos; since Athens is in the position of unjustly demanding the death of Socrates, it has put itself in the position of Crete, and not even of all of Crete, since the good side of Cretan organization serves Plato frequently as a model of good government.

The situation cannot be changed, but it can be modified by the delay brought about by chance (τύχη). The chance is actually a double one: that the beginning of the embassy should happen to fall the day after the condemnation of Socrates, and that the winds should delay the round-trip voyage of the ship. (Socrates cannot make any trip out of Athens, and he has refused a one-way trip in the *Crito*.)

Before the summary of the long discussion is given, the mood is described; Socrates is "happy" or "blest in being happy" (εὐδαίμων). Consequently he evokes no pity. And the first answer to the initial question, "how did he die" (the expression is repeated, 58e4), describes his mode, a mixture of pleasure and pain which is spoken of as "unusual" (ἀήθης). The possibility of such an unusual mixture makes it analogous in its fullness (συγκραμένη) to the later attunement of elements, the "harmonia" in the soul. The unusualness associates Socrates to those of heroic virtue who enjoy the higher salvation in the *Gorgias* and the *Republic*. This mood is spoken of as modifying the accustomed "pleasure" of philosophical discussion—an assertion that shades the mood into the flow of the discussion while at the same time subjecting the discussion to the mood—a philosophy that will soon be characterized, but only provisionally, as "the highest music."

Remarking on his leg pains, Socrates comments on the "seeming opposites," the minimal variants of physical pleasure and pain that he calls the "sweet" and the "troublesome,"[11] describes them as "attached to one head," and projects a fable of Aesop that does not exist about them; if Aesop had written such a fable, it would tell about how the god had tried to separate them but could not, and so he attached them. Aesop, too, is analogous in some ways to the Socrates who is then declared to have set Aesop's fables to verse (and perhaps also to music), after first writing a hymn to Apollo.[12] The Delphians, citizens of that other city sacred to Apollo, falsely accused Aesop of the crime of sacrilege, as Socrates has been accused of impiety; they then, citing an oracle, absolved of guilt anyone who would kill Aesop, as one man finally did (Herodotus 2. 134).

The poems are written to discharge a sacred obligation enjoined upon Socrates by a repeated dream "to make this music" (60e). The whole activity is further explicitly connected to the fact that "the festival of the god prevented me from dying" (61a), so that he could then make "that which people call music."[13] He claims that to obey this injunction is safer, thus linking the act of poeticizing to the presumptive redemption of the philosopher acting as poet, making "mythoi but not logoi,"[14] since he is not a "mythologikos."(61b). Evenus, to whom he is imagining this reply, in his personal situation presents the same two constituents, philosopher and poet, in a slightly different mix, since he is a Sophist and an established elegist. Yet there will be a slight revision when Socrates says (61e) that it is fitting to mythologize about the beyond—a declaration that turns "philosophy is the highest music" once more back on itself. All the intricacies of these connections are matched by the ambiguity, noted by Hackforth, in the *logos* about suicide. Suicide is more simply forbidden by the Philolaus who had been the master of Simmias and Cebes when alive. A further answer is given by the adduced analogy to "the logos spoken about them in the acts about which it cannot be spoken" (ἀπορρήτοις, "the mysteries").

The question about suicide, to begin with, is a sort of countercase to the *Crito*, since there Socrates opts for what could be called a passive suicide. But more precisely here he simply welcomes death (63b) because he will be in the presence of (1) gods who are (2) wise and (3) good, an attribution repeated later (80d-81). At a later point (99a) the *Crito*'s question about the causal relation between body and action is ironically glanced at.[15]

The injunction not to commit suicide is backed, first of all, by the argument that the gods are good masters (62a), and Socrates asserts that in this connection he will give a better apology than he did to his judges—a reference that places this dialogue in connection with the *Apology*, and as superior to it. All this discussion about what the philosopher will do when facing death is prior to the question of what death is. The very preparation for death will lead him to have knowledge (65e)—the philosophical attitude, rather than the pursuit of philosophical questions. The ensuing φρόνησις is a "wisdom" far more powerful here than the "practical intelligence" later ascribed to the term.[16] This will put him in a position of overcoming the desires, fears, loves, and phantasms of the body (65a), and as a purified spirit to comprise virtue itself in such virtues as courage, "prudence," and "justice" (68), here offered as a simple list guaranteed in their true (as opposed to false) manifestations by "purity," where the whole of the *Republic* is concerned with ascertaining what δικαιοσύνη may be, and large portions of other dialogues devote considerable elenchic energy to the others—to courage (*Laches*), to σωφροσύνη (*Gorgias, Protagoras*), not to speak of the large, intricate question of ἀρετή itself.

Here these virtues are easily comprised in an attitude rather than an *elenchos*, and they are sketchily listed as the result of a purification attained through attitude, and through a mood of the "hope" Socrates speaks of. "Fair is the contest, and the hope great" (καλὸν γὰρ τὸ ἆθλον καί ἡ ἐλπὶς μεγάλη, 114c). Perhaps echoing the earlier reference to hope (70a), the very intonation pattern of this sentence almost seems to assimilate to the term's Christian sense, but in any case it radiates a confidence, of equanimity and something more than equanimity, that must be accounted a rich base for the message of this dialogue. The concept of "purification" keeps recurring here, having first been introduced casually and, as it were, routinely, in the account of what the embassy to Apollo does for the city. This purification, bringing the deathlike philosopher who is almost free of the body to his φρόνησις, allows for a principle of "exchange" beyond the simple trade of pleasure for pleasure, pain for pain, fear for fear, etc. (69a). And all of these attainments come about through the detachment from the body, rather than from the proper philosophical definitions which, in this presentation, it precedes.

The philosopher, or rather "those who have philosophized rightly" (πεφιλοσοφηκότες ὀρθῶς) are effectually compared to Bacchants; it is not clear that there is not some commutative spillover, since being a Bacchant may also purify, notably for the few successful Bacchants among the many who aspire to that state (69d). In fact this whole passage condenses the intellectual, the religious, and the spiritual affirmations of Socrates, since the φρόνησις which is alone the "right coin" allowing for "exchange" (of "pleasure for pleasure, grief for grief," etc.) is incommensurate with that which it "buys and sells," and that incommensurability, taken logically, presents insoluble puzzles as a calculus of pleasures is at once invoked and transcended. The overriding term "intelligence," applied to elements of exchange, recalls the Heraclitean formula in which fire is an overriding term that governs the exchange of gold for goods and goods for gold (B90). And there is a further Heraclitean echo in the full reference at the end of this passage to Heraclitus' connection of Hades and Dionysus, and perhaps also to the mud which Plato here has Socrates say the uninitiated will lie in (69c6) when they come to Hades. These Heraclitean echoes, of course, are themselves in turn fused into the Pythagorean echoes, themselves indistinguishable here from the more regular references to initiations into the mysteries (τελεταί).

In this dialogue as in others one can largely derive Plato's differences of emphasis, refinements of definition, and even implied contradictions about anamnesis, the immortality of the soul, the moral constituents of the soul, and even the Forms, as readily from the structure of the dialogue in question as from a "development" in Plato. And these four dialogues insist on their structure, and even on their connection to each other, by their dependence on Socrates' actual trial. Of course the context-specificity of the dialogue does not contradict the notion of a development from dialogue to dialogue, but keeping that context-specificity in view has the advantage of focusing on the whole utterance, rather than on the runs of reasoning within it, however brilliantly worked through and centering for the dialogue itself these may be.

The kinship of the soul with the Forms is most fully stated here in Plato's work, and it is oddly appended to the doctrine of recollection, called a frequent subject for Socrates (72e), and now applied to much more than the mathematics of the *Meno*—to equals, to similar objects, to the Forms, and even to the possibility of recognizing defectiveness in the match of an individual with the Form. The optimism of the dialogue culminates here too, embracing anamnesis not only as a proof of immortality, if combined with the distinction of opposites, but as an organ enabling participation in the highest kinds of realization, in "the beautiful, the good, the just, and the holy" (79). It easily assimilates to the philosophy which is the means to break out of the threat of a bad transmigration (82d), a question more pressing here than the need to prove transmigration itself, which is taken for granted, even if not with full certitude.

There is in fact a play of certitudes through this dialogue, and the shift into a "second sailing," the "*deuteros plous*" of hypothesis, is only one among many, though especially emphasized by modern commentators who are attracted by the subtlety of the ensuing definitions about how one does build from hypothesis in Plato's fullest statement of the subject. Since Socrates undertakes the second sailing in the first place because of the impossibility of allowing Anaxagoras' causes, which even Anaxagoras seems to misapply by looking for physical causes instead of the presence of his "Mind," the second sailing is preferable in the immediate context for its applicability, though at the same time inferior as to certainty. But kinds of certainty are qualified constantly throughout the dialogue. The superlative assertion "philosophy is the greatest music" is not refuted, but it is contextually qualified as an inference mistakenly applied by Socrates to the injunction of the dream figure. His self-correcting change to "setting" fables of Aesop is also a false trail for him because he is neither poet nor "mythologos"; and the ensuing distinction between *mythoi* and *logoi* cannot be disentangled from the stated subjective limitations of Socrates or from the undispelled force of either if it were taken separately. In the passage about the "right coin" of phronesis to govern exchanges, phronesis is the result of a purification, and one that can most fully come when the soul is wholly released from the body. This is stated at the conclusion of the passage; he will know with full certainty when he gets there (69e). It is a contingency for the future as well as a possible realization for the philosopher in the present, who, in still another qualification, risks the state of being a hater of reasonings, a "misologos," if he allows mere reason to take over (84d). This confrontation of uncertainty comes at the end of a demonstration that had begun by asserting the completeness of a proof arrived at by combining the doctrine of anamnesis with the doctrine of the generation of opposites (77a). Again, without preamble a simple story, a mythos, depicts at some length (107–114) the physical and spiritual characteristics of this world and the next in a conclusion that is itself qualified as an approximation under doubt (114d). In the light of all these qualifications, and many minor ones, the *deuteros plous* of substituting propositions for sense experience (99d) is just a high point of shift in a constantly shifting presentation, one governed, as always, by the circumstance that the speaker stands imminently on the threshold of death. These are "last words."

Yet on the other hand, as in "philosophy is the highest music," there is a tone of assertion here that dominates the dialogue throughout. It rises to implied assertions in addition to the obscure foreshortening in the leap from cause to hypothesis. The θεῖος λόγος, discussed on page 43, is a possible firmer support, but one not likely to be available, though at the same time its superior *logos* is here at least envisioned. And even in moments of qualification the affirmation comes through. Socrates characterizes his discourse as one of ongoing joy, a swan song (85a). There is a persistent superlative cast to the language, even more pronouncedly than usual in Plato. So, for example, the positive terms in it give a eulogistic cast to the prevailingly cautionary sentence, "Simmias, I think, disbelieves and fears that the soul, though more godly and beautiful than the body, may nevertheless perish first, as being in a kind of attunement" (91c–d). This is true of "more godly and more beautiful," in their tone signature. It can even be said that a strong sense of "the Form of harmony" shadows the weak, main sense in the phrase "the condition of attunement." The phrase ἁρμονίας εἴδει, even though given in a summary of why Cebes thinks the soul may perish, carries a very strong undercurrent by bringing the terms of two systems into intersection. The first system comprises Plato's version of Greek harmonics in music, developed positively elsewhere, though here negative. In 89a Phaedo's reference back to the strength and beneficence of Socrates—*logoi* is itself stronger than the suggestion in ἁρμονίας εἴδει. That phrase itself in this context must be heard as preserving, under the sense of a passive attunement, a faint suggestion of the more general sense of harmonia—proportion, balance, and the like—in a dialogue where it is combined with the honorific term for the Forms which have here already been invoked (though not under that name) and will soon be named and subjected to prolonged and intense discussion. The Forms themselves stand firm as a measure for memory and a guarantee of the possible purity and permanence of the soul. Putting the two together as ἁρμονίας εἴδει grazes both systems, and it does so by way of beginning to frame a more comprehensive system in which this combination is embedded, while caught in a denial. All this is by way of advancing (and refuting) the notion that the soul is to the body as the tuning of a musical instrument. Harmony is further linked playfully to myth in the later reference to Harmonia and Cadmus (95a), a mythic residue left as a sort of affirmation in the equanimous spirit of the (prevailingly negative) summary; and it is never clear to what "Cadmus" may be taken to refer—a failure of application which is not at all bothersome in context, since both the naming of the myth and the adduction of a wholly new topic testifies to the serene inventiveness of the philosopher under stress.

The notions of the soul in its relation to the body are themselves, in turn, and specifically here, connected to the relation between knowledge and virtue, as these two will define the disposition of the soul after death. Virtue even without philosophy and mind (ἄνευ φιλοσοφίας τε καὶ νοῦ, 82b) can still bring salvation to a man who uses it, even unreflectively, in general and political life (δημοτικὴν καὶ πολιτικήν).

In these four dialogues, in abundant implied refutation of the charge of impiety against Socrates, the godly remains steadily in view. And at least four notions of the godly bear upon, modify, and possibly transcend the philosophical demonstrations: 1) the millennial embassy to Delos, and all its possible analogies to Socrates, 2) the Pythagorean ideas insofar as these are religious as distinct from philosophical, 3) the *theios logos* to which Socrates refers, as a supersession of the philosophical discussions, and 4) the simple, popular gesture at the end of Socrates' last words, "I owe a cock to Asclepius."

None of these four notions overlaps exactly with the large piety into which the Socrates of the *Apology* swells as he receives the death sentence. The view of the afterlife then, a wise conversation of spirits in the realm of Hades, matches not one of the possibilities of salvation and restriction that are laid out in the *Phaedo* (leaving accounts in other dialogues aside)—not even the long discussions about the realm of Hades which amplify the possibilities of the afterlife without suggesting that happy conversation would be included among them. Nor is any of these five notions of religiosity coterminous with the elaborate *elenchos* about the holy in the *Euthyphro*, where Socrates is engaged in conversation with someone who ignores the very large distress he himself allows to pass by, thus proving the selflessness of a devotion to framing good citizens and men with a respect for the very gods he was condemned for contemning.

In the *Phaedo* the whole discussion about logical procedures with hypothesis is, among other things, metalinguistic in constituting a description of the *elenchos*. This fullest of Plato's accounts of hypothesis here has the character of an introspection about already existing method rather than a search for a new one, and it is not clear that the *deuteros plous* is really a second best.[17] Coming before death, it simultaneously gives up on arguing the tentativeness out of inquiry, settles for that tentativeness, and declares a nobility to inhere in the tentativeness which the auditors are seen—at a great distance of time and place—to share. The immortality of the soul is thus enacted in a discussion about it, by a man unjustly condemned to death, glancing indirectly off the gods, if with many strands of assent, that in some ways go beyond Sophocles, Aeschylus (108a), and Euripides, and in other ways do not. Since Plato contents himself with their explorations, fails to extend them, and stays indirect while being syncretic about the gods, he is intellectually more exploratory but at the same time more archaic than they (as Homer is more archaic than his time) and more advanced (as Homer also is).

"It is not easy to show, nor is time sufficient in the present circumstance," "οὔτε ῥάδιον δηλῶσαι οὔτε ὁ χρόνος ἱκανὸς ἐν τῶι παρόντι" (114c). This is a pair of reasons that are themselves conditions of, and also constraints upon, discourse—and both vague. Does "not easily" mean "it could be done with difficulty," or is it litotes for it can't be done? A middle term puts it in an athletic-eschatological metaphor, "Fair is the contest, and the hope great." This seems to match with radiant equanimity the "fair danger," the *kalos kindunos*, it would be to believe. Which is not at all the same thing as saying it would be false to do so. All this amounts to a further level of qualification from the *deuteros plous*. But the match between the soul disposition in the concluding myth and that offered earlier in the *Phaedo* might be taken to extend the qualification backward, equanimity encompassing all dangers, including that of logical gaps and even possible errors, bringing to a large coda, at once questioning and optimistic, Plato's act of connecting this great range of topics to four points around the trial and death of Socrates. Thus is implicitly asserted a relation between the questions raised and an actual life—or between ideas and history. That, too, is a connection Plato addressed complexly, so much so that to assess that connection would involve an even longer discussion.

Notes

1. Nonce references to the trial, like the explicit one at the very end of the *Theaetetus*, or implied ones, like the presence and posture of Anytus toward the end of the *Meno*, do not orient those dialogues but merely import still another qualification.

2. R. Hackforth, *Plato's Phaedo* (Cambridge: Cambridge University Press, 1981 [1955]), 7, "The *Phaedo* is notably silent regarding political institutions and government; its ethics are wholly individualistic." This can be the case only if we ignore the situation and do not bring the argument of the *Crito*, set just hours beforehand, upon this dialogue. Socrates' situation is

a public one; he is held after a trial, and his execution has been delayed because of a rule that no public killing can take place while the annual embassy to Delos is underway. The word for "public," δημόσιαι, is the standard word in Plato for the contrast with "private," ἰδίαι. W. D. Ross, who treats doctrinal variations as a main factor in dating, well summarizes and tabulates the various views on the sequence of the dialogues, in *Plato's Theory of Ideas* (Oxford: Clarendon Press, 1951, 2), though to see these dialogues in a dated sequence with all the others will obscure their connection with one another.

3. They include Phaedo himself; the reported inquirer Echecrates, a Pythagorean; Cebes, who is possibly an adherent of the Megarian school, designated along with Simmias as a pupil of Philolaus; Apollodorus, associated with Socrates; Aristippus, called by Diogenes Laertius a hedonist Cyrenaic; Critoboulos and his father Crito; Euclides; Terpsion; Hermogenes; Epigenes; Aeschines; Antisthenes; Ctesippus of Paeene; Menexenus to whom a dialogue was devoted; "and others." (59b). Aristippus and Cleombrotus should even be counted in the census, since they are named as potential auditors who happen to be absent in Aegina, and so should Plato himself, who "was sick."

4. For a discussion of Socrates' attitudes in the complex legal situation of his conviction, see Richard Kraut, *Socrates and the State* (Princeton: Princeton University Press, 1984).

5. Indeed, like father like son, the father has also tied up a murderer, as Euthyphro is metaphorically doing to his father, whatever might be the outcome of the trial, something of which we have no hint. Euthyphro connects his situation to that of Zeus "whom men consider best and most just of the gods," who also tied up his father who had in turn castrated *his* father (6a).

6. See Martha Nussbaum, *The Fragility of Goodness* (Cambridge: Cambridge University Press, 1986), 25. She stresses that Socrates in the *Euthyphro* (7e-8e) questions the traditional Greek notion that the gods press divergent claims. These questions about priorities are elaborated in Paul Elmer More, *The Religion of Plato* (Princeton: Princeton University Press, 1921).

7. M. I. Finley offers no evidence for his conjecture that these are not Socrates' actual words other than the fact that legends did accrue to his person. See "Socrates and Athens," in *Aspects of Antiquity* (New York: Viking, 1968), 58–72. But speeches were also regularly written, and regularly preserved, even in far less famous trials. Why would Socrates not have used his rhetorical skills to follow the regular routine, and why, given the fame of the trial at the actual moment, would his speech have been lost when so many trivial ones were preserved? The burden of proof for having the *Apology* be an invention of Plato's—as are all the other dialogues—

would rest on those who would assert that it is not the recorded speech, even if perhaps modified along Thucydidean lines. One balanced account is offered in R. Hackforth, *The Composition of Plato's Apology* (Cambridge: Cambridge University Press, 1933), 1–7. Another is offered by W. K. C. Guthrie, *A History of Greek Philosophy* (Cambridge: Cambridge University Press, 1975), IV, 72–79. For its rhetorical structure, its parody of rhetoric, its essential accuracy, and its service as a later model for Isocrates' *Antidosis*, see Reginald E. Allen, *The Dialogues of Plato* (New Haven: Yale University Press, 1984), I, 63–75.

8.   This is a real back-reference, rare in the dialogues, to Socrates' connection with specific political events, where other back-references tend to be to personal involvements, like Socrates' history with Alcibiades in the *Symposium* or philosophical ones like his training under Prodicus in the *Protagoras* and the *Meno*.

9.   Jean Van Camp and Paul Conart in *Le Sens du mot theios chez Platon* (Louvain: Publications Universitaires, 1956) often trace a mythological or hyperbolic sense in the word. But in the *Phaedo*, it acquires "une étonnante souplesse" (63). It is especially complicated when love is in question, in the *Symposium* (75–88).

10.   L. R. Farnell lists a number of ancient references to such embassies in antiquity, most of them not so full of detail as the one here (which he includes in his citations), *The Cults of the Greek States* (Oxford: Oxford University Press, 1909), IV, 417–419.

11.   The question comes up again (83c-d). The rudimentary philosophy here keys this passage to many discussions of pleasure in the *Philebus* and elsewhere. (Hackforth gives a list, 49.) The general Greek context is discussed by J. C. B. Gosling and C. C. W. Taylor, *The Greeks on Pleasure* (Oxford: Clarendon Press, 1982). Their chapter "Bodily Pleasure in the *Phaedo*" (83–95), in their generally enlightening emphasis on the tradition of a physiological basis for pleasure, concentrates on the rejection of bodily pleasure, and on "the attack on hedonistic calculation," rather than on what is implied by the "seeming opposites" (which they do touch on, 86), on *phronesis*, and on *katharsis*. Their focus cannot let Socrates' strong emphasis on the soul as opposed to the body, or his optimism and superlative language about "purity," come much into the picture.

12.   In 85b Apollo is once again associated with music, this time to the swan song which the whole dialogue is effectually declared to be. The last reference to Apollo may be conceived to be that of the last words of Socrates, "I owe a cock to Asklepius," since that god is the son of Apollo and closely associated with him. Such a sacrifice would be in a medical context the more purely pious because of no immediate use to the dead man who is having this debt discharged after his death. (With Hackforth [1981, 190] we may second Wilamowitz in rejecting the notion that Socrates is

being cured of the sickness of life, a notion he nowhere advances.) The arresting irrelevance of this statement complicates the question about the analogies, beyond the pious act, which might bring it into relevance here. This could be the only explicit reference to a sacrifice in all of Plato, to which in general he avoids referring. (Just the *Seventh Letter*, the *Republic* and the *Laws* use the root "sphag", in addition to a reference at *Menexenus* 242c7).

13. A more popular sense of singing is used metaphorically in the expanded reference to the necessity of "singing (charms to the child) every day until you have sung away (the bogey-tale that the soul also dies at death)," 77e-78a.

14. Ronna Burger states the alternatives as those between mythos and logos, though by the series of implied propositions referred to above, poetry and the logos (of philosophy) are emphatically of the same kind and so cannot in this context be given the normal contrast of opposition so common in Plato as to be a recurrent phrase. "The Aesopian mythos thus assumes what the Socratic account makes into a problem: What is the so-called pleasant or the painful? It is because it implicitly raises this question—at least once it is contrasted with mythos—that Socrates' account can be labeled a logos." Ronna Burger, *The* Phaedo: *A Platonic Labyrinth* (New Haven: Yale University Press, 1984), 27.

15. Crito's arrangements return the discussion to practice where the recommendations lead to their future, and there are, Burger reminds us (115), references to law, (encapsulating the *Crito*) and to religion at the very end (a further capping answer in the *Apology*).

16. So, for example, stronger than mere practical intelligence is the φρόνησις of 76c, which the souls have before birth, and which then allows them to take up "knowledges" (ἐπιστήμας) in the plural. In 79d φρόνησις is a "reception" or "experience" (πάθημα) of what is pure and immortal.

17. Gregory Vlastos' discussion on reasons and causes "Reasons and Causes in the *Phaedo*," *Platonic Studies*, 76–109. for all its great discrimination and sharpness, cannot cut the simplicity and ambiguity of this phrase. Further, the whole discussion of 109–110, about what Socrates has been brought to believe (πέπεισμαι), about man's position in the heaven and earth of a mythical cosmology, may be taken to qualify Vlastos' argument. The *deuteros plous* is classified as only one of three levels of certainty—or better, of bearings towards solutions—and the governing posture of Socrates, as demonstrated before death, supervenes over even so clear and intricate a series as Vlastos has taught us to see. The series is irrevocably subordinate as well as toughly worked out. Further, as Julius Stenzel says (*Plato's Method of Dialectic*, 47): "In the Phaedo ... the 'chorismos' ... between experience and the Idea ... is at its widest ... but ...

the question what are methexis and parousia is pronounced to be entirely irrelevant" (100d). As Hans-Georg Gadamer more positively puts it, in *Dialogue and Dialectic: Eight Hermeneutical Studies on Plato*, translated and with an introduction by P. Christopher Smith (New Haven and London: Yale University Press, 1980):

> It is true, of course, that it is not until the *Parmenides* and the *Philebus* that the *methexis* problem is developed so radically that the participation of the many particulars in the one idea converts into the participation of ideas in one another. *However, the role played by the hypothesis of the eidos in the argument of the* Phaedo *implies this very solution.* There it is shown that "soul" is always together with "life" and never with "death," "two" always with "even" and never with "odd," "warm" always with "fire" and never with "snow" (137–138).

Chapter 3

Dialectic, Irony, and Myth in Plato's *Phaedrus*

1.

"Surely at this point," Socrates says near the end of the *Phaedrus*, "let it be that matters about *logoi* have been played through for us proportionately"[1] (278b). The verb "play"[2] cannot be confined to any utterances less than the whole dialogue, though the immediate reference is to a discussion about *logoi* in the writing and speech. Socrates treats not just this speech playfully; playfulness pervades the dialogue.

Socrates in the *Phaedrus* goes on further to qualify by suggesting a future logical test (*elenchos*, 278c) of the writings of Lysias or anyone else, and among the writers put on a par for future testing, Homer, the writers of odes, and Solon. His doing so introduces within this one dialogue three different, and irreconcilable, views about poetry—one that places it higher than other utterances (245a),[3] another here that puts it on a par, and a third (259c-d; 264e) that somewhat denigrates it, in terms different from the censure on poetry in the *Republic* and the *Laws*. The first and second views, indeed, can be found in this one passage, since Phaedrus is to go tell Lysias that he and Socrates got these *logoi* empowering them to question and judge where they "went down into the vale of the nymphs and the Muses and heard their words" (278b).[4] Again, the irony that hovers over the reference to the nymphs and the Muses does not vacate the relation of the religious and mythical domains to Socrates' propositions, embedded, we may say, always in much different material, rather than enchained, as modern philosophers would organize them. Moreover, the linking of their utterances to the fact of their betaking themselves to a particular spot frames them and further qualifies them, by a dramatic context.

2.

Eros is the subject under discussion, and the discussion is conditioned by being offered not in the form of an elenchic discourse between Socrates and Phaedrus but rather in the form of a speech that Socrates fashions to compete with the prior speech of Lysias. It is aimed, then, ambiguously at the form of Lysias' speech, to which Socrates refers, and at the content.

So far as the content is concerned, it discusses only two main topics, rhetoric and love, though these prove to entail notions of large import for Plato elsewhere—poetry, the gods, good and evil, prudence (σωφροσύνη), the Ideas, and the transmigration of souls. And it presents *aporiai* for all these topics. Socrates begins with a story about a lover of youth, in whose mouth he then places a speech. Within the speech Socrates has the lover himself begin with the very same thesis (τοῦτ' αὐτό, 237b) that Lysias has propounded—though it is soon qualified. The speaker is made to begin, in rudimentary Socratic fashion, at square one. The beginning he enjoins (ἀρχή, 237c) asks for a definition of ἔρως, and produces one without elenchic intermediation: "It is apparent to all that eros is a desire [ἐπιθυμία], and even non-lovers desire things that are beautiful [τῶν καλῶν]." He then quickly expands to "two primary and leading characteristics" (ἰδέα ἄρχοντε καὶ ἄγοντε, 237d) that are to be found in lover and nonlover alike, an innate desire (ἐπιθυμία, again, soon defined as ὕβρις) for pleasures and an acquired judgment (δόξα, soon defined as σωφροσύνη), that aims at the best. Socrates' imagined lover allows that the lover himself can pretend disinterest. This possibility, as applied back to either Socrates or Lysias himself, leaves open the question as to whether either or both have erotic designs on Phaedrus as a defining impetus for their speeches. Indeed, both Socrates and Lysias offer speeches that can be treated as generalized specimen addresses to a beloved. The designs of either speaker are in any case muted, but they cannot be discounted, since Socrates' imagined speaker himself raises such a possibility (237b, 256e). To apply such possibilities to Socrates' own utterances would at once bring the delicacy of a combined indirection and frankness into play—and "play," once again, is a term he uses to define his discourse (278b). Such delicacy easily shades into irony, but it would belong to a larger range of effects, a range that would include irony but not be confined just to irony. Lysias' speech is notable for lacking just such effects. It is rigid in tone, while Socrates' conversation provides a constant demonstration of psychological and rhetorical flexibility. Lysias' earnestness carries the implied claim that he at every point has moved from square one. In the contrast Socrates is besting Lysias philosophically, rhetorically, and poetically. Is he also proving himself the better lover?[5]

All that Socrates says, as doctrine, does not really contradict the principle of continence or chastity in Lysias' speech, since he finally recommends a sublimation that rarely, but emphatically, permits physical fulfillment.[6] Instead of just contradicting that speech, or testing it dialectically, Socrates amplifies it by other considerations while he is outdoing it in rhetorical variation and subtlety.[7] Along with offering a large theory of psychology to implement his discourse, Socrates puts into words an example of a fuller and more acute psychology by marshaling his "nuanced" presentation through "irony", myth, and drama, rather than just by straight contradiction or disproof.[8]

"The lover" (ὁ ἐρῶν) is called "a lover (ἐραστής) of things beautiful" and "every human soul by nature has beheld things as they are" (τὰ ὄντα, 249e). The last expression can be taken as also reflexive; among τὰ ὄντα would be the nature of love, in the gradual exaltation brought to comprise philosophy, the immortality of the soul, and the ideal of the beautiful. Socrates exhibits, and dramatically exemplifies, a corresponding participation in these ideals, and a demonstration of himself as a lover (ἐραστής), by the inspired trenchancy of his definitions, by the clarity of his charioteer myth, and by the exuberant effusions he employs when addressing Phaedrus.[9] Eros, to begin with, is revered as a god (243), and the speakers' mutual exchanges are characterized as close to dithyrambs (238d).

3.

Poetry leavens the discourse of Socrates, helping it to surpass the discourse of Lysias; just so does inspired poetry, and Socrates invokes inspiration (237a), surpass uninspired poetry. Still, Socrates' speech remains rhetorical, a contest speech. It competes with the speech of Lysias not only to the end of philosophical exposition for preferable ideas but also as a demonstration of superior rhetoric. It is offered as the sort of oral performance that in some ways surpasses a written one, though ironically it will have been written down in the *Phaedrus* of Plato, where we read it rather than hear it. Part of its rhetoric is to invert the conditions of Lysias, as it expands and qualifies the assertions of Lysias about love. As Lysias' speech is a real one written for oral delivery later, Plato's speech, attributed to Socrates, is an imaginary one, taken down, as it were, in writing after having first been delivered orally.

Socrates' switch from a version of Lysias' praise of the nonlover to a positive praise of love is mediated by abjuring his "error" (ἁμάρτημα, 242d) against the "god." "The customary sign" (his *daimonion*?) nudges him, and he compares his action of reversal to the verses Stesichorus wrote to expiate his denigration of Helen (243a-b). All of this rhetorical complex modifies the doctrine to be expounded by irony, by lightness, and by a version of piety toward the gods quite removed from straight devotion. At this rhetorical turn Socrates performs one of the two functions of logical discrimination he later classifies; he is subsuming his discourse, all under one heading of inspiration, poetry, and prophecy (εἰμί...μάντις, I am a prophet, 242c). The *Phaedrus* in general exhibits, but intermittently, at controlled rhetorical positions, a penchant for classification. As a counterpart to this fusion of discourse-types, Socrates toward the end of the dialogue urges the desirability of distinguishing types of auditors (271–73), in a context where rhetoric has at last become explicitly the topic under exclusive discussion, and where a share in truth (ἀληθείας μετέχειν, 272d) and similitudes of truth (ὁμοιότητα τοῦ ἀληθοῦς, 273d) are at issue.

Lysias' speech stands as a constant counterexample, to be pointed at explicitly or to be contrasted implicitly by what outdoes it. On the one hand its completion of technique implies a lack of adaptive technique: it is as finished as a piece of joinery (234e). On the other hand, it has no proper order and could begin anywhere (253–54). These seemingly opposed defects are aspects of the same lack. It is not just that Lysias is tendentious. We may say that Plato, as opposed to his represented character Socrates, is comparably tendentious in the irreducibly rhetorical cast of his own discourse. The tendentiousness of Lysias assumes that its object has fixed attributes and can thus be rounded out like joinery and completed. Plato's differing practice has to mean that he values the contrary of these qualities. Lysias' very last word, "ask" (ἐρώτα, 234c), advertises an open-mindedness about further questions, but it actually implies a closure, whether actual (if all questions turn out to have been adduced) or possible (if it turns out that there are some left). "I consider for my part that what has been said is sufficient," he says, "But if you desire further and consider something has been left out (παραλελεῖφθαί), ask." This one-dimensional notion of completeness, in which something might be "left out" or "omitted," helps to underscore, by contrast, the discourse of Plato—and that of Socrates, which it contains—open-ended on all sides because its rhetoric is *not* confined by a single relation to the truth which remains at the same time its constant objective.

Socrates says that this speech has filled him like a bucket (235e), touching satirically on the quantitative assumption in Lysias' presentation.[10] He begins his qualifications with a reference to the old wise men (σοφοί) who are not sophists or even philosophers but poets like Sappho and Anacreon. Their discourse will soon be adduced as offering the inspiration to which he will aspire (235c). Quite late, when Socrates takes up his characteristic definition-by-questioning (263), he has begun by continuing his assessment of Lysias' form. The method applies also to Lysias' content. Lysias began where he should end (264d); Eros should have been defined at the outset (263d).

4.

Lysias, too, is himself fixed in place as he is imagined to deliver his speech. There is no interplay between him and his auditors, the sort of interplay that gives life to the Platonic dialogue. Particles—which Lysias' speech employs sparingly—touch in these delicate qualifications, and a fine air of self-deprecation, often not measurable or sometimes even traceable, turns Socrates' statements reflexively back on the speaker. In something like courtship he must show himself somewhat bold while at the same time being somewhat modest.

Socrates certainly shows not only the irony of understatement, traditionally the root meaning of the term, but what might be called the irony of hyperbole, and notably in this dialogue. Nor are hyperbole and modesty necessarily at odds. Hyperbole is the extra effort of the man here dramatized as modest, just as modesty is the come-on that sharply frames his philosophical assuredness.

Possibly Socrates is courting Phaedrus—they are after all reposing on a riverbank in the country, as Plato emphasizes (230b). This possibility shadows every statement Socrates makes with a qualification of its assumed impartiality—a faint infinite regress that would turn him into a case that could be subsumed under his version of Lysias' point, the lover tendentiously acting as the nonlover. Whether or not this is so, there is a momentary playfulness, even at such points of definition as the summary of an earlier speech (265), which suggests delectation as well as philosophical definition. Or it would do so, were it not for the fusion of delectation and definition in Plato's discourse, itself to be understood as an instance of his stated principle that love entails philosophy and vice versa (256a).

When he speaks of "Sappho the lovely (καλή) and Anacreon the wise" (σοφός), Socrates speaks of himself as "hearing" them (235c), and therefore in a sort of silent and admiring subordinate position. Their discourse is stated to be superior to the prose he has just been discussing—and at the same time, by implication, to the prose he has so far been uttering. Moreover, the term σοφός, applied to Anacreon, picks up and ironically redeploys the other uses of the word with which it partly overlaps. Anacreon is a σοφός in the old sense. Σοφός is a Pindaric word for poet.[11] Anacreon, though a mere twitterer about pleasure, is still wiser than the sophists, to whom the name may be applied. His devotion to love in the very act makes him wiser in some respects even than the philosopher, to whom the term could also be applied. Yet, by the principle applied to Lysias, it is not enough just to celebrate love; the true σοφός must define it.

And this is not all. Being paired with Sappho the beautiful, Anacreon the wise can only admire what she actually embodies, unless wisdom attains to beauty—which poetry also does. So the adjectives could also be reversed. The terms apply to the poetry and not to the persons here; the poetry of Sappho is beautiful. Is there an ironic suggestion that the beauty of her verse makes her not only Anacreon's equal but his superior? If so, it is only a touch. Socrates moves past it quickly.

When he mounts his very first myth, however, before even the introduction of Lysias, it is framed by no less than five ironic qualifications. Questions about physical location quickly yield Socrates' much-modified reply to Phaedrus' direct question about belief. I underline the terms of qualification:

ΦΑΙ. οὐ πάνυ νενόηκα· ἀλλ᾽ εἰπὲ πρός Διός, ὦ Σώκρατες, σύ τοῦτο τὸ μυθολόγημα πείθηι ἀληθές εἶναι;

ΣΩ. ᾿Αλλ᾽ εἰ ἀπιστοίην, ὥσπερ οἱ σοφοί, οὐκ ἂν ἄτοπος εἴην, εἶτα σοφιζόμενος φαίην αὐτήν πνεῦμα Βορέου κατὰ τῶν πλησίον πετρῶν σύν Φαρμακείαι παίζουσαν ὦσαι, καί οὕτω δή τελευτήσασαν λεχθῆναι ὑπό τοῦ Βορέου ἀνάρπαστον γεγονέναι—ἢ ἐξ ᾿Αρείου πάγου. λέγεται γάρ αὖ καί οὗτος ὁ λόγος, ὡς ἐκεῖθεν ἀλλ᾽ οὐκ ἐνθένδε ἡρπάσθη.

Phaedrus. I hardly noticed it [the altar of Boreas]. But tell tell me, by Zeus, Socrates, do you *believe* this mythologeme[12] to be true?

Socrates. But if I *disbelieved* as the *wise* do I would not be out of place if I should speculate[13] and then *say* a gust of Boreas had pushed her while she was playing with Pharmakeia down from the neighboring rocks and that she *be said* thus to have met her end *being* seized by Boreas—or else from the Areopagus. For there is this account, too, that she was seized from there and not from here.

(229c-d)

This myth, from the common stock, teems with foreshadowings of conditions contrary to the loves that will shortly be under discussion. At issue here is a heterosexual affair involving a god and a mortal woman, or nymph, not a homosexual one involving men. Its consummation is doubtful and in the past, not in a hoped-for future. It was brought about, if at all, by force and not by persuasion. The myth, thus heavily shot with ironies in its relation to the theme of the dialogue and through the qualifications of its telling, was brought up lightly, as a feature of the landscape (229b). When Socrates has passed beyond it they return to the landscape; having led out from the waters, they pause to admire a tree (230a).

Before they do so, however, Socrates—who will be involved in rich mythologizing for the rest of the dialogue—ironically forswears attention to myths. To try to attain greater certaintly about this myth would soon involve one in others, he says. A man thereupon would have to set straight (ἐπανορθοῦσθαι) a species or form or idea (εἶδος) of Pegasuses, of Hippocentaurs, of the Chimera, of Gorgons and a host of other prodigies. He declares that he himself—who is here at great leisure—does not have the leisure (σχολή) to do so. What prevents him is that he cannot yet follow the adage of the Delphic oracle, "Know thyself." It would be laughable, he says, to examine other matters before knowing that. He does not yet know—he here dovetails his own identity with the very mythical terms he is abjuring—whether he "happens to be some wild beast (θηρίον) more multiplex and swollen than the Typhon or a tamer and simpler creature, partaking of some divine and unpuffed (ἀτύφου, "non-Typhon") destiny" (230a). Now we hear nothing more directly in this dialogue about the famous Socratic and Delphic self-knowledge. Indirectly the psychologizing about love, and the mythologizing, fill out such a general picture—thereby ironically contradicting the assertion here that mythology is a distraction having nothing to do with self-knowledge.

5.

Here the introduction of a fragment of a myth, and then the bare names of mythical creatures, at once activates several systems of ironic qualification. Further, as the richness of mythologizing in the *Phaedrus* particularly demonstrates, no one of the several myths that this dialogue raises has a similar dramatic impetus, a similar ontological set, or a comparable complexity, with respect to any other myth in the dialogue. Such a variety of myths in itself can be taken at once as an ironic demonstration of the instability in myth and also as an indication of the delicate insight, tinged with untrustworthiness, that inheres in this supreme linguistic resource of Plato's. That is, the myth is ironic in function while at the same time hyperbolic in expression.

So later (264–65) Socrates introduces his principles of classification, when he explicitly says he has been playing. He does so in a context where he assigns the good madnesses to separate gods, and when he distinguishes between the "not wholly unbelievable account" (λόγος) and the "mythic hymn." He then offers under one heading the two principles (εἰδοῖν, 265c9) of association and of subcategorization. These Stenzel calls "the plainest statement of the method of abstraction from particulars that can be found anywhere in Plato."[14]

The myth itself is earnest and playful at the same time. And some myths would seem to be more playful than others; in this way too they differ from one another. The most earnest would seem to be the longest, the myth of the charioteer who drives the winged horses of the soul, one white and one black. The final myth, that of Theuth, strikes me as a little less earnest, though nearly as long. It is hard to produce evidence for this view; yet the sun and charioteer are honorific, whereas Theuth is exotic, and there is much byplay with particles— often a telltale sign of levity—at the introduction of this myth. The seed-plants of Adonis would be more earnest than Theuth, less so than the charioteer. Most playful of all is the myth of the endlessly chirruping grasshoppers. Actual grasshoppers sing in the grass, linking the mythical ones to ones that can be simply seen. They function as simple analogues for discourse or music, an aspect of their love. That grasshoppers somehow live for the pleasure of the day, perhaps recalls Aesop (mentioned by name in the *Phaedo*, 60c). The grasshoppers have been brought up in the discourse about discourse as an example of discourse. This recursiveness and simplicity are mutually reinforcing.

The myth of the charioteer is adduced as a demonstration (ἀποδειξις, 245c) and after a preliminary demonstration of the immortality of the soul. This myth does not map a homology of resemblances, even though names could be given to the charioteer and his two horses. On the one hand his task is quite simple: to move them ahead and on a celestial path. But in another way the difficulties arising from the mismatched team lead to millennial cycles of trans-migrations. In accounting for these Socrates himself shifts ground, and the wings become those not of horses but of the soul. The details of sprouting new wings (250) in turn provide another myth, which opens up another angle on love and the celestial strivings. The final return to the horses (254) engenders a graphic physical description of the black one, which does then have allegorical applications, but partial ones, and only to one undesirable psychological state. Before that, the unfolding transmutations of the myth have produced a typology of souls defined, in still another modality (252), by their attendance to, and dominance by, some particular god, Zeus or Ares or Apollo or Hera. This assignment in turn redirects the typology of the eleven-gods-plus-Hestia, which had been brought in as a contrast to the striving human charioteers (246c–247b). As for credibility, "it is possible to believe it and also possible not to" (252c).

The complicated Theuth myth offers an account of origins, along with a typology of the intellectual functions enabled by writing. It comes up to fill in the insufficiency of an account of rhetorical expression. While the distinction between technical skill (τέχνη) and its lack (ἀτεχνίας) has been sufficiently established (274b), that between seemliness (or decorum, or that which is fitting—or handsomeness) and unseemliness (εὐπρέπειὰ / ἀπρέπεια) has not. The myth of Theuth, unlike the others, in avoiding its introductory topic, has little to say about εὐπρέπεια. It is as though the solution of how writing will work carries with it a solution to other problems related to expression.

The last myth, that of the seeds in the garden of Adonis, serves more as a metaphorical parable than a myth. It arises from, and is addressed to, the problem of making what one learns permanent. Since it fuses memory and expression, the intellectual and the moral, as well as a technique of care, what it includes in its reference is more complex than its elements. Hence this small myth may be said to recapitulate the large myth of Theuth as the grasshoppers myth partially recapitulates the charioteer. But all these myths differ among themselves so much in function, status, origin, structure, and tone, that such correspondences as these would only provisionally apply.

6.

The parable of the seeds is brought in to clarify a refinement not possible through the myth of Theuth. Qualifying and supplementary, it provides a measure to discriminate among kinds of writing. What is written down, including speeches for delivery (λόγοι) like those of Lysias, do permit recall. But they will not answer an auditor (274–75): they lack the suppleness of the "writing" engraved on the living memory, the "knowledge" (ἐπιστήμη) that is written on the soul of a learner" (276a).

Such orally revived "writing" has the advantage of being re-membered, and at the same time of allowing for dialectic—for the decision "toward whom it is necessary to speak and to be silent"[15] Of such a "living" piece of writing the actual physical writing is, prop-erly considered (δικαίως), just an image (εἴδωλον). "Since the power of λόγος happens to be soul-leading (ψυχαγωγία), it will be necessary for the would-be rhetorician to know how many forms the soul has" (271c–d).

The argument brings dialectic to the fore as a resolution of speech modes, but a discrimination is still needed between what merely amuses, like an eight-day garden of Adonis, and what is serious (σπουδή, 276b) like the seeds a husbandman tends for eight months.[16] The eight-day garden is to the husbandman's seeds as play to earnestness. But the dialectic quickly takes over this distinction as well, since Plato recommends not the solemnity of Lysias but an ad-mixture of play in a higher seriousness. The "serious" man (σπουδή is repeated, 276c) will not write his words on water. Having treasured them in "the garden of letters" he will spend his days "playing" (παίζειν) with them. At an earlier extreme of play, the grasshoppers are fancied as produced by the Muses (259c).

The dialectic in itself is not enough, however. Socrates has earlier indicated that even the skill (τέχνη) of "the Eleatic Palamedes" (Zeno) can be used to convince hearers that "the same things are like and unlike, one and many, abiding and fleeting" (261d). This defini-tion supersedes itself also by a playful touch: in calling Zeno by the name of the legendary discoverer of the alphabet and many other things, Socrates assimilates him to a parallel of the later myth of Theuth. In being called a Palamedes, Zeno is treated to the irony of hyperbole. At the same time, higher uses are attributed to him than the paradox-mongering of court controversy (ἀντιλογικ ή) for which it is here said his technique can be used. The mere rhetor is defined by a plain contrast between the horse and the ass (260), itself adduced as an example of false and superficial classification.

When Socrates is conducting his surely playful etymology connecting the prophetic (μαντικ ή) with inspired madness (μανικ ή), he is engaging in a dialectic that leads him shortly to a whole repertoire of intellectual functions—investigation (ζήτησις), mind (νοῦς), conception (οἴησις), inquiry (ἱστορία), and thought (διάνοια). Yet all these are playfully, and dialectically, caught up in a discussion of how bird-signs may be interpreted. In the charioteer myth a pure thought (διάνοια) and knowledge (ἐπιστήμη) nourishes the good horse so that he can see justice (δικαιοσύνη), prudence (σωφροσύνη) —and, once again, knowledge (247). These are the horses of the gods, whereas human souls "scarcely catch sight of things as they are (τὰ ὄντα)."

The very beginning of Socrates' first speech is caught up in drama and dialectic, as well as irony. Phaedrus' swearing by the plane tree, and his declaration that he will never say another speech, lays a "necessity" (ἀναγκάσω ἀνάγκην) on the "unwilling" Socrates (236d–e). He professes that shame will induce him to gallop through his discourse, and he invokes the Muses at once (as Lysias will not have done). "I shall speak under a veil," he says, "ἐγκαλυψάμενος ἐρῶ," and the word ἐγκαλυψάμενος points ambiguously both to the drama of hiding one's face and the indirect speech of the veiled stories and myths he will begin forthwith. Drama and indirectness perpetuate the dialectic on another plane, extending it, and keeping it playful.

7.

Much has been said about the transition from oral to written expression in Greece, and Havelock has impressively demonstrated how intimately such conditions are bound up into Plato's outlook and expression.[17] However, these main conditions are not exempt from dialectic—or for that matter from contradiction. Much in Plato substantiates Havelock's contention that Plato was striving for a preponderance of the written over the oral. Yet in the passages surrounding the seeds parable he gives primacy to the oral—an oral that at the same time is defined as a kind of writing in the head.

Plato's very vocabulary in this dialogue seems aimed at combining the oral and the written into dialectical complications. Elsewhere, as Havelock has persuasively shown, Plato associates poetry with oral transmission. Here in one instance he applies the less common sense of ποιητής, "writer," not only to prose but to the uninspired written prose of Lysias (236d), which he contrasts throughout with inspired writing, oral effusion, and verse. The other nine uses of ποιητής and its adjective in the dialogue all refer either to lyrical poetry or to dramatic poetry, or at least to highly imaginative writing inspired by the Muses and by the divine madness (especially in 245a). Socrates' own discourse, pretends to this higher form of writing, as against Lysias', though it is a kind of prose that in dialogue form carries some of the character of theatrical discourse as well as of the divine inspiration he repeatedly invokes. Furthermore, the term συγγράφειν ("compose in writing") and its cognates, habitually applied to prose writers, and usually by prose writers, from Herodotus on, occur sixteen times in the *Phaedrus*, where Plato unusually applies them not just to prose—though he sometimes does that (as for example 272b, 258a, 258c). Rather he uses συγγράφειν terms in the sense of "writing in general" or even applies them in cases where only poetry is in question. At the point of their highest frequency (257–58), they are called into dialectical use, meaning "writing in general" but at the same time applied back recursively to Lysias. Since the *Phaedrus* itself is a written presentation of an imagined oral conversation, it both incorporates and contradicts its own final recommendation of informed oral discourse as the highest form. Even if this recommendation is taken as aiming at Plato's unwritten doctrine, it retains its qualifying dialectical force within the statement of this particular dialogue itself.

The very act of reading is dramatized at one explicit point (230d); and the reading-recitation of Phaedrus himself, the speech of Lysias, is prepared for dramatically at the outset of the dialogue. The procedure vaguely resembles the way the client of such a λογογράφος would read a memorized speech in the law courts. Oral and written are combined in the later designation of Lysias' text as having been "delivered orally from a book," ἐκ τοῦ βιβλίου ῥηθείς (243c).

8.

One can apply back to Plato's dialogues, as a template of testing and sometimes modifying principles, two complementary notions developed in the *Cratylus* (385–86): Plato's version of Protagoras' notion that the truth is individual to every man, and Euthydemus' notion that all men are equally right. Both of these follow from the differentiation of persons through the byways of self-consciousness. Still, the community of language, which Socrates forces upon his auditors, implies a concord to be envisioned, if never reached, through various kinds of such testing. In the *Phaedrus* Lysias is out of reach, but the dialogue concludes, as always semi-ironically, with the praise of a young Isocrates. Thus Plato has Socrates act as though he were falling back to the rhetoricians, but in a form that will include potential philosophers, since Isocrates ran a rival school. The very semantic spread of the word σοφοί in the *Phaedrus* carries with it such a possible tolerance. The word "to agree" (ὁμολόγειν) and its derivates occur eight times in the *Phaedrus*.

Socrates' critique of Lysias' dialogue as lacking order refers us back to the order of his own discourse, which slides in and out of myth and permits all sorts of qualifications and interruptions. Then there is the overarching order of the *Phaedrus* itself, with a return to the initial topics, physically symbolized in the return to Athens at the end of the dialogue. Socrates and Phaedrus go out from the city at the beginning and return to it at the end. "Let's go," is its very last word. The dialogue is almost wholly circular in beginning with Lysias but almost ending with the encomium of Isocrates. At the very end, poetry, myth, and love are delicately touched on by the concluding prayer to Pan, which seals it as a kind of triptych honoring as well as exhibiting all three. A conclusion has been reached about the nature of rhetoric, and another about the nature of love, but the connections between them have only been sketched by comparison. Nor do these topics have the obvious relation to one another that, for example, rhetoric and virtue do in the *Gorgias* or proper classification and proper government do in the *Republic*.

It is, however, Phaedrus, who first mentions "Isocrates the fair" (τὸν καλόν, 278e). Does this mean that he is ironically shown not to have fully assimilated Socrates' teaching? Socrates takes up the praise up and agrees with him. Does this mean he is somewhat tired, or somewhat infatuated, or both? Again, here at the end the dramatic relations, and positions, all sorts of interplay perfuse the notions presented.

The term εἶδος, Form or Idea, a large one in Plato, runs casually through this dialogue, as I have shown above, sometimes as a place-marker for categorizations, sometimes in a weak sense that cannot be pressed. The dramatic presentation, the irony, and the very dialectic, permit it to remain fluid while other notions are set complexly into place. Plato's form in the *Phaedrus*, as sometimes differently elsewhere, serves also not only to keep questions open, but to let them participate in various degrees of being open, from the faintly ambiguous hint to full closure.

Notes

1. Οὐκοῦν ἤδη πεπαίσθω μετρίως ἡμῖν τὰ περὶ λόγων.

2. G. J. DeVries, *A Commentary on the Phaedrus of Plato* (Amsterdam: Hakkert, 1969), 18–19. Citing H. Gundert, "Zum Spiel bei Platon," in L. Landgrebe, ed., *Beispiele* (1965), 188–21, and his own earlier book *Spel bij Plato* (1949), DeVries lists six different senses (from Gundert's nine) in which play is used in the *Phaedrus*: "playful social conversation, playful song and dance in the service of the gods, a playful element in rhetoric and eristic, the dialectical play in Socratic irony, the general play in human existence." (One might question the last; all of the citations are from the *Laws*.) However, Plato's play among his many concepts is one procedure. An interpreter's play among Plato's given terms does not have unlimited latitude, or Plato's words make no sense at all. Jacques Derrida in "La Pharmacie de Platon," *La Dissémination* (Paris: Seuil, 1972), 69–197, rightly stresses the importance of internal "writing" to Plato, though there would seem to be no reason to enlist Plato as a supposed support for Derrida's own doctrines of absence and difference, when the *Phaedrus* argues for writing in the consciousness as a supreme *presence*. No concept

of "play" will allow for so clearly erroneous a reading of Plato's text. Moreover, with respect to Derrida's title, φάρμακον in the *Phaedrus*, each of the eight times it occurs, it always means unambiguously "healing drug" rather than "poison," as Derrida himself admits (109–112). This singleness of unambiguous meaning is the more marked as, in ways I shall indicate, Plato does tend in the *Phaedrus* to play on some ambiguities in this dialogue, and to play in general. Φάρμακον can serve only as "la différance de la différence (as it is called, 146) if it parts company entirely with Plato's text. (In which case why bring up Plato?) The fashionably resurrected neo-Frazerian term φάρμακος, "scapegoat," can still less be applied to this text, or to Plato in general. The word does not occur once in all of Plato, and it does violence to much that he says to enlist it reductively under the heading of this anthropological commonplace. As it happens, Derrida does not permit anything like such liberties with his own text, scolding those who would anachronistically translate Marx's *aufgelöst* as his *déconstruites*. See *La Carte Postale* (Paris: Flammarion, 1980), 285. Such a translation, Derrida asserts, would "égarer le lecteur."

3. "Putting into order and adornment (κοσμοῦσα) myriad actions of the ancients (τῶν παλαιῶν) it instructs the coming generations (τοὺς ἐπιγιγνομένους)."

4. νὼ καταβάντε ἐς τὸ Νυμφῶν νᾶμά τε καὶ μουσεῖον ἠκούσαμεν λόγων.

5. The distinctions and blendings about love merge into those of philosophy and poetry, as Martha Nussbaum discusses these in "'This Story Isn't True': Poetry, Goodness, and Understanding in Plato's *Phaedrus,*" in J. Moravcsik and P. Temko, *Plato on Beauty, Wisdom and the Arts* (Totowa, N.J., 1982), 79–24. She points out that the *Phaedrus* shares with the *Republic* the presentation of a contrast between poetry and philosophy: "A new understanding of philosophy ... reinterprets the distinction between philosophy and poetry." As she says (89), "Philosophy is now permitted to be an inspired, manic, Muse-loving activity."

6. Gregory Vlastos effectively demonstrates the presence of some physical fulfillment in the ideal Platonic love, drawing heavily on *Phaedrus* 254–56 ("Sex in Platonic Love," in *Platonic Studies*, 38–42). Plato's insistence on the ideal of near chastity is not just negative; love is the highest of his four forms of divine madness.

7. Giovanni R. F. Ferrari, in *Listening to the Cicadas* (Cambridge: Cambridge University Press, 1987), derives philosophical conclusions from the physical setting and circumstances of the dialogue. "The aims of philosophy are ill-suited to the restrictions of a single format in any case and can be most strikingly captured by the peculiar multiplicity of formats exhibited in the dialogue as a whole ... Where, then, is the 'philosophy' in this dialogue? I am saying that it lies in *both* halves of the dialogue and, just

as crucially, in the articulation between them" (30). "[Plato] holds that if rhetoric must become philosophical, then philosophy must acknowledge the extent to which it is rhetoric" (38).

8. K. Dorter (in "Imagery and Philosophy in Plato's *Phaedrus*," *Journal of the History of Philosophy* 9, 1971, 279–288) traces contrasting patterns of imaging in the dialogues. As T. Dalfen says ("Gedanken zur Lektüre Platonischer Dialoge," *Zeitschrift für philosophischer Forschung* 29, 1975, 169–194), "The inner, and indeed the decisive basis for the choice of the dialogue form was a certain interpretation of the essence of philosophizing: philosophy as permanent conversation" (171), "als ständiges Gespräch" (171). This notion involves "various dispositions toward philosophy" (187).

9. De Vries (*op. cit.*, 186) lists some of Socrates' many exuberant effusions towards Phaedrus. In addition Socrates playfully refers to him in the third person (261, 257b).

10. The term λογισμός, judging from the lexicon (L-S), would appear to be a favorite of Lysias'. The repetition of προσήκει, "it is fitting," from Lysias' speech by Socrates (238b), may be a somewhat mocking echo.

11. Σοφός=poet in Pindar O. 1.116; O. 9.38; P. 3.113; I. 1.45.

12. Μυθολόγημα is a rare word, possibly a coinage of Plato's, not far in meaning from the modern "mythologeme" or a group of mythologemes.

13. Σοφιζόμενος, judging again from the lexicon, is a favorite word of Lysias, and also of Isocrates. The word, we may say, proleptically links the two orators who begin and end the *Phaedrus*.

14. Julius Stenzel, *Plato's Method of Dialectic*, 17. These are defined as "seeing them under one idea to bring together particulars that have been scattered in many places (εἰς μίαν τε ἰδέαν συνορῶντα ἄγειν τὰ πολλαχῆι διεσπαρμένα, 265d) and "to be able to divide them again into separate ideas according to the ligatures they have by nature (τὸ πάλιν κατ'εἴδη δύνασθαι διατέμνειν κατ'ἄρθρα ἧι πέφυκεν, 265e). I have left "eidos" unglossed, rendering it each time as "idea," though the shift of senses is clear, and still clearer if we adduce the third use of the word in this passage, the question of Phaedrus, "What is the other idea (eidos) you speak of, Socrates?" (265d). Εἶδος in fact changes its meaning throughout the dialogue. We may consider the passage in 229d, "τὸ τῶν Ἱπποκενταύρων εἶδος ἐπανορθοῦσθαι" is being paralleled with "ὄχλος τοιούτων Γοργόνων καὶ Πηγάσων, ἄλλων ἀμηχάνων, πλήθη" and "ἀτοπίαι τερατολόγων τινῶν." The term has an almost periphrastic status of rough equivalence to the other three words used to govern monsters. This weaker use occurs in the two uses at 253c8 and another at 253d4, as well as perhaps also in "κατὰ τὸ εἶδος ἑκάστης τιμῆς," 259d2. In 237a7 ὠιδῆς εἶδος is paired with γένος μουσικόν in a stronger sense approaching a technical one, as Socrates uses

the term while invoking the Muses. The sense is still stronger in 249b6–9 when understanding, *logos*, memory and psyche are all brought to bear as needed to grasp the perception occasioned by transmigration. (Δεῖ γάρ ἄνθρωπον ξυνιέναι κατ᾽ εἶδος λεγόμενον, ἐκ πολλῶν ἰὸν αἰσθήσεων εἰς ἓν λογίσμωι συναιρούμενον). Comparably strong but more liberated from αἰσθήσεις, is the πᾶν τὸ τῆς ψυχῆς εἶδος of 251b7, and the uses in 263c1. All in all the word occurs twenty-five times in various forms, and it never stays fixed for long in this dialogue, a flexibility with terms that characterizes Plato's usage generally.

15.   ἐπιστήμων δέ λέγειν τε καί σιγᾶν πρός οὓς δεῖ.

16.   The antithesis between the systems of luxuries associated with Adonis and the necessities associated with the husbandmen are substantiated in Marcel Detienne, *Les Jardins d'Adonis* (Paris: Gallimard, 1972), though he does not mention Plato there.

17.   Eric A. Havelock, *Preface to Plato; The Greek Concept of Justice* (Cambridge: Harvard University Press, 1978). In the large literature on this subject one might signal Charles Segal, "Tragédie, oralité, écriture," *Poétique 50*, April 1982, 131–54. See also Ronna Burger, *Plato's Phaedrus, A Defense of a Philosophic Art of Writing* (University: University of Alabama Press, 1980); and P. Lacoue-Labarthe, "Typographie," in *Mimesis des articulations* (Paris: Flammarion, 1975), 167–70. As Burger says, "The dialogue's reflection on its own character as a product of writing results ironically in the apparent deprecation of the activity of writing" (2). "The sweet speech of the divine lover which washes away the bitter taste of the speech of the nonlover, cannot uncover the tension within the condition Socrates lays down for the true art of speaking" (69).

Chapter 4

Plato and Poetry

1.

Plato banishes from his commonwealth much poetry, as well as some music, for reasons ingrained in his conception of proper discourse. He does so on a notion of mimesis, a notion connected to music, and, through orality, to what could be called the music of words.[1] But he also draws on poetic texts as though they were authoritative. To say what poetry might be for Plato, in all its cross-currents of complexity, requires reconciling what are on the face of it contradictory assertions in the dialogues. Carrying through an adequate account of this situation would entail getting beyond the single, cohering oral function from which Havelock well shows that Plato is trying to release himself.

The direct use of poetry in Plato is simple to begin with, neutral in presentation and positive in effect. That is, Plato has a habit of citing verses to support, or even to introduce, some position or other that he has Socrates adopt. Dozens of times in the dialogues Plato has recourse to a poetic citation as though it has an authority beyond contestation. As the occasion seems to demand, he uses and sometimes even sets such authoritative lines into a structure, like the citations in the *Protagoras* of Simonides and Pittacus. He never, or rarely, questions a view propounded in a poem, and the adjudication of how to interpret one line of poetry is a central philosophical puzzle in the *Protagoras* (339a–347b).[2] When in the *Phaedo* (113c9) Socrates uses the expression "as the poets say," he is amplifying the poets, but relying on them. Poetry is even used as an "authority" for banter in the *Symposium* (174).

Even in the *Republic* (545a–547a), the Muses emerge as deliverers of the true information, on the stated analogy of Homer, defection from which causes debilitation (φθορά). "The Muses must answer, since they are muses."[3] Hesiod is also brought in, and a new definition of his epochal periods, since mixes of them are now said to be allowed. In the *Laws* (810e–811a) a characterization of poetry is offered which involves multiple experience (πολυπειρία) and multiple knowledge (πολυμαθία). Adimantus in the *Republic* (363–66), in a context of a supposed last judgment about acts of justice, makes a general statement about "the children of the gods, poets and prophets, who show forth that this is the way things are" (366b), and Socrates praises his speech. In the *Euthyphro* (6c) it is alleged that poets make up stories about gods, and it is asked if they are true. This set of questions effectually inverts the earlier charge that Socrates poeticizes the gods, "They say I am a poet about the gods"[4] (3b). Homer is quoted as an authority on naval management (*Laws*, 706b), and very soon (707b) the battle of Salamis is brought up. The meters of poetry, and very likely the modes of music, modify for the Greece of Plato at least three millennial traditions, Ionic, Doric, and Aeolic.[5] To subject effects of those metrical traditions to moralizing examination and then to exclude most of them is radically to divorce the society from tradition, with which at the same time it is Plato's project to realign it.

This disparity, or even contradiction, between the special authority of poetry and its special threat, is never directly resolved in Plato, and it would be hard to construct a consistent argument that would reconcile the two views, since one cannot simultaneously validate and invalidate an authority.[6] Plato's dialogues, where he adduces quotation from poets, could be thought of as complete without such quotations, so far as their philosophical substance is concerned, and even so far as their dramatic structure is concerned. These quotations do not, interestingly, ever work in the resolving way that myths do, long or short, when they are introduced into the dialogues, nor do they work in a way resembling the source of myths, religion—the very religion, in turn, of which the poems are a chief, or sole, verbal evidence and about which Plato himself is repeatedly at pains to make pious reference. In the *Apology* (22b) after consulting the oracle, Socrates consults the poets.

The use of religion intersects with the use of myth and the use of poetry. All three, for example, bear on the quotation from Pindar in the *Meno*, which is introduced to validate the doctrine of the transmigration of souls.

A close look at the chain of argument in this dialogue would show that the citation from Pindar is a principal argument of the *Meno* in supporting the doctrine of *anamnesis*, transmigrating memory. The demonstration following the quotation, which elicits geometric axioms from a slave who has never studied geometry, in some ways depends on the citation from Pindar, though Socrates conducts his demonstration more in the spirit of modern philosophy than might seem to obtain in connection with citations founded on a religion that has now been dead for a millennium and more.

Even the quotations from Theognis and from Simonides in the *Protagoras*, if possibly ironic, are still based on a sense of their authority. They are taken as though the poetic line has a kind of authority not open to the kind of examination to which Socrates regularly subjects philosophical statements. In fact his hermeneutic attempt to probe the poetic question so as to determine what it may be made to yield implies the opposite, and even Theognis' views are supplemented rather than refuted.

It is not easy, in short, to separate religion from poetry in Plato, or either religion or poetry from myth, even the myths that Plato invents or adapts. The inextricability of poetry from myth and religion reflects not only a specifically Greek situation and not only a general condition of human utterance. Since for Plato philosophy conditions poetry and myth, and since religion in a sense initiates them and also interacts with them, his multiplex sensitivity to poetry contributes to signaling that he offers a powerfully comprehensive, and also a uniquely special situation in the range of human utterance.

On the negative side, in the *Republic*, the first discussion of poetry, from Book Two (377–401), is adduced in the context of what would be the place of poetry in an education. While imitation is brought up (391–95), it is brought up in the context of two other criteria, the moral valuelessness or untrustworthiness of a poetry, and its propensity for telling lies about the gods.[7] Only the "simple" style has the balance that could lead to harmony (399), and the discussion proceeds to gymnastics. The second discussion begins abruptly in Book Ten, after the states of the soul and appropriate pleasures have been discussed, though a passing reference to Euripides' praise of the tyrant had come up in the blaming of tyranny (Book Eight, 568). This second discussion has to do not with education but with the state of soul of an individual man. Yet in the *Laws* the state itself is a mimesis, like a tragedy (817b). Poetry in the context of marriage is appropriate for places of breeding (459e). Homer is quoted in the *Phaedo* (112) as an authority on geological cosmology. In the *Gorgias* (502) tragedy engages pleasure and also politics, serving as an unwitting bridge between them—with meter and the rest subtracted as just *logioi*. The *Laws* compares real public life to tragedy (916b).

In the *Republic*, Book Ten, poetry is rejected because it is an imitation of an imitation (595), and also because it is bad for the soul, leading it to muddle and imbalance. In this different set of criteria and different context, all poetry is rejected, not just some. It is bad for the soul (604), and there is a modest interval between that statement and the prose fictitious-anecdotal-mythological account of Er. It seems potentially contradictory that at the end of the dialogue it is a mythos which "was saved ... and saves us."

The severe restrictions on poetry in the *Republic* are of a piece with its entire model for a regulated society. The principles of these restrictions contradict the use to which Plato puts actual poems there, as well as his use of the imaginative processes of myth. But such contradictions are part and parcel of the work of Plato, contradictions of doctrine in addition to contradictions of procedure. The strict control of erotic activity enjoined by the family regulations in the *Republic*, for example, contradict the access to love, open on principle, in the *Symposium* and the *Phaedrus*.[8]

The victory of Agathon in a tragic, and so a poetic, competition is the occasion for the *Symposium*, and a comic poet is given a significant voice there, as is the beloved of the tragic poet who is host, and the tragic poet himself. Poetry in the *Lysis* (204d) is used as a means of courtship. Where philosophy itself is under discussion there, Socrates recommends that "a man inquire of the poets; for they are as though fathers of wisdom (*sophia*) for us, and guides" (214a). A line of poetry begins the discussion of the affinity of like person for like. And later, easily and on a contrary doctrine, Hesiod is quoted, with equal authority, on the grudge of like against like (215d).

The poet's inspiration often appears in Plato as linked to not-knowing. However, not-knowing at another angle, if brought to awareness of itself, gets a kind of positive valuation as the Socratic ignorance that is the beginning of wisdom. But normally, as in the *Ion*, the inspiration betrays a nonconsciousness on the part of the inspired. Still, Ion is not himself a poet, but a reciter of Homeric poetry, a Homerides. That dialogue, then, really reveals the unconsciousness of the actor rather than the poet. Using the categories of the *Republic*, we may put the actor-reciter at a third remove from the reality of the Forms, since he is one remove from the poet, who is at a second remove.

2.

Plato's ways of using poetry are partially framed by the ambivalences governing his presentation of it in the *Ion*. These ambivalences appear even in Plato's use there of a single word that appears fairly often in the *Ion*, the word *theios*, often a positive term for him. In the *Ion*, however, he tends to use it to modify poetic perception in a sense that gives it a strong negative cast.[9]

The handling of poetry in the *Phaedrus* (245) is given a complex positive function which the *Ion* reflects in the general notion of enthusiasm.[10] As it relates to the god, this notion is positive in the *Ion* and reflects the valuation in the *Phaedrus*. However, in so far as it derives from the ignorance of the rhapsode, as against a Socratic tradition that values knowledge, it stands at the opposite, negative pole in the repertory of Plato's notions about poetry. Poetry in the *Ion* is now negative, now positive, and it admits of this polarity even though the dialogue is short, simple, and conducted by a fairly thick-headed interlocutor. It may be said in passing that these features of the *Ion* recall other dialogues before thick-headed interlocutors, like the *Euthydemus*, the *Laches*, the *Hippias Minor*, and the *Euthyphro* (a resemblance which could help support the authenticity of this dialogue). Even the *Ion* has a logic internal to the dialogue, a sequence of ideas and of dynamic relations between the two persons which presents a network, if not a system, in which is developed a true complexity of perceptions and affirmations.

First of all, it should be noted that it is Socrates, and not Ion, who catalogues and summarizes the subjects with which Homer concerns himself, and in a manner quite different from the discussion on *techne* which dominates the end of the dialogue:

> Ὅμηρος περὶ ἄλλων τινῶν λέγει ἢ ὧνπερ σύμπαντες οἱ ἄλλοι ποιηταί; οὐ περὶ πολέμου τε τὰ πολλὰ διελήλυθεν καὶ περὶ ὁμιλιῶν πρὸς ἀλλήλους ἀνθρώπων ἀγαθῶν τε καὶ κακῶν καὶ ἰδιωτῶν καὶ δημιουργῶν, καὶ περὶ θεῶν πρὸς ἀλλήλους καὶ πρὸς ἀνθρώπους ὁμιλούντων, ὡς ὁμιλοῦσι, καὶ περὶ τῶν οὐρανίων παθημάτων καὶ περὶ τῶν ἐν Ἅιδου, καὶ γενέσεις καὶ θεῶν καὶ ἡρώων;

> SOCRATES: ... Does Homer treat of matters different from those that all the other poets treat of? Wasn't his subject mainly war, and hasn't he discussed the mutual relations of men good and bad, or the general run as well as special craftsmen, the relations of the god to one another and to men, as they forgather, the phenomena of the heavens and occurrences in Hades, and the birth of gods and heroes?   (531c1–6, tr. Lane Cooper)

Actually, this passage constitutes an answer to the argument of Ion, which Socrates implicitly claims to refute, that Ion can only recite and criticize Homer because Homer differs from other poets. On the other hand, Socrates says that Homer's subjects are the same as those "of Hesiod and the other poets." In this light, the list has been drawn up with reference also to Hesiod (though the most immediate reference is of course to Homer). Yet Hesiod, in his numerous "phenomena of the heavens" (*pathemata ourania*), does not refer exactly to "Hades." The case of Hesiod complicates the question, and Socrates remains equivocal when he speaks finally of "Homer and the other poets." If the subjects were tabulated, the list for Homer would be longer than that for Hesiod. Other poets would not seem to enter easily into such a list. Possibly for this reason Socrates must leave them anonymous and stay preponderantly Homeric (as well as Platonic in his Homer) when he alleges that other poets share Homer's subjects.

To be sure, this statement is an answer, and a refutation, of Ion's contention that he can recite and criticize only Homer, because Homer is distinct from other poets. Socrates could also be taken to be referring to the whole epic tradition, but even so, it is remarkable that poets from that tradition come in for virtually no citation in the dialogues, while here in the *Ion* he makes no mention of the many poets whom he does cite in the dialogues.

It is also noteworthy that this catalogue makes no reference by name to any character from the Homeric poems, although in the dialogues Plato often brings in an Achilles, an Ajax, a Priam, or an Odysseus for illustration. Here, aside from the reference to Hades, his presentation of Homer strangely slights the *Odyssey*. The conception of accidents or events (*pathemata*) suggests more the visions of another world in the *Phaedo*, the *Republic*, the *Phaedrus*, and the *Gorgias* than it does the world of the eleventh book of the *Odyssey*, where virtually no event takes place. Above all there is no match in the Odyssey for *pathemata ourania*. The point of view in this passage remains persistently, if vaguely, Platonic also in the light of the human activities it details. The emphasis on a collectivity, and on a nearly absolute distinction between *agathoi* and *kakoi*, is closer to the collectivities of the *Republic* and its moral imperatives,[11] and also of the *Gorgias* and the *Protagoras*, than it is to the *Iliad*, and the actions military and moral in that poem. Nor is the distinction between *agathos* and *kakos* so clear in the *Odyssey*. Of course the distinction between *agathos* and *kakos* does find clear and elaborate expression in the dialogues of Plato. In brief, this list is also so general that it ill prepares the terrain for the specific qualities in the discussion that follows, and it barely touches on those qualities.

Later, too, when Socrates again resumes the genres of Greek poetry, their repertory is so diverse that it leaves Homer somewhat aside. Socrates speaks of enthusiasts, *enthousiazontes*, as like the magnetic force that passes through a chain of iron links (533e). Further, it is after having begun with the particular poetic genre Homer practiced that Socrates forms his list of its concerns:

Πάντες γάρ οἵ τε τῶς ἐπῶν ποιηταί οἱ ἀγαθοὶ οὐκ ἐκ τέχνης ἀλλ' ἔνθεοι ὄντες καί κατεχόμενοι πάντα ταῦτα τὰ καλὰ λέγουσι ποιήματα, καί οἱ μελοποιοί οἱ ἀγαθοὶ ὡσαύτως ... κοῦφον γὰρ χρῆμα ποιητής ἐστιν καί πτηνὸν καί ἱερόν ... ἕως δ'ἂν τουτὶ ἔχηι τό κτῆμα, ἀδύνατος πᾶς ποιεῖν ἄνθρωπός ἐστιν καί χρησμωιδεῖν. ἄτε οὖν οὐ τέχνηι ποιοῦντες ... ἀλλά θεῖαι μοίραι ... ὁ μὲν διθυράμβους, ὁ δὲ ἐγκώμια, ὁ δὲ ὑπορχήματα, ὁ δ' ἔπη, ὁ δ' ἰάμβους.

For the epic poets, all the good ones, have their excellence, not from art, but are inspired, possessed, and thus they utter all these admirable poems. So is it also with the good lyric poets; ... And what they say is true, for a poet is a light and winged thing, and holy, ... So long as he has this in his possession, no man is able to make poetry or to chant in prophecy. Therefore, since their making is not by art, ... but is by lot divine—therefore each is able to do well only that to which the Muse has impelled him—one to make dithyrambs, another panegyric odes, another choral songs, another epic poems, another iambs.   (533e-534c)

First of all, this list is remarkable in that, while at the same time denying *techne* to poets, it begins by already having judged the poets in advance, admitting only good ones—a point Plato repeats in having Socrates speak of *melopoioi*. In any case, moreover, the discussion proceeds a little to one side of Ion, who is not himself a poet but a reciter of the poems of Homer,[12] and "interpreter or critic" ("Ὁμηρίδης" and "ἑρμηνεύς").

By a Jesuitical sleight, Plato here sets the poet at a distance a degree still further from reality than the poet of the *Republic*. There the poems that remain "pure" (*katharoi*) would be in a great minority. But one could choose candidates for such purity among three or even four of the six genres named here by Socrates. So the census of poems that are acceptable is implicitly greater in the *Ion* than in the *Republic*. Further, the term "*entheos*," which is in view here, has positive overtones, even at the moment when this text takes a negative posture towards *techne*, which is seen in a positive light when Socrates concludes by demonstrating a lack of *techne* in poetry itself and in Ion's perceptions about poetry. Here, *techne* has ambiguously negative overtones because it implies a lack of inspiration, the inspiration which is the necessary condition—and because *techne* comes into play, inspiration is also part of a sufficient condition—for the production of a good poetry.

As he continues, Socrates classifies the links in his magnetic chain, and as he does so he makes clear the distinctions among spectator (*theates*), rhapsode or actor (*hypocrites*), and poet. The rhapsodes are also possessed, some by Homer, others by Orpheus or Musaeus. Socrates once again refuses *techné* to the lot of them.

Still, there is an aspect of *"techne"* to Homer, and Socrates himself illustrates the point. Because he examines only cases where *techne* remains in question, it could be said that Socrates virtually lets pass Ion's affirmation that he posseses a *techne* of the "rhetorical" kind.[13] As Eric Havelock has abundantly shown, Homer is a sort of encyclopedia for the Greeks, and it is precisely this function, in his view, that Plato intends to refute. What better means of doing so than admitting that Homer has indeed well described the techniques of the charioteer, the doctor, the fisherman, or even the seer, but could not stand in for any of these experts? This is exactly the argument Socrates uses to cap his demonstration. If he denies *techne* to Ion, he leaves him *theios*, a term that both praises him and excludes him from an expertise in any other social domain.

Even in the *Ion*, then, and more emphatically in the entire work of Plato, it can be seen that there is a great diversity, and sometimes even a divergence, in the uses of poetry and the views of poetry to be found there. The *Ion* remains ambivalent in its own assertions, and even in its attempt at precise definitions, because it does not escape these diversities and divergences.

3.

Yet such inspiration as the *Ion* quizzes, even when it bears what is on the face of it a pejorative designation ("mania"), is still accorded praise. "Poetic mania" or inspiration is also inducted for utilization, in the *Phaedrus*, where poetic madness is the chief one under discussion of four kinds, all praised[14]—prophetic madness, therapeutic madness, love madness, and poetic madness. Indeed, in this instance poetic madness may be said to combine two kinds, since its power is enlisted to turn its excessive powers to love (*Phaedrus*, 244–45). It is poetry that is to be a future logical test (*elenchos*, 278c) for the writings of Lysias or anyone else. They are to be measured by Homer, the writers of odes, and Solon.

The first discussion in the *Republic* (376d–400c) begins positively: and it is qualified by its own mythic character, as if "mythologically exposed in a story" (ἐν μύθωι, μυθολο-γοῦντες, 376d). The first part of the guardians' education—"musical"—is to proceed before "gymnastic" education. The rejection of the poets comes by way of restricting the stories to be told, which are to be judged by the "pattern" (τύπος, 377b) used to "shape" or "stamp" them (πλάττεται). In this assertion, the most authoritative poets, Homer and Hesiod, do not give the right pattern. They are rejected not just because their stories are "false"; the education of the guardians is to begin with false stories rather than true ones. Their fault is, rather, that their fictions lack correspondence to the way the gods and heroes are—and the comparison to the painter (whose painting is wholly unlike) differs from the later rejection, which hangs on likenesses at too great a remove, rather than on unlikeness.

The representation of the gods, in all their aspects, is at this point the governing criterion. Homer is guilty first of all of theological distortion, and at this point one bearing on "the patterns with respect to theology" (τύποι περὶ θεολογίας). Plato deepens and focuses his argument by switching from Uranus and Kronos, Hera and Hephaestus, to "the god" (379a). At the same time he widens his net from specifically Homer to "epic and lyric and tragedy"—and the satiric iambic also (380a).

In one sense the subject here is as much theology as it is the poetic handling of it. The "second point" has to do with attributes of the god, his lack of deception and his changelessness. This discussion doubly undercuts Homer and Aeschylus (the poets named this time, 380–81), because they show stories embodying the opposite of these attributes, and they refer to Zeus rather than to "the god" in general who "least of all departs from his Form" (380e). And there is the further assertion that the god has nothing false in him (382e)—which would lead to a contradiction, if consistency were being sought here, since (a) false stories should first be told (b) the gods are, it is assumed, the object of stories but (c) the god does not admit of falsehood.[15] The exposition, through this slippage, betrays a tentativeness which befits the dramatically hurried sketchiness of this very inception of principles for the education of supposed guardians.

Then, a third point, the poet must pass on encouraging, and not discouraging, notions about Hades (as Homer does, 386); "the more poetic they are," he says, "the worse they are for children and men to hear," and the reason given is, oddly, not social control but 'freedom,' the *'eleutheria'* of the citizen's civil status in the city state—"men for whom it is necessary to be free rather than terrified into slavery to death" (387b).[16] Self-control, though, is implied, since it is shameful for Achilles (as the son of a goddess) to react agitatedly to the death of Patrocles, for Thetis to lament, for Zeus to be saddened over Hector, and for the gods to laugh (388a–99b).

As for poetry about men, Socrates here changes the standard from veracity about specific behaviors to the universal principle it is still the ongoing task of the *Republic* to determine, the nature of "justice" (*dikaiosune*). *Dikaiosune* is broader as a conception than any word that can be used to translate it—broad enough, it can be argued, to be retained as a measure for poetry, if of course it were applied more liberally than Plato here wishes to apply it.

Again shifting perspective, he uses this principle, aided by "imitation," to test kinds of poetry, rather than individual poets—dithyramb, tragedy, comedy, and epic. Here these genres are ruled out from fitness for educating guardians. Yet in other dialogues, all of these are referred to freely as implicitly valid modes of expression, a fact which throws into special relief the context of the *Republic* as a determinant here. The guardians are to be kept from undertaking imitations, as well as from hearing them, except for the unmixed, pure sort that will keep a guardian from being a "variegated man," (ἄνδρα παντοδαπόν, 398a). For lyric, all will be excluded, with the exception of songs for the brave under pressure and for the peaceful afterwards in worship and instruction (399b–c).

Much later, when Socrates resumes the discussion, even though he summarizes his rejection of a poetry that is mimetic (Book Ten, 595a4), mimesis is again introduced as a criterion.[17] This time, though, the term itself means not the simulation of the voices of other persons as opposed to straight narration (ἀπλὴ διήγησις), but rather, more generally, the correspondence of a literary representation to actual ideas, wants, and objects, and then to the guiding Forms beyond these. In the earlier discussion the proper imitator was to be brought through "speaking and narrative" to a "form in which what was in reality good and beautiful would be told" (396c)—a strongly positive, if severely restricted view that is here dropped (595a–608b). Indeed, Socrates relaxes virtually all the restrictions on poetry at the very end, allowing in his last words for a possibility of range that may said to match the contingent possibility that defines the whole constructed structure of the *Republic* in the first place (Book Five, 471c–73b). He is verging on the program for an educational syllabus well based in intelligence, prudence, excellence, and justice (*phronesis, sophrosune, arete, dikaiosune*), much like the one offered by Diotima in the *Symposium* (209c–d). That program *does* include Homer and Hesiod without qualification, and also "all the good poets," especially Solon.

The final discussion of poetry in the *Republic* is located between praise for the just and harmonious philosophic man and the myth-amplified exposition of the immortality of the soul. It is as though in such a framing context the discussion of poetry—if it not be regarded as a compulsive digression—takes on more optimistic coloring, in spite of the very limitations deduced about it. Indeed, Socrates begins with recalling his lifelong "love and respect" for Homer as a constraint against his speaking what he thinks to be the truth (595c). The discussion is now given the benefit of the discriminations around the doctrine of Forms in Book Seven. And he has now moved from gods and "the god" to the demiurge as the fashioner of Forms (596a–d)—or of himself, of heaven, of earth, and of the gods themselves. He is a "maker"—a *poietes*—just as the poet is a *poietes*, and by the measure of such supreme fashioning, the poet might well stand at two removes and still be conditionally admissable; as, again, he finally is. So far as the painter is concerned, it can be said that to show the object as in a mirror (*katoptron*, 596d7), and faintly (*amudron*, 597a) with respect to truth, is still to show it—as against the misrepresentation charged to the poet in Book Three. Further—and not consequentially in logic— Homer is joined in a short imaginary dialogue (599d–600c) in which his being at a second remove from Forms, for all his knowledge, would prevent him from answering the very question of the *Republic*, "which among cities has been better instituted because of you?" He cannot claim to be a civic founder like Lycurgus or Solon, a "wise" man like Thales, or the founder of rules for living, like Pythagoras.

This inadequacy is followed up by a partially commensurate triad of activities, "making, using, and imitating" or "making an image" (*eidolon*), for the three possessions, knowledge, correct opinion, and mere charm (*kelesis*), respectively. In this respect the poet is at a "third remove (602c) from the truth," not just a second. Then, in still another demonstration (602c–603), distortions of perspective are shown to be uncorrectable without a principle of measure, which the mimetic cannot of itself furnish, and especially not of "the thousands of oppositions with which our soul teems" (603e). Rather, poetry tends towards playing these up instead of pacifying them by a measured law (*nomos*). So, in the conclusion, only "hymns to the gods and encomia of good men are to be admitted into the city" (607a5). But "there is a sort of ancient variance between philosophy and the poetic," he says, and he urges that, now minimally, poetry be examined for being "useful" as well as "pleasurable," before being admitted to the city.[18]

Now the actual use of poetry in the dialogues admits of a wide variety that is at variance with a strict application of these canons, though it is reconcilable with their spirit, since the goal in view almost always involves some aspect of virtue or knowledge or justice or some combination thereof. Still, the means that is regarded as mostly dangerous or treacherous in the *Republic* is regularly given its key Greek authoritative place in other dialogues. The *Hippias Minor* bases itself on an interpretation of the actions of two Homeric heroes, Achilles and Odysseus,[19] beginning with the question of which is the more beautiful (*kallion*, 363b), the *Iliad* or the *Odyssey*. The gist of the discussion fortifies an identification between the beautiful and the good, without questioning at all the appropriateness of the evidence that is brought under examination, the poems themselves and the particular intentions the heroes reveal in their speeches.

In the *Seventh Letter* (345e), Plato makes an easy cultivated allusion to Scylla and Charybdis (*Odyssey* 12, 428–46), lightening the mention of the pressure placed upon him at his third voyage to Italy. Even though generally the *Laws*, in this as in other respects, supplements the *Republic* in the wholesale condemnation of poetry, still it is in the *Laws* (680b–c) that the *Odyssey* is quoted as a historical authority on the kind of government obtaining among the Cyclops, and a little later on the mountain settlements that preceded Troy (681e). Homer is quoted as a religious authority at the beginning, middle, and end of the account of judgments in the afterlife at the end of the *Gorgias* (523–27).

A host of passing references to Homer permeates the dialogues—and these are by no means confined to Homer's central position in Greek religious institutions nor to his corollary function as a sort of encyclopedia of information in a culture recently oral, comprehensive as both of these are. It is not just Homer, moreover, but the whole Greek poetic tradition, on which Plato constantly draws.[20]

In the *Theaetetus* (173e) Pindar is quoted for a passage that will glorify the reach of the philosopher's intelligence. Euripides' depiction of the very buffeting of the passions that is decried in the *Republic* does not prevent the *Symposium* from posing as a high example the Alcestis probably modelled on the *Alcestis* of Euripides.[21]

The *Protagoras*, which also examines at greater length the question about the teachability of virtue, turns at a key moment not just on an authoritative quotation from Simonides but on an *elenchos* directed at the correct interpretation of this quotation. As in the *Meno*, the quotation is introduced at an impasse in the discussion. It is Protagoras himself who quotes Simonides at a point where he has agreed to continue the discussion only if he can ask the questions. The irony that plays through the whole of the *Protagoras* is not absent here, but it does not markedly qualify the status of Simonides, though it does so somewhat indeterminately.[22]

The respect that Protagoras is given, and the qualifying self-limitation he exhibits, both condition his opening assertion, "I consider

that the greatest part of culture (*paideia*) for a man is to be skilled
(*deinon*) about verses (*epon*, 339a)." The reference to *paideia* sets
the assertion in a deep cultural context from which Plato's practice, I
have been arguing, does not dissent, though one set of strictures, those
of the *Republic* and the *Laws*, would deeply revise the role of poetry
in *paideia*. Poets, Protagoras goes on, have expressed themselves on
the very topic under discussion, on virtue. Simonides addresses a certain Thessaleus as follows:

> It is hard for a man truly to become good,
> Foursquare in hands and feet and mind, framed without blame.

Socrates claims that it does not need elucidation—and is well-ex-
pressed. If so, Simonides then says, as the poem proceeds it
contradicts itself:

> What the saying of Pittacus sets out does not ring true,
> Though said by a wise man; he says it is hard to be noble.

The statement has now become not only complicated by Simonides' alleged denial of what he has said earlier; it is further
complicated by his putting it in the metalinguistic form of criticizing a
saying of one of the Seven Wise Men; Simonides is shown to be engaging in the very literary-critical *elenchos* that Protagoras has
invoked. But Socrates resolves this proposed contradiction by distinguishing between "becoming good" in the first quotation and
"being noble" in the second. That the distinction is serious is indicated by its direct relevance to the main question "Is virtue
teachable?" This critical exposition could have no basis, not even an
ironic one, if the possibilities of the *Republic* were allowed that poets
can generally be mistaken and typically are.

The satiric overtone about Protagoras' excessive reliance on poetry remains an overtone. Socrates both jokes about this and evokes
multiple contexts when he calls on Prodicus, who is present, to help
with a defense because he is Simonides' fellow-citizen; Socrates calls
on Prodicus, he says, the way Homer has Achilles call on the river
Scamander—a hyperbolically joking evocation that assigns a mock-
heroic dimension to the heroic *Iliad* (339e–340). Socrates quotes
Hesiod to substantiate Simonides' first statement (340d) and
Prodicus' defense. Two quotations, three speakers, and three poets are

now involved, as well as the "godly wisdom begun long ago by Simonides, or even earlier" (341a). More angles of the quotation are examined, briefly, and then Socrates (342) brings the discussion back to the main distinction, relating the question of virtue to what he claims to be the ancient tradition of philosophy in those very polities that will later in the *Laws* embody political ideals, Laconian and Cretan. They hide this tradition, however, as understaters in what could be called a supremely Socratic fashion. This is what "to be laconic" really means (342). It leads directly, he claims, to the pithy utterances (*rhemata brachea*) of the Seven Wise Men, of whom the seventh in his list is the Spartan Chilas (343).

Then come the utterances of the Delphic oracle—"Know thyself" and "Nothing to excess." In quoting these Socrates has created a sound if somewhat fanciful bridge between the kernel utterances in the poetry under question and the basic proportions with which philosophy began—notably his own: especially in the *Apology*, he will rely fundamentally on the Delphic "Know thyself." Pittacus' utterance is one of these (343b7). Simonides' aim, he declares, was to better the apopthegm of Pittacus; and so he sets up "It is hard to be novel," so that it can be bettered by "It is hard to become good." Socrates then creates a sort of *elenchos* of the saying of Pittacus (344b4) and proceeds to substantiate this reading with other, relevant verse quotations. It is possible to *become* noble, but impossible simply to *be* so, since an activity of process (*praxis*) must always be involved.

Since the exegesis here leads to and supports the fundamental Socratic principle that no one knowingly and willingly acts wrongly (345d), it is impossible not to grant some earnestness to this discussion: it means what it says. But it inextricably presents that meaning through digressive overassertion and modifying byplay, through still another twist of irony that invests all the conditions here derived from poetry—and philosophy—indeterminately with a hint of sportive contingency. It concludes with the somewhat irrelevant corollary that Simonides may sometimes have had to praise a tyrant against his will, and is forced by Pittacus' oversimplification to blame Pittacus when he would prefer not to have done so.[23]

Further interplay, founded on an unequivocal, and here double, recourse to the authority of poetry is undertaken at the main turning point of the *Phaedrus*, where Socrates appeals to the parallel case of Stesichorus in abjuring his own version of Lysias' proposition that the beloved would do better to listen to the nonlover than to the lover. In a case where indeed love and its possibly disastrous consequences are at issue (part of Socrates' point), the legendary case of Helen, Stesichorus saves himself from temporary blindness by writing:

> This story is not genuine,
> You were not in the well-decked ships
> Nor came to the towers of Troy.

Thus he was able to gain his sight, Socrates says (ironically, it must be), "because as a devotee of the muses (*mousikos*) he knew the cause," as Homer did not (243a), who thus remained blind. So Stesichorus wrote his palinode, his recantation, and Socrates proposes to write his own palinode.[24] He then outlines the kinds of madness, one of which is love-madness, another the madness of the Muses. He is proposing to expound the madness of love, by the madness of poetry, madness being a necessary ingredient in both cases, so that a "palinode" on love would a fortiori gain from its recourse to such possession: "The lover is mad ... The greatest goods come to us from mania, a gift of the gods ... and the mania of the Muses ... teaches as it adorns them, ten thousand deeds of those of old" (244a–45a).

The quality of maniacally inspired poetry, it is here asserted, consists in its communicating "deeds of those of old." It memorializes heroes, as Homer did. Stesichorus picks up this thread at the point where love enters the fabric; and Socrates has, so to speak, both covered that tradition and passed beyond it as he proceeds to his own poetic speech, which begins on a subject quite different from both, though connected logically for the wise to the fact that love is a "gift of the gods": "All soul is immortal" (245c5).

The discussion will begin not only, of course, in a prose that is characterized as analogous to poetry but in a prose that utilizes arguments very much along the lines of the discussion about the immortality of the soul in the *Phaedo* and the *Meno*. Thus by implication Plato has associated his procedures generally not just with poetry but with inspired poetry (which he has distinguished from uninspired in the introduction about *mania*). The transition to the myth of the soul as a charioteer drawing a team through the heavens with one white-winged horse and one black retains the connection between the prose demonstration and the myth's ontological extrapolation beyond it. All this is characterized as poetic, as from the domain of inspired poetry, and as true doctrine, substitutive and corrective of false doctrine, the way the poem of Stesichorus was. This demonstration, indeed, has the authorship of Stesichorus playfully assigned to it (244a).

After an eschatological demonstration, the discussion gradually shades back into the abstractions with which it had begun. At a still later point, as a sort of descent from these lofty identifications into which poetry and the origins of poetry are intimately and indissociably integrated, there is a casual, more ordinary testing of the views of Sophocles and Euripides (268c–69a). As often, an irony veils the heart of the questioning. The *Phaedrus*, with unmistakable playfulness, touches on a myth that the poets are grasshoppers ravished into carelessness of their very survival by the charm of the muses.

In the *Phaedo*, one argument against defining the soul as a harmony is that it does not accord with the view of the emotions that Homer expresses (94e–95a); and Socrates will shortly say that he will try to carry out a discussion about the soul "Homerically" (95b7). In a discussion of the depth and purity of impressions that the heart of a person may take, Homer is spoken of as "riddling" (*ainittomenos*), and as "the all-wise poet" (*passophos poietes*, *Theaetetus* 194c–e).

From the *Charmides* to the *Laws*, Solon, the statesman-poet, is brought in as what amounts to a countercase to the socially vitiating poets censured by the *Republic*.[25] Solon's life is integrated into his writing, but his political activity, in the *Timaeus* (20–25), is valued as more important than his poetry. In the *Phaedo* (60d–61a), using terms that include both poetry and music ("*mousike*" allowing for both activities of the Muses), Socrates, who has been setting Aesop's fables to verse and writing hymns to Apollo at the injunction of a dream visitor,[26] introduces the more comprehensive possibility that "philosophy is the greatest music"[27] This possibility, turned back on the variety of Plato's confrontations with poetry, and indeed with music too,[28] would subsume that variety as providing the constituents of a range of valuations and interpretations, positive and negative. It would strain them, and in a sense oversimplify them, to try to reconcile them—or even to leave them in a sort of fragmented and random divergence. This abstracting maxim from the *Phaedo* on the one hand, and the employment on the other hand of what is claimed in the *Phaedrus* to be poetic inspiration as the basis for confecting a myth with an explanatory function, means that we cannot detach the activity of poetry from Plato's constructions themselves, though we cannot identify them with it wholly either, since the component of philosophical inquiry remains primary in them, fighting against the very poetry it utilizes, interprets, rejects, and in some ways imitates.

Notes

1. Plato's situation of contesting the encyclopedic thrust of the authoritative oral poetry in his tradition is well detailed by Eric Havelock in *Preface to Plato*. The *Laws* (669) summarizes another set of criteria for the "image" (εἰκών) in poetry and music and all the arts: 1) "that which is" (ὁ τε ἔστιν) 2) "how it is rightly presented" (ὡς ὀρθῶς), and 3) "how well it is presented" (ὡς εὖ). Again, what is puzzling is the lack of a sense that these criteria in themselves are in need of far fuller demonstration.

2. The range of Plato's use of poetry, beyond implicit contradictions, is pointed up by Bruno Gentili's summary in another connection in *Poetry and its Public in Ancient Greece* (Baltimore: The Johns Hopkins University Press, 1988), 153), "Poetry of absolute values and human perfection on the one hand, and, on the other, poetry of relative values and human perfection—these are the two opposed positions taken up by Pindar and Simonides." But Plato seems to assign equal authority to both (assuming that any irony about Simonides in the *Protagoras* is an overtone). This is striking, even if one does not go all the way with Gentili's schematic opposition.

3. ἀποκρίνεσθαι ... ἀνάγκη Μούσας γε οὔσας.

4. Φῆσι με ποιητὴν εἶναι θεῶν.

5. M. L. West, *Greek Meter* (Oxford, Clarendon Press, 1982), 29–55.

6. Unless we provide, as we should, that the context of a given dialogue is determining. Kenneth Dover in *The Symposium* (Cambridge: Cambridge University Press, 1980), 82, points out that the Greeks when they cite poetry usuually do so out of context. As Hans-Georg Gadamer more positively puts it, (*Dialogue and Dialectic: Eight Hermeneutical Studies on Plato*, 49), "Thus Plato's purification of traditional poetry can be understood only in relationship to the purpose of the whole of this paradigmatic constitution in the *Republic*. And the proposed purification of poetry, like the constitution, is not to be taken literally, i.e., as a set of instructions for

reconstructing traditional education, a purification of the curriculum according to new standards."

7.   As Gadamer says (43) "Exactly why does Plato reprove Homer? First, for his picture of the gods, i.e., the human appearance, so well known to us, which he gives the gods—gods who in the heights of their Olympian existence quarrel and transgress, plot and scheme in much the same way that men are forever doing. And second, he resists Homer's image of Hades, which must necessarily arouse the fear of death. He objects to the excessive bewailing of the dead, the excessive scorn and ridicule, and the wanton passions and desires in Homer's gods and heroes. All this seems to be more a critique of myth such as it exists in Homer than a critique of poetry per se. And Plato is not alone in his criticism of myth. His predecessors here include philosophers such as Xenophanes, Heraclitus, Pythagoras, and Anaxagoras, all of whom had similar criticisms of Homer's theology. But above all it is the later poets, Pindar and the tragedians, who are in agreement with Plato. It is they who purified and exalted the imagery of the gods and heroes by building upon the old myths while expressly rejecting the traditional form of the legend." And further (40–41), "Homer, it is said, had not founded a better state than Charondas or Solon. Nor did he have any ingenious discoveries to show for himself like those of Thales or Anarcharsis. Nor was he influential in the private sphere; unlike Pythagoras, who established a Pythagorean way of life for the few, Homer created no Homeric life as the leader of a circle of followers. Nor could he even compare to the great sophists in being an effective and successful educator, but instead he found himself living an unstable rhapsodic existence."

8.   For example, the guardians are to pursue a good not "deceived by sicknesses or erotic loves" (ἢ ὑπό νόσων ἢ ὑπό ἐρώτων ἐσφαλ' μένον, 396d1–2). See also the rejection of *aphrodision*, *Republic* 606d.

9.   That the *Ion* is at once clear and ambiguous is indicated by the efforts that have been made, never carrying full conviction, to translate this dialogue into an explicit doctrine. Hans Diller addresses these difficulties in "Probleme des platonischen Ion," *Hermes* 83, 1955, 171–81. For the limitations of the dialogue in its attempt to separate literary criticism from the expertise of specific techniques, see Steven Lowenstam, "Is Literary Criticism an Illegitimate Discipline? A Fallacious Argument in Plato's Ion," *Ramus*, 22, 1, 1993, 19–32.

10.   Enthusiasm is amply discussed by Hellmut Flashar in *Der Dialog Ion als Zeugnis Platonischer Philosophie* (Berlin: Akademie Verlag, 1958). André Delatte, *Les Conceptions de L'Enthousiasme chez les philosophes présocratiques* (Paris: Belles Lettres, 1934), traces the history of the conception. Delatte cites Heraclitus on the Sibyl and on Dionysus; Empedocles, Democritus, and the Hippocratic texts on "the sacred malady." Plato applies the term "ἐνθουσιάζειν" to politicians and philosophers, as

Flashar has indicated (120–21). Plato gives the term only once in the substantive, in the *Timaeus*. Otherwise Plato uses the verb, never the noun. He discusses enthusiasm in the *Laws* (719c). Socrates in the *Apology* links the poet to *"theomanteis"* and *"chresmodoi"* who perform not by skill but by nature, "οὐ σοφίαι ... ἀλλὰ φύσει τινὶ καὶ ἐνθουσιάζοντες" (22c). It is in a context where Socrates claims to be the wisest because he knows he is ignorant. In this light is can be said that poets are neither better nor worse than the politicians and the technicians that he has also consulted. See also J. Verdenius, *Mimesis, Mnemosyne* II, 11 (1943), 233–62; 12, 1944, 118–50.

11.   As Hans Diller indicates, "Probleme des Ion" (186), the dialogue addresses the relations between "man and woman, slave and free, guardian and subject," as they are discussed in the *Republic* (600d).

12.   *Ion*, τὸν γὰρ ῥαψῳδὸν ἑρμηνέα δεῖ τοῦ ποιητοῦ τῆς διανοίας γίγνεσθαι τοῖς ἀκούουσιν, "the rhapsode must become an interpreter of the poet's thought to those who listen" (530c1–3). To be sure, the theory of the magnetic links does assimilate the reciter and the interpreter to the poet himself. A passage in the *Laws* identifies them all, "Is it not the case that all poets and listeners and actors would admit that poetry in its relation to music is wholly an imitation and production of images?" (ποιήματα μίμησίς τε καὶ ἀπεικασία; καὶ τοῦτό γε μῶν οὐκ ἂν σύμπαντες ὁμολογοῖεν ποιηταί τε καὶ ἀκροαταὶ καὶ ὑποκριταί ... 668b10–c2).

13.   In the course of his presentation, Ion answers Socrates with respect to the subjects "of the other *technés*" that he believes should treat that which is proper "to man, to woman, to the slave, to the free man, to him who is governed and to him who governs," (ἃ πρέπει, οἶμαι ἔγωγε, ἀνδρὶ εἰπεῖν καὶ ὁποῖα γυναικί, καὶ ὁποῖα δούλωι καὶ ὁποῖα ἐλευθέρωι, καὶ ὁποῖα ἀρχομένωι καὶ ὁποῖα ἄρχοντι, 540b3–5).

14.   Often, of course, mania has a common negative valuation in Plato as at *Rep.* 9.573a; *Rep.* 382 (where he discusses poetry but does not specifically apply the term); *Phil.* 45e; *Prot.* 323b. The guardians are to avoid "being brought to mania in word and in deed" (*Rep.* 396a3; repeated also at 396b).

15.   The inconsistency would be diminished if an absolute distinction were made (though Plato never makes one explicitly) between the Olympian gods and Plato's abstract "god."

16.   The term "the free city state" is adduced in this connection again at 395c; again, the guardians are to imitate "what is fitting to them from childhood—the courageous, the social, the holy, the free."

17.   This criterion can be discussed on its own merits, or it can be isolated so as to produce a definition of what Plato means by mimesis. Such

a consideration might begin with the objection of Julius A. Elias, in *Plato's Defense of Poetry* (Albany: SUNY Press, 1984), 11), "The counterclaim on behalf of the artists which does not appear to have occurred to Plato, or perhaps he was merely being disingenous, is that it is the form itself they attempt to copy, not the physical copy of it."

18.   See also Jacqueline de Romilly, *Magic and Rhetoric in Ancient Greece* (Cambridge: Harvard University Press, 1975), with quotation of erotic effects in *Gorgias* (fgt. 9, *Helen*). A considerable psychology is developed for "charm" (θέλγειν), by Charles Segal, in *Harvard Studies in Classical Philology*, 1962—but for Plato the term appears only once, of singing in *Symposium* 197e. Further, as Guthrie (IV, 451) points out, this is just a *moral* education; intellectual education comes later.

19.   There are different degrees of appositeness in Plato's assignment of authority to poetry. Jules Labarre, in *L'Homère de Platon* (Paris: Belles Lettres, 1949), 49 and passim, presents four classes for Plato's citations of Homer, based on the "nécessité plus ou moins grande" of the citation.

20.   This is richly elaborated by Paul Vicaire, *Platon Critique littéraire* (Paris: Klincksieck, 1960).

21.   Vicaire (172). He notes that the dramatic date of the dialogue is close to that of the production of the play.

22.   Guthrie disagrees (*History of Greek Philosophy*, IV, 227), as do others whom he cites. But in substantiating what he calls "outrageous," Guthrie has the Spartans here, whom Plato much admired, supposedly subjected to irony. As Michael C. Stokes, who takes the use of Simonides seriously, well says, "It is well to assume until proved mistaken, Plato's consistency of purpose throughout the dialogue." *Plato's Socratic Conversations* (London: Athlone, 1986), 315. The play of irony over the whole dialogue, and its consistency of tone, would further militate against our bracketing the presentation of arguments about the quotations from Simonides into a self-contradicting, exaggeratedly satiric posture, as is argued by Gregory Vlastos, "Does Socrates Cheat?" in *Socrates: Ironist and Moral Philosopher*, 132–56 (135–39).

23.   Michael C. Stokes (*Plato's Socratic Conversations*, 195) connects the classification here to Protagoras' own assertion (316c–d) that poets, mystery-purveyors, gymnasts, and musicians were all really Sophists *avant la lettre*. Among poets he lists Simonides, Homer and Hesiod, all three quoted in Socrates' discussion.

24.   As Charles W. Griswold says in *Self-Knowledge in Plato's* Phaedrus (New Haven: Yale University Press, 1986), 77, "The complexity of the status of poetry is also clear from the fact that the palinode of recantation is itself a kind of poetry." See also Martha Nussbaum, "'This story isn't true': madness, reason, and recantation in the *Phaedrus*," *The Fragility of Goodness*, 200–34. Nussbaum well frames the deductions one can make from

this dialogue, while allowing "literature" and "philosophy" to separate too definitively.

25. Vicaire, 117–19, discusses the passages in Plato where Solon is considered.

26. As Hackforth points out, the term "enteinontes" would mean too that Socrates is setting the fables to music—a strange idea.

27. ὡς φιλοσοφίας μὲν οὔσης μεγίστης μουσικῆς (*Phaedo* 61a).

28. In the *Cratylus* "Muses" and "music" are derived from the Doric word *mosthai*, a desire. The data on Plato's ramifying references to music are presented in Evanghélos Moutsopoulos, *La Musique dans l'oeuvre de Platon* (Paris: Presses Universitaires de France, 1959). For a discussion of the pervasiveness of Plato's views, through Aristoxenus, as they governed technical descriptions of musical practice and effect, see Flora R. Levin, *The Manual of Harmonics of Nicomachus the Pythagorean* (Grand Rapids: Phanes, 1994); and her forthcoming book on Aristoxenus.

Chapter 5

Plato's Handling of Myth

καὶ χρὴ τὰ τοιαῦτα ὥσπερ ἐπᾴδειν ἑαυτῶι, διὸ δὴ
ἔγωγε καὶ πάλαι μηκύνω τὸν μῦθον.

And one must, as it were, sing such things to oneself; for that reason
indeed I have been lengthening out the mythos, and for a long time.

Phaedo, 114d5–7

The story or mythos for Plato will lengthen out a dialogue but also
wind one up. It is not even clear here whether by "mythos" Socrates
means the story he has just told of the rivers of the underworld and
the Last Judgment, or much of the whole of the *Phaedo*. In any case
this myth's freedom of combination matches the freedom of invention with which he brings it into his argument, performing upon it the
fusion which revises and redefines the separation from myth that
Xenophanes and Heraclitus and Hecataeus in their various ways had
taken as a beginning of philosophy. They sought a freedom which
Empedocles, and after him Parmenides, found within the domain of
myth itself by writing their philosophical systems in the framework of

cosmological allegories. Both Herodotus and Thucydides found it necessary to draw a line between their inquiry and foregone myths. But Plato boldly conducts his inquiry neither by staying within the realm of myth nor by eschewing myth, but rather by deepening the nature of philosophical discourse through playing fast and loose with myth, making it subserve the logos that had seemed antithetical to it, while at the same time enlisting its power to extend the logos.[1] As Julius Stenzel says of Plato, "He gives to mere mythology the dignity of a religious metaphysic, and demonstrates that it is the foundation of that synopsis of the whole of knowledge for which he strives."[2]

Since Plato often invents his myths or composes them from a variety of sources, it is easy for the modern interpreter to forget that one aspect of his doing so is that he exercises the same creativity toward myths and myth-making that is generally exhibited by the Greek poets, though in a far more forceful and original manner. It has long been argued that the selection of myths in Homer slants them away from the chthonic practices that were in vigor in his era; Homer has an Olympian bias, Hesiod a slightly different one. Among philosophers, Empedocles invents but also deeply recasts his myths. In a society that had no separate scriptures other than literary texts, any important literary text could take on a religious tinge. And so could even oral arguments, a situation which could be taken as offering a corollary to the indictment against Socrates, that he "does not esteem the gods the city esteems, but other, new daimons" (*Apology* 24b7–8).

Behind Socrates is a Socratizing Plato. The turn inward and "personal" takes the dramatic form out of the realm of myth, initially—and then restores it elsewhere in this rhetorical repertoire. The dialogue installs myth in "remembered" reality, a key nearly always given in time to a specific time, as in the Sparta of the *Laches* (424). In all this Plato drastically revises the use of myth in the poems, prose treatises, and aphorisms of the pre-Socratics, as well as the received range of myth in the culture from folk tale to ritual, embracing the literary uses in epic, lyric poetry, comedy, and tragedy.

It is perilous either to connect the myths in the dialogues too closely to the rest of the demonstration or to separate them too definitely. Sometimes, to repeat the musical analogy ("philosophy is the greatest music," *Phaedo*, 61a), the mode changes, sometimes the melody, and sometimes both. One of the longest and most traditional of Plato's myths, that of Epimetheus and Prometheus in the *Protagoras*, serves just to slant the topic towards an anthropology in which shame and justice (δίκη) can be connected to social need as givens; as an "evidence" (τεκμήριον) that "you should not get the notion of being deceived that in reality all men consider that every man participates in justice and in every political virtue."[3]

We are accustomed to Plato's invention of myths, and also to his distortion of prior myths, even in regularly straightforward instances, like the Prometheus of the *Protagoras*, where fire is obscured by its being put on a parity with public activity, and before that with private subsistence. The public activity turns out to require the supplemental agency of Hermes, where fire had been stolen not (as traditionally) from Zeus, a god who here is strangely in the background, his name not mentioned until halfway through the story. Rather, fire is stolen from Hephaestus and skills from Athene, and the punishment of Prometheus seems here to be that he is simply barred from Olympus. This is a strangely mild fate, especially in view of the fact that Protagoras is shortly to recommend that human beings who lack a "justice" and "shame-respect" (*aidos*) are to be put to death as a pestilence (*nosos*, 322d). In this situation, indeed, the myth puts Prometheus close to the point of view of the gods.[4]

All these interpretive details may be regarded as either Plato's modifications, or his representation of Protagoras' modifications, and the form of the dialogue prohibits our distinguishing these two alternatives. But we are left with a modified myth, as often in Plato, who usually offers one that has been either invented or heavily adapted. Often, and characteristically, the references to mythical figures from the tradition are so succinct that they have the force of references to a piety that Plato rarely singles out, again, for distinguishing the elements in it. More characteristically he conflates his components, so that both Orphic and Pythagorean constituents are melded in the *Phaedo*.[5] Or else, as in the *Meno*, he separates these elements, so that the authority of Pindar and the mathematical demonstration are distinct, if mutually substantiating. Mathematics and music were at the heart of the Pythagorean system, whatever it may have been, but Plato's abundant citations of mathematics and music in the points made about a *paideia* never connect these "skills" to religion, even though there is much evidence for a mystique about mathematics in Plato, as Konrad Gaiser demonstrates,[6] and even though mathematics, in the *Meno*, the *Republic,* and elsewhere is used in a nearly theological way; and even though the references in the *Phaedo* and elsewhere to harmony in the soul have to be intended as something more than metaphors, and therefore to be taken for some sort of transposition of Pythagorean doctrine.

In the *Phaedrus*, for example, the initial mention of myth is linked to a specific place, and to the ordinary Greek religion, seen in low profile because Boreas is not a major god. Geography switches to mytheme when the question is raised as to whether in a sort of love triangle (Boreas, Pharmacia, Orythuia), Boreas abducted Orythuia. The "scientific" answer, that she was blown off the cliff by the north wind, is attributed to *sophoi* and declared unsatisfactory.[7] Difficult cases would really puzzle the *sophoi*, Socrates says, and the ones adduced, unlike the myth (with its love-analogy), are all composite beings—centaurs, gorgons, chimeras, and Pegasuses.

The last figure, in fact, provides a long-range thematic link in this dialogue to the winged horses driven by the charioteer of the sun. But meanwhile the two speeches of Lysias and Socrates have been matched and then dropped on the principle of "this story isn't true" in Stesichorus.

The limitations of the *sophoi* get shifted when later they (in a different sense) are contrasted with the *deinoi* (245d2), who by definition are "terribly skilled," and so are much the same as those of the *sophoi* in this passage. Yet they do not believe what Socrates is recounting of the soul, when the *sophoi* do believe. *Sophoi*, that is, in one context are implicitly opposed to *sophoi* in another.

That later opposition, combined with the earlier one applied to Boreas, validates myth. It makes myth an approximation-stab through resemblance at an explanation of what would otherwise be inexplicable. This is here stated to be all that a human being can do, as opposed to a god who could expound the idea.

The more curtailed a myth, it may be said, the more it departs from the ideal account which a god could give, of which a human account is at best an approximation. This important principle, a sort of narrative or diegetic corollary to the theory of Forms, is formulated distinctly, if briefly, as Socrates is about to begin the myth of the Charioteer:

Περὶ μὲν οὖν ἀθανασίας αὐτῆς [τῆς ψυχῆς] ἱκανῶς· περὶ δὲ τῆς ἰδέας αὐτῆς ὧδε λεκτέον οἷον μέν εστι, πάντηι πάντως θείας εἶναι καί μακρᾶς διηγήσεως, ὧι δέ ἔοικεν, ἀνθρωπίνης τε καὶ ἐλάττονος· ταύτηι οὖν λέγωμεν. ἐοικέτω δή συμφύτωι δυνάμει ὑπο᾽ πτέρου ζεύγους τε καὶ ἡνιόχου.

About the immortality of it [the soul], that is enough. But about its Form [*idea*], we must speak as follows. What it is would be wholly and in every way a narrative for a god, and a long one. But what it is like [is a narrative] for a man and shorter. So in this way let us speak. It is like the congenital force of a winged team and a charioteer.   (246a2–7)

These differentiating traits are offered here to distinguish a god's account (*diegesis*) from a human one. The god's deals with the subject "wholly and in every way" (πάντηι πάντως), in the redundancy of emphasis; a man can do it "in this way" (ταυτῆι). A god's account deals with "what sort it is," a human one with "what it is like." And a god's is long, a man's shorter.

Such "limiting" conditions persist in the dialogue; in a different perspective, they govern the superiority of oral presentation to written. Here the myths start both with a negative condition of human limitation and with a positive capacity of exceeding the *sophoi*. The opposition madness-sanity, with the four types of madness, is likewise conditioned. And the explanations stand on a par of "seriousness" within the definition of play for the whole dialogue, whereas in the *Symposium* the mix of seriousness to play can be felt to change, measured by the terms *spoude* as opposed to *paizein*, coming to a head at 197e6–8. As Dover says, "Agathon describes his speech as partly παιδία ('sport,' 'relaxation,' 'entertainment') and partly σπουδή μετρία, 'seriousness in the proper measure', 'a degree of seriousness.'"[8] Aristophanes is playful on the surface; he behaves as though he is guessing psychology through approximations. Alcibiades is buffoonlike in his behavior but straining earnestness through intoxication in his desperation about Socrates, who himself has waxed, from a playful beginning, into an earnestness like that of

Eryximachus. The *Phaedrus*, by contrast, keeps its mix of earnestness and play in an even tone throughout. But play (παιδία) remains for Plato a term associated with myth as late as the *Statesman* (265b–d). The force of the association, given the way he uses myth, works not to undercut myth but to dignify play.[9] Traditional myths are frequently given playful passing mention in the dialogues, as the joking reference to Amphion and Zethon in the *Gorgias* (506b) or the reference to Cadmus and Harmonia in the *Phaedo* (95a–b).

In the *Laws* (898b), speaking of the mind (*nous*) in which resides the single principle of motion, the Athenian says "we would not appear to be insignificant demiurges in the *logos* of beautiful images"[10] Here the Athenian is comparing the collective dialogue to the work of supreme craftsmen, and the "logos of beautiful images" grazes myth without exactly taking it up fully. The cosmology here, in so far as it exemplifies pure spirit, parallels the myth of Er in the *Republic*. But in so far as it is physical rather than psycho-spiritual, it conforms pretty much to the structure joined when in the *Theaetetus* (180d) the myth of Oceanus and Tethys is interpreted as figuring the truth about the transitoriness of things.

The terms themselves shift. In the *Republic* at one point (382c–d), *logoi* is used of the words in a context where the term "mythologies" is also used—a casual overlap which demonstrates, at the point of diction, that on one tangent the terms, and so the conceptions, admit of convergence. "Falsehood in words ... and [it may be useful] in the mythologies we just spoke about, through not knowing the way the truth obtains about ancient things, likening the false to the true so that we may make it as useful as possible."[11] In the *Gorgias* (523a) Socrates says what he calls *logos*, Callicles calls *mythos*. Such equivocation, and even sometimes a reversal, of these two large terms is rendered possible because Plato has placed them into interdependence, and an interdependence new to the Greek philosophical and literary worlds. The interplay between *logos* and *mythos* testifies to the indissociable function of both in the full Platonic presentation.[12] "The myth of Protagoras died" Socrates says in the *Theaetetus*, referring by "myth" here to a doctrine of perception (164d). He continues, adding what in its sense is a metaphor but with the same reference, "it wouldn't have died if the fathers of the first myth had lived" (164d–

e).[13] In the same dialogue (173–74), after a number of metaphors have been applied to the use of language in the contemplative life, there is introduced the pattern-story of the Thracian girl mocking Thales for falling into the well when he looked at the stars (174). This is not called a myth, but it is interpreted also as touching on both the function and the subjects of philosophy. It is another submythic illustrative anecdote.[14]

Plato's invented myths draw, as they must, on the repertoire of mythical staple elements, sometimes incorporating traditional myths while reshaping them in a way that itself is traditional, as he does with the Prometheus myth. His overall patterns, too, accord with the underlying syntax of the recursions in neolithic mythic thinking, in their adaptation for millennial cycles of the seasonal cycles connected to sun and moon by the Indo-European and various other mythic systems. And this is so for the largest of his myths, the eschatological ones in the *Republic* and the *Gorgias*. It is the case, as well, for the complex myth of human origins in the *Timaeus*. In the *Timaeus*, a cosmic myth of the creation of the human soul at once explains fantasy, the structure of the eye, and how images get reversed in mirrors (45c–e). It also lays this explanation out in relation to the invisibility of the soul as against the visibility of things: "For of beings it is fitting that for this thing alone, mind, be established; it is called the soul; and it is invisible" (46d5).[15] As Ronna Burger points out, myth in Plato's presentation tends to get associated with ontology.[16] When he employs traditional myths, usually in passing, Plato takes them fairly straight, and as though he is giving them the standard credence of his culture. He does not raise pointed questions about them, as Heraclitus does about the oracle at Delphi, the Sibyl, and the relation between Hades and Dionysus. There is little or nothing in his work that would allow for an examination in the contradictions, say, of an Apollo who is at once murderous and benificent.[17] On the other hand, even the stern *Laws* (603d7) envisages a polymorphous situation for the human psyche that the myths in other dialogues may be taken to address, "soul teems with myriad oppositions (ἐναντιοματῶν)." And the *Laws* sees a taming function for mythology: "Now it seems well to testify to your account ascribing their ancient way to their wildness through telling a story/myth about it" (680d30).[18] In the

Laws (663e) one must also believe even the strange "Sidonian mythologeme" (τό τοῦ Σιδόνιου μυθολογήμα) about hoplites sown from teeth, the sort of myth that, when invented, like the one Aristophanes offers in the *Symposium*, is covered in the glow of fictionality.

In his inferential process Plato sees the very sources of springs and rivers as sacred signs remaining to us showing that what is said "now about it (the earth) is true" (*Phaedo* 111d5–7). By inference, then, a credence is assigned to the Greek gods, but a blind credence that later in the *Republic* (for example) will monotheize before it examines—in contradistinction to either Sophocles or Aeschylus, of whom the first is mentioned and the second quoted early in the first two books of the *Republic*. In the *Statesman* (268e), the myth of Atreus and Thyestes opens out to the stars and the demiurge, and then to the startling idea of reversing the life-course: the young become babies and then disappear. As Burger says (27) of the reference to Aesop in the *Phaedo*, "The Aesopian mythos thus assumes what the Socratic account makes into a problem: What is the so-called pleasant or the painful? It is because it implicitly raises this question—at least once it is contrasted with mythos—that Socrates' account can be labeled a logos." But the *mythos* inextricably extends and complicates the *logos* here in the *Phaedo*, as elsewhere.

To ask about Plato's own belief points up that question but also deflects and complicates it. All the evidence of the dialogues leads to the conclusion that he believes the traditional myths somewhat the way his pious contemporaries did—which is by no means an easy resolution in itself, as Paul Veyne has shown. As Veyne says:

> How could all these legends be believed, and truly believed? The question is not of the subjective order: the modalities of belief refer back to the modes of possessing the truth; a plurality of programs about truth exists through the centuries which comprise different distributions of knowledge, and it is these programs that explains the subjective degrees of intensity for belief, bad faith, and contradictions in a single individual. We believe Michel Foucault on the question [It is of course Nietzsche's point originally]: the history of ideas begins truly when the philosophical idea of truth is historicized.[19]

This modality, then, is a complex anthropological question, but it feeds into the still more complex modality of the question of the credence, within his system and generally, that Plato would wish to assign to the myths that he invents in his dialogues. They are not simply the tales of an anthropological informant, on however large a scale. But they must also be treated at least initially as such.

The significative structure of an invented myth, however, may translate easily point for point into the abstract argument it is designed to illustrate,[20] and still it may reach deep into the confluences of religious tradition, as is the case with the story of those condemned to carry water in sieves in Hades because they have not mastered the passions (*Gorgias*, 492e–94). This is again a counterexample to Callicles' retort that if those are blessed who want nothing, then stones and corpses are most blest. Socrates introduces his reply with the Borges-like quotation from Euripides (the lost *Phrixes* or the *Polynices*) that makes what may be called a super-Heraclitean[21] point about the distinction between life and death in the first place: "Who knows if living is to die, dying to live."

"We may already *be* dead," Socrates says, "and the body be a tomb" [*soma*=body/*sema*=tomb], so that part of the soul where the desires happen may be such as to be influenced and to reverse up/down, as some high flown mythologizing man, perhaps a Sicilian or an Italian, adduced in the name 'jar' [*pithos*] comparing 'obeying' [*pithanos*] and 'persuasive' [*peistikos*]: and imaging through their insatiability the senseless and uninitiated, ... and their desires, unreproved and not 'watertight,' to be like a perforated jar." Then this image, in turn, is compared to the wretched in Hades who must carry water in a sieve over to a perforated jar. One image overlaps the other, and the central conception combines a mystic tradition and philosophical speculation. Yet what is "left over" in the correspondence between the image-vehicle of the sieve and the correspondence-tenor of the desires will yield no further significations than a sense of hoariness and awe about the whole. That sense, however, gives an apocalyptic overtone to the lightness of Socrates' banter and an oracular impenetrability to the lucidity of his *elenchos*. It does not carry us far toward interpretation that there are many sources for this myth.[22]

In so far as Socrates has once more resumed the normal distinction between life and death, the final myth of *punishment* in the afterlife that he tells (523–27) is less speculative in its overall significative dimensions than the sieve-watercarrier story. It is also more conventionally Orphic, and less isolated, in its congruence with the accounts of the disposition of souls in the afterlife that are offered by the *Republic* (614a–621d), the *Phaedrus* (246a–57d), and the *Phaedo* (107d–15a). But the repertory is larger; and so it opens out to a greater specificity than the "desires" of the earlier tale, beginning with the Isles of the Blest (523–27). While its significative structure remains the same, its metalinguistic characterization does not, being defined by Socrates' introductory suspension of a definition, "Hear, then, a beautiful *logos*, which you, I think, may consider a *mythos*, but I a *logos*, since I shall tell you what I am to tell you as something that is true" (523a1–3). In a sense this scheme preserves the indiscriminateness between life and death, since the corpse and the soul of the dead man retain here the features of the body while it was alive, as well as a correspondence to its psychological features.

Since this *mythos-logos* ends a dialogue concerned with reasons for avoiding wrongdoing and eschewing the primacy of desires, it is meant, as the peroration shows, to serve as a capping demonstration and conclusive argument (it is called a " *logos*"!) to the *elenchos*, for the same effect. But, again, it draws on the somewhat different structure of story fortified by religious tradition. As Ronna Burger says, "Socrates uses the word *mythos* for the first time when he offers to tell Simmias something worth hearing about the things on the earth beneath the heavens."[23]

Protagoras' invocation of the Prometheus myth is negative and reductive. It posits a society where, instead of the repertoire of interrelated virtues with which the dialogue concerns itself later, the two implanted principles of shame and justice do the whole work of empowering the citizens to manage their state.[24] The question being asked, whether the virtues are teachable, is removed by this transfer of shame and justice through Hermes at Zeus' behest. There is no question of educating a citizen who happens to lack these; he is simply to be put to death. To cast all this in the form of a myth has the effect of removing it from argument, and Socrates does not directly contest it.

Now as I have argued at greater length above, the myths of the *Phaedrus* differ among themselves in topic and in ontological set. In the Sun, the Line, and the Cave of the *Republic* a group of myths is brought to bear on the same topic, and adjudicating the relations between their figurative and their propositional structures is a task of enormous intricacy I shall not undertake here. In the *Symposium*, more expansively, virtually the entire dialogue is given over not just to the dialectic of argument but to a sort of dialectic of myths, accounts brought to bear on the one topic of love, most of them with enough overlap to one or more of the other myths to be felt as supplementations, and to be illustrating the *Phaedrus'* principle of approximation ("what it is like"). Moreover, the length and intricacies of the nesting accounts may be taken as an effort to vie with the desirable principle of length for the account, in which a god exceeds a man. While it cannot be convincingly demonstrated that the myth-charged accounts are ordered into a strict hierarchy, the fact that the last one, "reported" by Socrates, is attributed to a semi-divine narrator, Diotima, would bring it on the way to the criterion of a god's account of "what sort it is"; and so it would be hierarchically preemptive as well as supplementary to the other accounts. At the same time Diotima's myth is bathed in the contingency of the ironic possibility that Socrates has invented her. In this case, to continue applying the strictures brought to bear in the *Phaedrus*, the account would be offering a (human) "what it is like" in the form of an invented, divine "what sort it is."

When Socrates enters, the transmission of wisdom is joked about as a mystery. "It would be a fine thing, Agathon, if wisdom were the sort of thing that would flow from us as from the fuller to the emptier if we just touched one another" (175d). Agathon, who has just won in the Dionysiac contest, proposes Dionysus as a judge between them (175e), thus playfully associating poetry and the drink of which Dionysus is also of course a sponsoring god—and of which they are both to partake and partially to abstain in order to hold their dialogue.

Aristophanes is postponed because of hiccups—and so full mythmaking is postponed in favor of comprehensive science, expounded by the physician Eryximachus. His tracing of love through the entire universe covers the body, music, meteorology, astronomy, piety, and virtue. This encyclopedic account is exhaustive from one point of view; it is possible, as Eryximachus maintains, to fit Pausanias' discourse into it (and so Phaedrus' as well). But from another point of view his limitation is indicated by the fact that his sober earnestness has broken the tone of the dialogue. It follows from this circumstance that levity has the important function of leading to myth. This structure asserts, through its change of tone, that the compensatory need for sportive moderation, as generally in the Platonic dialogue, is an aspect of the need for an indirection that only myth can provide when approaching imponderables like the nature of Eros.

Aristophanes then appends his myth to an initial assertion that "love is the greatest pleasure for the human race as a physician of what he has cured in them" (189d)—a departure from Eryximachus in the guise of a compliment to the art of the physician. In its range the myth Aristophanes tells can be subsumed under all three of Frutiger's classes, the allegorical, the genetic, and the parascientific. Its narrative assigns to stages of prehistoric development what can be described for intuitive characterization of the psychological dynamics of love, rather than a comprehensive but essentially inert account of its force. The poignant and tragic cast of these creatures who become allegorical as they become only part of the lost "whole" human being is conveyed in a comic tone that anticipates Socrates' concluding remark that the comic poet and the tragic poet could be the same person. He could be the same person in the same discourse, we can deduce, if the discourse employs myth as this one does.

The mythical Diotima transposes all the complexities of the allegory of Poros (Sufficiency) and Penia (Want), into a *logos* that combines abstractions without allegorizing them—reminding us that Poros and Penia are so close to abstractions that the point could have been made about their interrelations without either allegorizing them or setting them in a causal narrative. But if this had been done, it would have been at the loss of the endowment of mystery that here the mere *form* of myth provides.

As it is, the allegorical narrative succinctly recounted by Diotima shades out of the *logos* about mediation and into a still more intense *logos*, to which it serves as a preliminary. The spirit of mythmaking comes through this speech in its hyperbolic, one could even say, its poetic, tone. And Alcibiades' comparison—which draws on myth—of

Socrates to a Silenus statue, acts almost so as to extend the myth-making spirit to the ultimate figure of Socrates himself, who is of course not allegorical.

There are also correspondences among the myths from dialogue to dialogue, and most notably among the four long eschatological myths, those in the *Gorgias* (523e–27e); the *Phaedo* (107d–15a); the *Republic* (614a–21d); and the *Phaedrus* (246a–57b).[25]

So wide and detailed is this particular group of myths, and so intimately connected to the *logos* of the dialogues where they serve characteristically as part of a climactic position, that it would be fair to derive from any of the myths some hint, at very least, of the religious-spiritual life. This impulse is always present in Socrates, and in what he says, because of his spirit, the *daimonion*. In the *Theages* (128b), Socrates says he knows nothing but a little about the erotic, then makes transition to "the way this is" (οἷον τοῦτο ἔστι) he speaks of the "daimonion with me since boyhood" (128d) and says that it always signals him a turning away (σημαίνει ... ἀποτροπήν) and never turns him toward anything (προτρέπει). He gives the example of a gymnast and a further example, including an oraclelike death prediction. The power of the daimonion replaces the object of becoming wise (σόφος) in the discourse. "This is my being (συνουσία)," he says (130d5) and he will try to "encourage the godly in you by prayers and by offerings" (131a5–6).[26]

A myth implies neither skepticism nor credulity. The myth, in one sense, does not admit of truth or falsity, but Plato himself does make the distinction, to assert the truth while admitting the possibility of falsity. He speaks of the myth in the *Timaeus* (26e) as "being indeed very great, not a shaped myth but a true account."[27] There are submyths in Plato, like the story of Gyges in the *Republic* (359). The shepherd who comes to Gyges in this parable now acts (justly) in a context of social authority, where in Book One proper shepherding was a *techne*-illustration. This is an illustrative story, not exactly a myth in the fullest sense; it provides a reassurance of a continuity between history and legend both in time and in the community of moral problems.

But in any case by combining the myth with the cross-questioning elenchic inquiry of his dialogues, Plato doubly or triply preempts the assertion of discourse, moving it to a deeper level at the same time that he keeps it open. First, the domain of myth does not admit of truth or falsity, and so by entering that domain Plato preempts the testing adduced by the *elenchos*. This is all the more the case because he has invented the myth himself, and so he need not turn his questioning back on that element in the culture, as Xenophanes and Heraclitus had done. Second, by confronting the *mythos* with the *logos* he raises their relation to a dialectical level that forces the reader to account for their interaction. And third, especially in the eschatological myths and such as the myth of Diotima, he leads the discourse into an area of visionary assertion that summarizes and also extends the logos into an area that proclaims itself to be final.

Myth envisages the soul of the individual man, but it also envisages the polity. Plato speaks of "the polity which we mythologize with a logos" (Rep 501e4).[28] As Marcel Detienne stresses, the city as the locus of application of myth is always in view.[29]

In the *Phaedrus*, having announced that he will "begin his demonstration" (*apodeixis*), which is at the same time already categorized as under the "mania" of the poets, Socrates has effectually prepared the way for an interdependence of *logos* and *mythos*. Delaying the *mythos*, he first gives an abstract summary of "all soul" as a principle of motion, and, conversely, of motion as a test of the presence of soul—a conception which can be taken to undergird the motion of the Charioteer and his horses through the heavens. At the same time, the Charioteer allegorizes not that motion, which is a sign of soul but not a definer of the soul's activity. So in the shift from motion to Charioteer, Plato provides the frame for still other large shifts in this myth—shifts that are evidenced in none of the other myths in the dialogue. The shift is glossed over in this instance through repetition of the word "like," the subject being the Form of the immortality of the soul. Plato has Socrates offer, instead, a shorter narrative of "what it is like"—and "It is like the fused force of a winged team and charioteer."[30]

In the course of this narrative Plato ranges from Zeus and the conventional Twelve of the Olympian gods to his most austere conceptions of mind, and to an astral universe. Vagueness of time, place, and exact status in the transmigration cycle between life and afterlife, here accompanies the attribution of a census of virtues of the soul (247d) and a gamut of nine possible human roles (248d–e). These are seen as in effect mutually understanding the Forms, through *anamnesis*; "truth," which is a sort of recall of the soul's proper bearing, is also a precondition of human existence (249b–e). It turns out that the philosopher's intelligence (*dianoia*) alone[31] will grow wings (πτεροῦται). "For it is with those it is always in the memory with respect to the power; with them that a god who is one has the attribute of a god" (θεός ὤν θεῖός ἐστιν). The last sentence spreads its vision across the whole range of being and existence which had so far offered fairly clear distinctions—gods from men, this life from the afterlife. In the process this account obscurely furthers, and extendedly obscures, its allegorical mapping, whose byways turn so as not to be confined to a single set in its rich, seemingly improvisational modulations. We are reminded, so to speak, that the lauded *mania* of the poet is at work—and in fact that mania is now mentioned; the philosopher is like the poet for standing aside from "the many" in his enthusiasm (ἐνθουσιάζων), or being "disturbed" or "out of his senses" (παρακινῶν, 249d.)[32] Socrates goes on, indeed, to link his lover of beauty to the lover of wisdom in "divine madness" (249d). Then the growing of wings—emphasizing that they are the lover's (250e–51b)—are described in a vivid detail that effectually changes the perspective, and with it the significative intentionality, from the astral to the psychological. A long excursus on the fitness of certain souls to the domains of certain gods—Zeus, Hera, etc.—and another significative shift back to a more schematized version of the Charioteer (253c–56e), further dramatizes the erotic psychology by highlighting that the horses are one black and one white.

Yet in this dialogue we still have two brief myths to go—the cicadas and the Garden of Adonis—as well as a longer one—the myth of Thoth. For all their differences, every one of them is situated with respect to Socrates, and conditioned as bearing on the love-atonement of his discourse after the quotation from Stesichorus.

In an earlier discussion,[33] I located Plato's procedures globally at a third phase of mythmaking, after a first unitary phase and a second seasonal-constructive "binary" phase (of which the most elaborate theoretical exposition in the work of Lévi-Strauss, especially the *My-*

thologiques). However the modifications, attenuations, permutations, and ironized suggestiveness in Plato's use of myths is such that he not only—as would normally be the case—comprises the earlier phases. He also anticipates later ones, so powerfully that Ovid himself at best only parallels his subtleties, and it is not till the most delicate literary procedures evolved in the Renaissance that further modifications take place. Even these, which often advertise a derivation from Plato, could be understood to register a responsive ring in Plato's *mythos*, all the more for his steadfast, and quite original insistence on neither separating them from his *logoi*, nor allowing them to merge entirely.

In following the lead of adding inventive material to myth, which the tragedians and possibly their predecessors have done, Plato has crossed a line; he has appropriated their function of myth, in all its mystery and intensity. But by plunging myth into the crucible of free invention he has redefined it. He has further redefined it by setting it against the disproportionate and somewhat incommensurable *logoi* of his dialectic, itself a developed form of the tragedians' own dialectic. When the myths are inserted into the dialectic series as part of an argument, as in the *Phaedrus* and the *Republic*, or as wedded at every stage to the argument, as in the *Symposium*, then the interaction between the modes, and the power of that interaction, is insisted on. But myth is never a whole and separate domain for Plato, as it always is for his predecessors. He variously but steadily combines it, and this throws the interpreter to the second level of asking what the combination amounts to in a given case, what the principle of combination may be, and what the conception of whole utterance has been effectuated so as to give the combination its force. By inventing myths rather than just receiving them, Plato modalizes the whole domain of myth and all that is connected with it—religion, poetry, and also philosophy.

Notes

1. Henri Joly, *Le Renversement Platonicien: Logos, Episteme, Polis* (Paris: Vrin, 1985), 330–41. points out that dream, myth, and play are connected in Plato's view of political theory (Rep. 4., 433b–c).

2. Julius Stenzel, *Plato's Method of Dialectic*, 13.

3. ἵνα δὲ μὴ οἴηι ἀπατᾶσθαι. ὡς τῶι ὄντι ἡγοῦνται πάντες

ἄνθρωποι πάντα ἄνδρα μετέχειν δικαιοσύνης τε καί τῆς ἄλλης πολιτικῆς ἀρετῆς, τόδε αὖ λαβέ τεκμήριον. (*Protagoras* 323a5–7).

4. The myth may serve to soften the starkness here. The radicality of the proposition can be seen by measuring the discourse of the *Protagoras* against the large Platonic and Greek distinction between *nomos* and *physis*. Felix Heinimann (*Nomos und Physis*, 117–18) remarks that "For our problem the chief result is that in this doctrine *dikaion* and *aischron* ... the antithesis Nomos-Physis has no place. For when all ethical standards are only *nomo* then one can really not speak of a *physei dikaion*."

5. R. Hackforth, *Plato's Phaedo*, 172–73.

6. Konrad Gaiser, *Platons Ungeschriebene Lehre.*

7. As Charles Griswold says (*Self-Knowledge in Plato's* Phaedrus, 38), "Socrates' proposed demythologization of the Oreithuia story robs it of its human significance, replacing eros with death caused by natural factors, and so renders the story useless for self-knowledge."

8. Kenneth Dover, ed., *Plato's Symposium*, 23.

9. On "measured truth" versus "play" in Plato, see W. K. C. Guthrie, *History of Greek Philosophy*, IV, 56–66; V, 178–80.

10. οὐκ ἄν ποτε φανεῖμεν φαῦλοι δημιουργοί λόγωι καλῶν εἰκόνων.

11. τὸ ἐν τοῖς λόγοις ψεῦδος ... καί ἐν αἷς νῦνδή ἐλέγομεν ταῖς μυθολογίαις, διά τό μὴ εἰδέναι ὅπηι τἀληθές ἔχει περί τῶν παλαιῶν, ἀφομοιοῦντες τῶι ἀληθεῖ τὸ ψεῦδος ὅ τι μάλιστα οὕτω χρήσιμον ποιοῦμεν.

12. See Luc Brisson, *Platon: les mots et les mythes* (Paris: Maspero, 1982), especially "l'opposition: mythe/ discours vérifiable," 114–44.

13. καί οὕτω δὴ μῦθος ἀπώλετο ... Οὔ τι ἄν ... εἴπερ γε ὁ πατήρ τοῦ ἑτέρου μύθου ἔξη.

14. The story about Thales is told in the context of the discrepancy between lawyers and philosophers in court—the former are slaves to the scene, the latter impractical. This in the context that "public" truth sometimes meets Protagoras' requirement in some qualified way (as 172 begins to say). All this is a different angle on the Cave, and indeed [allowing for considerable foreshortening] on the entire *Republic*. Thales sees the stars but not what is at his feet. "And the gibe fits all those who are occupied with philosophy," "τ'αὐτόν δέ ἀρκεῖ σκῶμμα ἐπί πάντος ὅσοι ἐν φιλοσοφίαι διάγουσι" (174a)—except that shortly (175) the philosopher's life is praised.

15. τῶν γάρ ὄντων ὧι νοῦν μόνωι κτᾶσθαι προσήκει, λεκτέον ψυχήν—τοῦτο δέ ἀόρατον.

16. Ronna Burger, *The* Phaedo: *A Platonic Labyrinth* (New Haven: Yale University Press, 1984), 242ff.

17. Such ambivalences have been a staple, of course, in anthropological discussions for more than a century. For Apollo, see Marcel Detienne "L'Apollon meurtrier et les crimes de sang," *Quaderni Urbinati*, 22, 1 (Vol 51), 1986, 7–17. "Magna Graecia and its lands open to colonization see flow together in the same fever both Apollo the devourer of men and the god of paeans and white garments: the Archegetos, founder of altars and cities; and the god greedy for human first fruits, of the bodies that are theirs, is also the god of Crotona and Metapontum with whom Pythagoras wishes reincarnation to be pure and miraculous" (16). In the *Republic*, indeed (405), reference is made to the effectual polynomy of Apollo.

18. νῦν μὴν εὖ τῶι σῶι λόγωι ἔοικε μαρτυρεῖ, τό αρχαῖον αυτῶν επί τὴ ἀγριότητα διά μυθολογίας ἐπανενεγκών.

19. Paul Veyne, *Les Grecs ont-ils cru à leurs mythes*? (Paris: Seuil, 1983), 39. And Veyne also asserts, "Questions of method and positivity presuppose a more fundamental question: what is myth? Is it altered history? Aggrandized history? A collective mythomania? An allegory? What was it in the eyes of the Greeks? This gives us an opportunity to verify that the feeling of truth is very broad (it easily takes myth into its whole), but also that 'truth' means many things—to the point where it takes into its whole the literature of fiction" (27).

20. As Percival Frutiger well says in *Les Myths de Platon* (Paris: Alcan, 1930), 144, "There is, with Plato, no radical heterogeneity between the mythical and the dialectical." Frutiger offers three interesting categories of classifying myths: the allegorical, the genetic, and the parascientific (180 ff.).

21. See Heraclitus B62, "Immortals are mortal and mortals immortal, dying their own life, living their own death." ἀθάνατοι θνητοί, θνητοί ἀθάνατοι, ζῶντες τό ἐκείνων θάνατον, τὸν δέ ἐκείνων βίον τεθνεῶτες. See also B60 "the road up/down, one and the same." ὁδός ἄνω κάτω μία καί ὡυτη.

22. E. R. Dodds, ed., *Plato's* Gorgias (Oxford: The Clarendon Press, 1959). Dodds lists them. He cites Rohde, Frazer, and A. B. Cook with reference to Orphism, the Danaids (a painting of Polygnotus), a lekythos from Palermo, and a possible rainmaking rite. Further extensive parallels are discussed in Eva Keuls, *The Water Carriers in Hades* (Amsterdam: Hakkert, 1974).

23. Ronna Burger, *The* Phaedo, 196 (on 110b1–11c3).

24. Shame, however, interestingly, has considerable generalizing power in Plato, as a kind of holdover from the same culture that preceded his. See Richard McKim, "Shame and Truth in Plato's *Gorgias*," in Charles L. Griswold, ed. *Platonic Writings, Platonic Readings*, 34–48.

25. Frutiger (*Les Mythes de Platon*, 254–66) elaborately tabulates

parallels, among these dialogues with Empedocles, Pindar, and the Orphic texts; he lists as headings: the divine origin of the soul, the fall of the soul, expiation and metempsychosis, the law for soul-evolution, the body as a tomb, the virtues as liberating the soul, the ladder of lives, the meadow of the Blest, the road of Heroes, Forgetfulness and Remembrance, judgment and punishment, and the final liberation of the soul into blessedness. These correspondences between Plato and the tradition have been supplemented since, notably by M. L. West, *Orphism*, (Oxford: The Clarendon Press, 1982), 118 and passim.

26. τό θεῖον τό σοὶ γιγνόμενον παραμυθεῖσθαι εὐχαῖς τε καὶ θυσίαις. The *Theages*, to be sure, may not be authentic, but the daimonion is discussed elsewhere. The arguments pro and con the authenticity of the *Theages* are discussed in Guthrie, V, 393–94.

27. τό τε μὴ πλασθέντα μῦθον ἀλλ' ἀληθινόν λόγον εἶναι πάμμεγά που. As Paul Veyne claims, citing Pausanias VIII, 8, 3; "For the Greeks there is no problem about myth; there is only the problem about the improbable elements the myth contains. This critique of myth begins with Hecataeus of Miletus (who already made fun of the ridiculous things the Hellenes told, fr. 1 Jacoby); compare, in Pausanias himself, III, 25, 5, the criticism of the myth of Cerberus by Hecataeus." Paul Veyne, *Les Grecs ont-ils cru à leurs mythes?*, 143. However, Veyne does elide the differences between what would seem to have been Hecataeus' rudimentary somewhat summary approach to myth and the elaborately modulated approach of Plato. He also elides Plato's approach with that of Pausanias centuries later.

28. ἡ πολιτεία ἥν μυθολογοῦμεν λόγωι.

29. Marcel Detienne, *L'Invention de la mythologie*, 155–89.

30. ἐοικέτω δὴ συμφύτωι δυνάμει ὑποπτέρου ζεύγους τε καὶ ἡνιόχου. The language here, at the point of shift, is highly intensive and foreshortened. "Fused" is the translation of "συμφύτωι," which ties it most to its verb, "grow together." Other common senses are also present: "congenital," "natural," "kindred," "united." To have it modify "dynamic" verges on poetic usage. "ὑποπτέρου" can mean "soaring" as well as "winged." One cannot rule this sense out in such immediate proximity to δυνάμει. R. Hackforth, in *Plato's* Phaedrus (Cambridge: Cambridge University Press, 1952), 69, argues "that ὑποπτέρου belongs to ἡνιόχου as well as to ζεύγους follows from 251b7, πᾶσα γάρ ἦν τό πάλαι πτερωτή." However, in grammar ὑποτέρου is singular, and the rules of adjective agreement in Greek allow an adjective preceding two singular nouns to be either singular or plural; and so to go with either just the first one or with both. Here the usage is so delicate as to suspend these possibilities. It is precisely only after the massive shift that we learn of the Charioteer's wings. Moreover, the soul itself is spoken of shedding its wings

when it commands a body (246c–d). Till then we had been told only of the horses' wings. To make the distinction of the adjective here cover both team and Charioteer, and then wait for pages to discuss the other wings, is a sort of overemphasis. Here the possibility, I would argue, is no more than a hint easing us into the shift to come much later. And as Hackforth also points out, there is, strictly speaking, a comparable indeterminacy about the number of horses in the team, usually taken for a pair, but the word "often means a large number."

31.   An "inconsistency," as Hackforth notes (86). Among many others, here and throughout the play of the dialogue!

32.   The verb literally means "move aside" and its root, κινεῖν, echoes the κίνησις or motion which had begun the whole discussion as the test of the presence of soul.

33.   Albert Cook, *Myth and Language*, Chapter II, "The Large Phases of Myth."

Chapter 6

Suspension, Hypothesis, Digression, and Poetic-Religious Authority in the *Meno*

The doctrine of inherited memory, of *anamnesis*, is such a striking part of Plato's *Meno* that it is hard not to follow the lead of many commentators, the first of whom is Aristotle, in taking that doctrine as the most important element in the dialogue, when in fact if it has a subject, it is the question of whether or not virtue is teachable. But it does not stick close to that topic in the way that the *Laches*, say, sticks to courage. Nor does it come to any firm conclusion about the teachability of virtue. Even *anamnesis*, which seems a distinct doctrine easily summarizable, works far less comprehensively in the *Meno* than the way it is used, for example, in the *Phaedo*.

The *Meno's* doctrine of *anamnesis*, presented in the cross-examination of the slave boy, has itself been cross-examined by commentators in modern times, and so extensively that there is a tendency to isolate this cross-examination as though its results were fully equivalent to the doctrine that Plato was known to hold. Yet there are elements in the dialogue that introduce at least the possibility of qualification, and for effectually limiting the doctrine. The various suspensions in the dialogue, and the tendency towards self-cancellation in its whole presentation, as I shall try to show, amount to a qualification. The appeal to religious authority, which introduces and frames the cross-examination of the slave boy, constitutes a reassertion of *anamnesis* on another, prior basis.

Leading into the doctrine of *anamnesis*, Socrates first bases it not on the cross-examination of the slave boy, but rather on the religious authority of Pindar and other poets and priests. The cross-examination is appended to these as a corollary. Religious authority, indeed, is something that Plato rarely questions, even when he probes religious notions, as he does in the *Euthyphro* and at the end of the *Republic*. In this he differs both from the modern philosopher and the modern cultural anthropologist, who seek a prolonged examination of exactly how "religion" functions in a society.[1]

The *Meno* would seem to be a fairly straightforward dialogue in the light of how it has been scrutinized by analysts over the past several years for the exact implications of its presentation of the doctrine of *anamnesis*. Yet here, in a clearer and more schematic form than many other places in Plato's work, we are first of all confronted with the question of how seriously we are to take, and how extensively we are to apply, the *Meno's* suspensions, self-refutations, and dramatic presentations—all three modified by a persistent tendency toward digression. Starting with the question of the ways virtue may be transmitted, the dialogue fairly quickly gets to the paradox that you cannot learn what you do not already know and need not learn what you do know. *Anamnesis* is introduced to resolve this paradox, and after the lengthy discussion of it, the dialogue moves back to questions about the transmission of virtue, without really resolving them. If we take these qualifying presentational strategies in the strongest way, then, they reduce the function of *anamnesis* within the dialogue to its relation to virtue. And yet it is at the same time a doctrine, and one of Plato's, as Aristotle identifies it, attributing it to the *Meno*.[2]

Now, the close attention of interpreters to the reasoning process in this dialogue tends to obscure its circularity, and also its recourse to other forms of verification than logic or hypothesis.[3] In particular, interpreters rarely draw implications from its ascription of a comprehensive authority to Pindar, who is quoted at a key point on the central question of *anamnesis* before any other discussion on it is broached.

Except for this unequivocal appeal to authority, the elenchic procedure here abounds in shifts and qualifications. As Michael C. Stokes says, "We may find some guidance in a passage in which Socrates offers some questions and observations about his own questions and observations. It will not offer more than guidance."[4] He says further (of the *Meno*), "One might be tempted to suppose that the interlocutor's rejection, preferably with contumely, was meant to be a sign to us ... But once we have crossed that barrier, it is difficult to know where we stop. How do we distinguish interlocutors who do from those who do not represent Plato's thought?"[5] How indeed? But we need not share Stokes's assumption that there is globally a separate thought of Plato's here, to be identified with any interlocutor, even Socrates, and even if we do accept the strong evidence that Plato accepted the doctrine of *anamnesis*. Here, as elsewhere, these difficulties can be taken, and I believe should be taken, as indicating the exploratory and interqualificatory nature of the dialogue.

This dialogue ends where it begins, with a question about whether virtue is teachable. And the conclusion, since nothing has been solved, throws into some doubt the points that have been made through the whole dialogue, including the questions about *anamnesis*. "Can you tell me, Socrates," it begins, "Is virtue teachable; or is it not teachable but learned in practice; or does it come about in men not by being practised or taught but by nature or in some other way?" (70a).[6] This is a large census of possibilities. If one allows for combinations among them—and the "ors" logically suggest that expansion—then it could be taken for exhaustive. The subject has been posed with an unusual abruptness and completeness at the very outset of the dialogue. But this completeness has been elaborated only to be sidestepped, first by a long *elenchos* based on attempts to get the interlocutor to define the initial term, "virtue."

Among these listed possibilities, only the last is allowed for, and that in extraordinary fashion: the "some other way" is in one sense the *anamnesis*, the memory of what was known in another life. Further, as has been remarked by commentators, this kind of learning throws into an infinite regress the question of how learning comes about, if it is taken as a serious and logical answer: for how then was it learned in whatever was the first in the series of these other lives? Thus the *anamnesis* could also be taken to be classified under "taught by nature."

"Nature" (*physis*) is of course a large, overriding Platonic concept; taken with "law" or "custom" (*nomos*) it has been held to cover much or even all of his exposition.[7] The conception of nature is first introduced in a large, all-embracing proposition presented as self-evident in the context of *anamnesis*, "All nature being akin" (ἅτε γὰρ τῆς φύσεως ἁπάσης συγγενοῦς οὔσης, 81d1). The leap to the cross-examination of the slave is connected, through this mere genitive absolute phrase, to a stated condition even larger than *anamnesis*. In fact this startling aside is arguably of a generality greater than anything else in the dialogue. This quasi-Empedoclean, or even quasi-Parmenidean and quasi-Heraclitean (and possibly also Pythagorean), axiom is in fact the largest in the dialogue, and the more striking that it is presented in passing rather than as the culmination of the sort of deductive series that the *Phaedo* offers. It expands the term φύσις beyond any merely casual usage, and beyond the nature-nurture opposition of "by nature or in some other way" (70a). It can even be said to go beyond an opposition with νόμος, since by this axiom φύσις might be taken to include νόμος, along with everything else. The topic at hand is the *anamnesis* of *arete*, after all; it is that which "all nature being akin" allows. And *arete,* it can be argued, is in Plato's world and specifically later in this dialogue an idealizing force for νόμος as well as a goal for human nature.[8] Now this overarching condition actually does not entail either *anamnesis* or interconnections between one knowable set of ideas and another. All nature could be akin and *anamnesis* could be the case, and still a connection between one idea or fact and another would not have to be recoverable through *anamnesis*. As distinct from the close connection of *anamnesis* with the theses about the afterlife in the *Phaedo*, here it is suspended. Here it produces neither the near-certainty nor the hope of the other dialogue, but rather trailing off through suspensions in the approximations and the *faute de mieux* of "right opinion" at the end of the dialogue, a conclusion that is logically inconsistent with the suspended demonstration about *anamnesis* and mathematics—as well as with Plato's assertions about the connections between mathematics and the soul elsewhere. For if all nature is akin and exact knowledge in domain after domain is recoverable through *anamnesis*, there would be no reason for anything less than full certitude on everything. It might take a Socratic technique to elicit that certitude, but the path to certitude would be clear; no mere approximation like the "right opinion" of the end of the dialogue, no possibility of losing one's way on the road to Larisa, could long persist.

"If you yourself are persuaded of these same things, persuade Anytus, so he may be gentler, and if you do persuade him, you will benefit the Athenians too" (100b–c).[9] These are the dialogue's final words. Persuaded of exactly what? So one might ask, though it is in any case an injunction that the discussion have a modifying effect on Anytus, a man the reader of this dialogue would have to recognize as one of the judges who condemned Socrates to death. The reader would further have received Socrates' unusually positive reply here about the Sophists, and especially Protagoras, in response to Anytus' ignorant denigration of them, as an echo of the proceedings of the trial that will take place relatively soon—in 399, and the dramatic date of this dialogue is placed at about 402. It is not asked that Anytus *become* gentler, which would be more logical, unless the "be" is taken to refer to a particular point in time, such as the trial of Socrates. " ... so that if you persuade him of this, it will be the case that you benefit the Athenians too." This "too" must mean "in addition to myself and others present here." So it would also, by proleptic prophecy, refer to the trial without naming it. In any case, this conclusion, which returns almost to square one with respect to the teachability of virtue, is more than usually prospective. Such conclusions usually trail off, but Anytus has been brought in at the point where a long discussion is joined about the puzzle provided by the fact that the sons of the greatest men are often notably less virtuous than their fathers.

The two objects of the verb *"peitho,"* "be persuaded" or "believe," carry the strength of the term "conviction." Here the term cannot mean "believe just subjectively for yourself alone." And in that light, it is noteworthy that the first time it takes a plural object, "these things," "ταῦτα." The perfect tense of the verb declares them to have been achieved in the course of the dialogue—which is to be taken globally, and which is therefore more imposing as a whole than any of its separate propositions can be taken to be.

Now Meno's later military and political career, which ended in execution at the hands of the Persians to whom he had betrayed Athens, flies in the face of such knowledge, as does the later career of Anytus. Here, in congruence with what Plato's audience would have known about Anytus, he is not assenting to any of the propositions raised in the dialogue, except silently and therefore unquestioningly to the religious guarantee for *anamnesis.* The immediately previous propositions at the end, praised by Meno, are (1) "virtue is got neither by nature nor by teaching but arrives by divine fate and without thought (νοῦς) to whomever it arrives" (2) "unless he be the sort of political man who can make another political." But (3) such a person would be "alone ... as Homer says Tiresias was among the dead" (100a). Of this series, "nature" and "teaching" come in the list at the beginning, but the rest fall under the "some other way" of 70a and expand it beyond recognition. This occurs in a context where it is expressly declared that "virtue is not teachable" and that "virtue is not knowledge" (99a).[10] One could further add to the series by using this passage to adduce "knowledge" (ἐπιστήμη) and "opinion."[11] These are to be a "guide to the right" (τό ὀρθόν)—but their role is much in suspension here. These three propositions, or five, do not make a set, though they are presumably lumped together under the singular "this" of the terminal sentence.

"These things" and "this" must be equivalent, and in their local currency of grammatical usage they here solve the problem of the one ("this") and the many ("these things") which was raised earlier with respect to "virtue" (71c–72b). They only solve it in passing, and "ironically," since it was not solved as a topic in the dialogue. Among themselves they pose not only incommensurabilities but other possible puzzles: is not "divine fate" (θεῖα μοῖρα) the motive for "nature," especially since chance is ruled out? How large a scope must finally be given here to "politics":—not much mentioned in the dialogue, since political men were the ones cited as not being able to inculcate virtue in their sons. The pair mentioned here as guides for cities are also incommensurate, the old heroic Themistocles and the ominous and small-minded Anytus (99b).

At the beginning Socrates makes the question "Is virtue teachable?" yield to the question "What is virtue?" and he soon gets Meno to offer enough examples of virtue for a "swarm of bees."[12] Skillful propositional manipulation does not get them past this question of the many and the one (71c–72b), nor will it get them past the question of the part and the whole (78–79). The introduction of defining an entity that seems not analogous (except for its susceptibility to definition), the "figure" or "schema," provides a hint that in the cross-examination of the slave there will be an analogy between the knowledge-through-memory of geometry and the knowledge of virtue. Yet this is only a hint, and it is strangely not picked up. That virtue can be known through memory is also a question attributed here wholly to religious authority, since the slave's cross-examination concerns geometry rather than virtue. As Martin Andic shows, though, there are many possible connections between geometry and virtue in the ensuing discussion.[13]

Another entity mentioned, not analogous to virtue or with no analogies to be drawn in terms of the dialogue, is color. This, too, is successfully defined with the help of terms from Empedocles, as though to adduce this heir of the Ionians would guarantee the irrelevance of the question, except insofar as it offers practice (learning by practice) of how to define the term with which one wishes to begin a series of propositions. Still, the definition of color is also sufficient unto itself; and here it is not brought to bear on anything else, whereas virtue is presented as bearing on many activities.[14] At Meno's protest over the part-whole impasse, Socrates, rejecting Meno's double-jeopardy trick about knowledge (you can't learn what you don't know or what you do), changes the subject drastically by bringing up "men and women who are wise about divine affairs" (σοφῶν περὶ τὰ θεῖα πράγματα, 81a).

Though Socrates has charged Meno with "breaking up and dividing virtue" (καταγνύναι μηδὲ κερματίζειν τὴν αρετήν, 79a10), his questions will soon use this fundamental break to produce a traditional, a poetic, basis for ascertaining what virtue is. Before this, though, Meno calls Socrates a "stingray" (νάρκη) and a "magician" (γόης 80a–b); Socrates playfully accepts this and intro-duces the possibility of discourse by trading such images (ἀντεικάζειν), only to dismiss it. At this point the entire first elenchos has been brought to a complete impasse. And then Socrates shifts to an entirely new approach, connecting a recourse to religion and poetry to the impasse in the discussion:

ΣΩ. ὁρᾶις τοῦτον ὡς ἐριστικὸν λόγον κατάγεις, ὡς οὐκ ἄρα ἔστιν ζητεῖν ἀνθρώπωι οὔτε ὃ οἶδε οὔτε ὃ μὴ οἶδε; οὔτε γὰρ ἂν ὅ γε οἶδεν ζητοῖ; οἶδεν γάρ, καὶ οὐδέν δεῖ τῶι γε τοιούτωι ζητησεως—οὔτε ὃ μή οἶδεν—οὐδέ γὰρ οἶδεν ὅτι ζητήσει.
ΜΕΝ. Οὐκοῦν καλῶς σοι δοκεῖ λέγεσθαι ὁ λόγος οὗτος, ὦ Σώκρατες;
ΣΩ. Οὐκ ἔμοιγε.
ΜΕΝ. Ἔχεις λέγειν ὅπηι;
ΣΩ. Ἔγωγε. ἀκήκοα γὰρ ἀνδρῶν τε καὶ γυναικῶν σοφῶν περὶ τὰ θεῖα πράγματα—
ΜΕΝ. Τίνα λόγον λεγόντων;

Socrates: Don't you see that this *logos* you conduct is an eristic one, that a man cannot inquire about either what he knows or what he doesn't know? For he wouldn't inquire about what he knows, for he knows it, and has no need of this sort of inquiry—and not about what he doesn't know, since he doesn't even know what he is to in-quire about.
Meno: Doesn't this *logos* seem to be well said Socrates?
Socrates: Not to me anyway.
Meno: Can you say how?
Socrates: Yes I can. I have heard of men and women who are wise about divine affairs.
Meno: What is the *logos* that they speak?   (80e–81a)

The same term, *logos*, is the hinge of authoritative equivalence between the reasoning process and the religious adduction. As Socra-tes goes on:

ΣΩ. Ἀληθῆ, ἔμοιγε δοκεῖν, καὶ καλόν.
ΜΕΝ. Τίνα τοῦτον, καὶ τίνες οἱ λέγοντες;
ΣΩ. Οἱ μὲν λέγοντές εἰσι τῶν ἱερέων τε καὶ τῶν ἱερειῶν ὅσοις μεμέληκε περὶ ὧν μεταχειρίζονται λόγον οἵοις τεῖναι διδόναι· λέγει δὲ καὶ Πίνδαρος καὶ ἄλλοι πολλοί τῶν ποιητῶν ὅσοι θεῖοί εἰσιν. ἃ δὲ λέγουσιν, ταυτί ἐστιν· ἀλλὰ σκόπει εἴ σοι

δοκοῦσιν ἀληθῆ λέγειν. φασὶ γὰρ τὴν ψυχὴν τοῦ
ἀνθρώπου εἶναι ἀθάνατον, καὶ τοτὲ μὲν τελευτᾶν—ὃ
δή ἀποθνήσκειν καλοῦσι—τοτὲ δὲ πάλιν γίγνεσθαι,
ἀπόλλυσθαι δ'οὐδέποτε

Socrates: A true [*logos*], as it seems to me, and a fine one.
Meno: What is this, and who are they who say it?
Socrates: Those who say it are all those priests and priestesses
whose concern it is and are able to give an account [*logos*] of what
they practice. Pindar says so too, and many other poets, all those
who are "godly."[15] This is what they say; and see if they seem to
you to speak the truth. They say the soul of man is immortal, and
when it comes to an end—what people call to die—then it is born
again and never destroyed.   (81a–b)

Pindar's account of Persephone's role and function in the process
of transmigration is then quoted as if it were authoritative. No irony
seems to be present, and the word "true" (ἀληθῆ) has been repeated. The soul, Socrates goes on to say, "has seen things here, and
those in Hades, and all things, and there is nothing that it has not
learned" (81c5–7). This comprehensiveness of the soul's knowledge,
here stated both positively and negatively, would certainly include the
segments of mathematical capacity that are shown in the *anamnesis*
experiment on the slave; which then follows. And indeed, Socrates
begins to assert as much in the rest of the sentence—"So that there is
no wonder that it can call up a memory of those very things it knew
before, both about virtue and about other things" (81c7–9).[16]
"Virtue," of course, has been the topic under discussion. "Other
things" will be instantiated by triangles and squares.

The coupling of "virtue" and "other things," has been shown
earlier in the dialogue to call for exact elenchic demonstration in defining abstractions that are much more obviously connected to
virtue—prudence (σωφροσύνη) and the like—than is mathematics.
Here the coupling, as well as the *anamnesis* itself, is first validated by
the reference to reliable poetic testimony about religious traditions.
"For since all nature is akin and thence the soul has learned all things,
there is nothing to prevent someone who recalls just one thing—what
men call learning—from discovering everything else, if he is courageous and does not tire of the inquiry; for inquiry indeed, and
learning, are entirely *anamnesis*" (81d1–5).

This staggeringly large sequence of propositions hinges, again, and hinges wholly, on the religious citation.

"All nature is akin," picks up, as it were, and universalizes Meno's opening question in the dialogue, which ended with asking whether virtue came to man by nature (φύσει) or some other way. And it also conditions the qualifications in the answers later on (89a–c).[17] The whole series looks backward easily to resolve Meno's paradox about the impossibility of learning something if you know it and also if you do not.[18] It looks forward to the *anamnesis*-demonstration, the cross-examination of the slave about geometry, which strictly speaking has the status of an example rather than a proof, though it is presented by Plato elenchically and its presentational structure as a proof has been the nearly exclusive concern of modern commentators.

The key argument of the dialogue rests on an appeal to authority, and to the "divine inspiration" of poets, Pindar in this instance, whose account about transmigration and the immortality of the soul begins the dialogue all over again, changes the nature of the questioning, and introduces the demonstration about *anamnesis* which it frames as the first in the hypothetical series, though not logically commensurate with it.

As Moravcsik points out, the discussion of *anamnesis* that follows through examining the slave about geometry is in two parts, themselves incommensurate, and incommensurate taken together with the questions about virtue in the body of the dialogue.[19] The first puzzle, about the relation between the length of the side of a square and the number of equal squares it contains, is different from the second, about how a line of irrationally measured length can be set as a diagonal for an exact way of setting inside a square another that is exactly half its area.

Reintroducing Plato's frequently broached connection between mathematics and the soul, if it were done in any forceful way, would reconcile the appeal to authority with the proof by cross-examining the slave. Konrad Gaiser shows that Plato presents the soul as a (mathematical) boundary of the body, and as a mathematical/physical equivalent for everything.[20] Yet this is not done at all explicitly in this dialogue, and no connection, poetic or Pythagorean, is made between

Pindar's account of the soul and the mathematics elicited from the slave. The connection between mathematics and the soul, elaborated in the *Republic*, is here suspended, like every other positive notion in the dialogue. Connecting mathematics and the soul could be an alternate route to the universal interconnections in nature, "all nature being akin," but it is a route that Plato here does not have Socrates take. The mathematics in the slave-*anamnesis* demonstration is not then given any of the extra force that the doctrine gets in the *Phaedo* to carry it beyond the immediate fact of the existence of the faculty.

Since in the *elenchos* Meno is himself shown to be obtuse, the slave is a) a weaker demonstration of *anamnesis*, b) more exact (for his passivity) than another might be, c) less dialectical, d) more specialized, e) implicitly not tragic. All these limitations increase the difficulty of relating the deductions about the slave to the doctrines of Empedocles or Pindar or the mysteries, or even the fuller Plato.

It is perhaps relevant to the large shift from Pindar to the slave that Aristotle cites the *Meno* on *anamnesis* specifically for failing to distinguish between particular and universal. The suspended close of the dialogue is congruent with the cross-examination of the slave in so far as both exemplify a structurally presented "feeling" to account for particular cases in relation to the universal. Plato, oddly, has it both ways by the circular presentation of virtue as it is paralleled by two incommensurate means of proof.

Now modern analysts, for all their vigor, simplify this presentation. They do so crucially by leaving out or underreading the passage from Pindar (81c–d) when in fact on the balance of the dialogue, that is all that really remains of an unquestioned assertion. For knowledge of virtue, if it really were accessible through *anamnesis*, would be much clearer and more distinct than any probability allowed for in the rest of the dialogue. If retrieving it were so difficult as to be beyond the sort of maieutic powers here exhibited—which go far beyond the cross-examination of the slave—it is not clear how the presence or absence of *anamnesis* would bear on the act of teaching. Yet nothing is said at any point to qualify or mitigate the authority of Pindar and the priests, and if we subject that presentation to any irony based on Plato's attitude towards poetry elsewhere, we would be obliged to throw out the baby of hypothesis with the bath water of authority.

So, for example, in his detailed and cogent exposition of the argument and propositional structure of the *Meno*, Terence Irwin at no point even mentions the Pindar-Persephone-wise men-and-women-argument from authority.[21] R. S. Bluck[22] speaks of this key passage as "strictly speaking a digression," which strictly speaking is exactly what it is not. The consonance of this passage with the long expositons in the *Phaedo*, the *Republic*, and the *Gorgias* might have given the commentators more pause. Sharples, quoting Klein in partial substantiation, states well the reliance on Pindar's authority, but he does not press the conclusion, as in any case a commentary for school use might well choose not to do: "In answer to Meno's paradox Socrates introduces an esoteric religious doctrine of reincarnation and, *based on this* [my italics], the theory that all learning is recollection."[23] In any case the argument has been replaced; and the authority of the quotation from Pindar remains unqualified.

By the time the cross-examination of the slave has taken place, Socrates is ready to jump back to the question of virtue (86c). Mathematics is now like virtue in so far as both are susceptible to hypothesis (86e–87c)—still another technique that has less than final results. Soon, indeed, there is another jump.

As Richard Robinson shows, the acute employment of hypothesis to sort out the how and the what of virtue, proceeding from still another mathematical analogy, reaches the conclusion that "virtue is a kind of knowledge" (86c–87d). But then, fairly soon (89a–89d) comes a demonstration that "virtue is not knowledge."[24] The keenness and originality of the hypothetical procedures here, on Robinson's showing, are the more remarkable in that they serve to suspend rather than to resolve the questions.[25]

The dialogue returns to the Sophists, with whom it began, and it finds them inconsistent on the teachability of virtue—as Socrates has been himself. He then goes on to allege inconsistencies on this very question in the poet Theognis (95c–e). So far as authority goes, these citations hold a middle ground. On the one hand they are inconsistent (though in fact they can be reconciled as Bluck notes, ad loc) but on the other hand if they had no assured authority, this would not be a problem. The distinction between knowledge (*episteme*) and right opinion (*orthe doxa*) gives the preference to the former but curiously associates the latter to the mobile statues of Daedalus, which seem to be valued as a technical achievement rather than deplored; and in fact they are praised as "wholly fine" (πάνυ γὰρ καλὰ τὰ ἔργα, 97e5)—though they at the same time are best tied down. Then—continuing the metaphor—the statues become knowledge through *anamnesis* (98a6; this closes the circle of reasoning differently). "Right opinion" turns out even to be a superior political guide (99c). The mention of the mobile statues of Daedalus, indeed, introduces the mediation which will result in political effectiveness; if true opinions (the term has now shifted from "right opinions" and has become "true opinions," ἁι δόξαι ἁι ἀληθεῖς), are properly tied down. If not, the opinions or the mobile statues are as useless as a runaway slave until they are bound by something that is called at once a reasoning process about cause and an *anamnesis*. So the *elenchos* and *anamnesis* are tentatively identified:

> οὐ πολλοῦ ἄξιαί εἰσιν, ἕως ἄν τις αὐτάς δήσηι
> αἰτίας λογισμῶι. τοῦτο δ'ἐστίν, ὦ Μένων ἑταῖρε,
> ἀνάμνησις, ὡς ἐν τοῖς πρόσθεν ἡμῖν ὡμολόγηται.
> ἐπειδάν δὲ δεθῶσιν, πρῶτον μὲν ἐπιστῆμαι
> γίγνονται, ἔπειτα μόνιμοι.

> They are not worth much until somebody ties them [the true opinions] down by reasoning of a cause, and this, Meno my friend, is anamnesis, as we admitted before. Whenever they are bound they first become knowledge, and are then stable. (98a3–6)

A rich series is offered here; the "reasoning of a cause" puts cause into a lengthy process; the reasoning must go on, and the cause cannot just be *ad hoc*. Also, the whole *anamnesis* argument, through the explicit back-reference, is brought to bear. The rich series will get someone from right opinion to knowledge, a term given in the plural to match "opinions," though "knowledges" is ambiguously a kind of superlative and at the same time an odd pluralization of what has so far been offered as one general term. In any case the possibility of being led from opinion to knowledge is not entertained for very long. Finally that possibility would be so extraordinary it would make a statesman who could carry it off like Tiresias among the dead. With teachability removed from men, and with ἐπιστήμη and φρόνησις ruled out, it emerges that—minimally but practically—all that is left is what is now called "good opinion," εὐδοξία" (99c). With this faculty alone "useful politicians keep the cities on a straight course," (οἱ πολιτικοὶ ἄνδρες χρώμενοι τάς πόλεις ὀρθοῦσιν). These politicians—Themistocles and others, who could not educate their sons—are now accorded the same adjective that designated the priests and priestesses: they are "godly" (θείους, 99c8), and they are compared with respect to "intelligence" (πρὸς τὸ φρονεῖν) with diviners and soothsayers. "They speak rightly many great things in a state of inspiration but do not know what they are saying"[26]

This identification, after the distinction has been made, nearly closes the circle between the domain of the *elenchos*—knowledge—and the domain of religion and poetry. "All those who are poetic" (99d1) are shortly brought in the list—perforce including the Pindar and the Theognis, who had been adduced earlier.

Anytus might be annoyed at the negative conditions here—"they do not know what they rightly speak." But if a politician could teach another politician, he would resemble Tiresias and be the only wise man among the dead. This comparison is richly extensible in itself; it effectually compares Anytus, and the type to which he belongs, to a failed Tiresias. It invokes a more abbreviated, and also a more traditional Homeric, form of the afterlife than the Orphic one of earlier description. It also puts the whole picture in the perspective of the most authoritative of poets. These are the very last assertions of the dialogue, except the injunction to persuade Anytus to be gentler. They are qualifying, suspensive, anticlimactic—and persistent in their adduction of poetry to continue qualifying an *elenchos* that has itself been suspended.

In one sense the *Meno* returns to its beginning; this itself demonstrates the "wisdom" of the Socratic *aporia*, as a clearing of the decks. In another sense, it has the argument both ways, having managed both a vigorous *elenchos* and an appeal to religion, poetry, transmigration, and inner sense, all flowing together. Or else, if we look at the whole structure of the dialogue, Plato has managed here to touch on many of his concerns without putting them through the *elenchos*, all the while structuring them as though they had been through it. The relative lack of yield from the *elenchos* as applied to *arete* and its teachability throws into relief the possible sharpness of the elenchic method. Once again it allows an interlocutor to find out he knows he does not know. At the same time it allows for the isolation, at the end, of an instinctual political wisdom as a substitute for an unattainable knowledge, an endorsement of a functional *orthe doxa.* This coexists with something that in fuller dialogues would be a far higher mental function, the participation in the cogeneration of everything (τῆς φύσεως ἁπάσης συγγενοῦς οὔσης, 81d1) that the immortality of the soul allows. Even the paradox that precedes the induction of Pindar and other wise men on immortality—Meno's puzzle that you cannot know what you know and cannot know what you don't—is amplified. To that degree it is accepted by Socrates before it is dismissed; by not being directly refuted, this radical skepticism coexists with the doctrine of immortality. In this way a number of doctrines about the capacity of the human intelligence are aligned and allowed by that mere fact to coexist, as well as to come about through the *elenchos,* rather than being hierarchized. Hypothesis is a second best in the *Phaedo,* but in this dialogue, for all its fits and starts,[27] it is not so characterized.

What are we to make, then, of the elaborate demonstration of hypothesis which occupies the center of the dialogue, attached though it is to the authoritative transmigration-immortality doctrines from Pindar and the wise, godly seers? I would submit that even in the light of the contingency for which I have been arguing, and also in the light of the criticisms, however severe, that can be made of its presentational strategies, it is meant to stand in the dialogue, but to stand in isolation. The same is true of the two long *elenchi,* one preceding it and one following it. The first comes to a halt when Meno says that he has been immobilized by the stingray, Socrates, and cannot get past the impasse about how to attain knowledge. In agreeing with him about the impasse, Socrates calls his point eristic not to dismiss it but to reassure him; which we know in context because Socrates immediately turns to the alternate account of transmigration and immortality, as though that will not only provide a sort of solution but also get the discourse going again. The progress of the discourse is somewhat suspended, however, because it leads to the hypothesis-exchanges, which themselves in turn lead to the second *elenchos.* That, too, is closed out by a sort of adequate second-best in the reliability of guidance from right opinion. On the positive side here, what has happened is that the impasse from *elenchos* has twice been resolved by the adduction of a human faculty to some degree independent of it, the first time by the *anamnesis* taken on authority (if buttressed by the cross-examination) and the second time by the appeal to the viability of right opinion. The first time the *elenchos* is stopped and gives way to something more, the soul and the capacities of *anamnesis*. The second time it trails off and is compensated for the failure to establish the teachability of *arete* by something less, the "right opinion," which has to be a poor second best to knowledge, however viable it may be for the practical politician (a figure who is given a sort of free rein here that is strange for Plato).

Anamnesis due to transmigration, *elenchos*, and right opinion are not tested against one another at all. It is not clear they could be. Here they coexist in a progressive suspension which has been engendered by setting the question of the relation between knowledge and virtue. The *elenchos* in a negative way closes out each time it approaches this question, leaving the positive residue of the alertness that the technique can produce, when the interlocutor is a nearly equal partner with the leader. Gorgias, Protagoras, and the Lysias of the *Phaedrus*, by contrast, do not set themselves up into a Socratic *elenchos* but rather engage a question-and-answer session of the sort that Thrasymachus abortively proposes in the *Republic* (350e). Here in the *Meno* the *elenchos* has, as demonstrated, an abiding value, even if—in characteristically Platonic fashion—the topics it addresses tend to be so large that they spill over into the area covered by other, related human capacities. The strategies of suspension permit all these attitudes to coexist without working out interrelations between them, and also without stressing their coexistence. That simply *happens* in the dialogue. By an extraordinarily wide survey Plato has here demonstrated the difficulty of establishing interconnections between the central Platonic topics of knowledge and virtue.

Notes

1. For Greece, and for other cultures too, these practices confront the investigator with an "iceberg," as Paul Veyne says in *Les Grecs ont-ils cru à*

leurs mythes?, 17. "Greek religion," Walter Burkert says, "is far from easy to know and understand." See Walter Burkert, *Greek Religion* (Cambridge: Harvard University Press, 1985), 1. See also Victor Goldschmidt, *La Religion de Platon* (Paris: Presses Universitaires de France, 1949).

2. Aristotle, *Prior Analytics*, 67a. Ὁμοίως δὲ καὶ ὁ ἐν τῶι Μένωνι λόγος ὅτι ἡ μάθησις ἀνάμνησις. οὐδαμοῦ γάρ συμβαίνει προεπίστασθαι τὸ καθ᾿ ἕκαστον, ἀλλ᾿ ἅμα τῆι ἐπαγωγῆι λαμβάνειν τὴν τῶν κατὰ μέρος ἐπιστήμην ὥσπερ ἀναγνωρίζοντας. "The same way, too, does the reasoning work in the *Meno* that learning is anamnesis. For in no way does it obtain for us to know each case beforehand, but at the same time by induction we can grasp the knowledge part by part as though we were recollecting it." If the qualifications work that may be deduced from the shifts and suspensions in Socrates' argument, they both do and do not qualify the doctrine, which it may be presumed Aristotle would have known from the longstanding oral traditions about the doctrine, and possibly also about dialectical method, in the Academy as well as from this particular dialogue. This curious, and logically intolerable, coexistence of certitude and qualification in the same large statement happens not just in the *Meno*, in fact, but characteristically throughout many of Plato's dialogues. Here Aristotle treats Plato's doctrine in a chapter that deals with cases of failing to distinguish between particular and general knowledge. "For when we look at particulars from the whole," he goes on, "we do not know them by what is peculiar to them, and so we can make mistakes about them." (Τῆι μὲν οὖν καθόλου θεωροῦμεν τὰ ἐν μέρει, τῆι δ᾿οἰκεία οὐκ ἴσμεν, ὥστ᾿ ἐνδέχεται καὶ ἀπατᾶσθαι περὶ αὐτά.)

3. Richard Robinson, "Hypothesis in the *Meno*," in *Plato's Earlier Dialectic* (Oxford: Clarendon, 1953), 114–22; Jakob Klein, *A Commentary on Plato's* Meno (Chapel Hill: University of North Carolina Press, 1965); R. S. Bluck, *Plato's* Meno (Cambridge: Cambridge University Press, 1961); R. W. Sharples, *Plato's* Meno (Chicago: Bolchazy-Carducci, 1985).

4. Michael C. Stokes, *Plato's Socratic Conversations*, 10.

5. Stokes, 17. The type of argument concerned is a set of syllogisms by Zeno of Citium, which "Malcolm C. Schofield ... has recently drawn attention to" (442, citing "The Syllogisms of Zeno of Citium," *Phronesis* 1983, 28, 31–58).

6. ἆρα διδακτὸν ἡ ἀρετή; ἢ οὐ διδακτὸν ἀλλ᾿ ἀσκητόν; ἢ οὔτε ἀσκητὸν οὔτε μαθητόν, ἀλλά φύσει παραγίγνεται τοῖς ἀνθρώποις ἢ ἄλλωι τινὶ τρόπωι;

7. F. Heinimann, *Nomos und Phusis*.

8. Φύσις is so comprehensive here as to be vague, but it cannot be restricted to physical nature. It also includes human nature in its first usage here (70a); and it is germane that at least nine of the twenty times that

Thucydides uses the word, he is referring clearly to human nature.

9. σὺ δὲ ταὐτὰ ἄπερ αὐτός πέπεισαι πεῖθε καὶ τὸν ξένον τόνδε Ἄνυτον, ἵνα πραιότερος ᾖ· ὡς ἐὰν πείσῃς τοῦτον, ἔστιν ὅτι καὶ᾽ Ἀθηναίους ὀνήσεις.

10. Οὐκοῦν ἐπειδή οὐ διδακτόν ἐστιν, οὐδ᾽ ἐπιστήμη δὴ ἔτι γίγνεται ἡ ἀρετή·

11. "Intelligence" (φρόνησις) has also been reasoned away from accessibility (88d–89a). Δόξα is a term stronger than opinion, especially since the term "right opinion" (ὀρθή δόξα) is used, elsewhere in the dialogue (97–99), and τό ὀρθόν comes up shortly in this context. On ὀρθή δόξα generally, see Julius Stenzel, *Plato's Method of Dialectic.*

12. Pierre Louis, *Les Métaphores de Platon* (Paris: Belles Lettres, 1945), finds that Plato uses the term swarm, σμῆνος, as a term for multiplicity (32).

13. Martin Andic, "Inquiry and Virtue in the *Meno*," in Malcolm Brown, ed., *Plato's* Meno (Indianapolis: Bobbs-Merrill, 1971), 262–314. Fortifying the connection between geometry and virtue in this presentation would indeed be a requisite task in a modern conception of what would be necessary to carry through the argument in order truly to centralize the geometric demonstration. Andic well performs that task, but Plato pointedly refrains from doing so. By skillfully deriving sets of propositions buttressed by arguments from other dialogues, and by scrutiny of separable statements in the *Meno*, Andic is able to show a notion of the *a priori*, and of possible knowledge in addition to actual knowledge, as underlying the *Meno*. Still, none of this comes to anything like full conclusion in the dialogue itself. Andic's initial characterization remains (263), "First, the theory of recollection does not seem to answer the question that prompts its formulation in the dialogue, viz., whether knowledge or inquiry is possible at all; and yet that question was dismissed as the raising of a 'trick argument,' implying that the question was a stock one among the eristics or debaters of the day, that the argument it raises was and was known to be fallacious. Socrates faces similar fallacies in other dialogues and apparently knows how to resolve them. Why then does he not offer a similar resolution here, in place of the vastly more ambitious and speculative theory of recollection and immortality, which appears not only gratuitous and vacuous but regressive, inviting the same eristic question it is meant to answer?" And further of the learning paradox (299), "It therefore appears that Meno's question was the right one to raise, whatever exactly he meant by it."

14. The term τραγικ́ή in the *Meno* applied to a color definition (Taylor, *Plato* [Cleveland: Meridian, 1966 (1926)] can mean not only stagey and imprecise but also given to that particular kind of poetic dialogue—a stated position instead of an inquiry (ζητεῖν).

15. Some translators render θεῖοι as "inspired"; but Plato himself

provides a clear gloss by having Socrates quote the Spartans (always good guides, according to Plato): "Women call good men godly. And when the Spartans praise a man as good they say "This is a godly man"" (99d 6–8). Of course "good" (ταγαθός) is the adjective corresponding to "virtue" (ἀρετή). The term θεῖος is a broad and comprehensive one in Plato, almost always deriving a a powerful idealization from the identification of (some qualities in) men with (those in) gods.

16. ὥστε οὐδέν θαυμαστόν καὶ περὶ ἀρετῆς καὶ περὶ ἄλλων οἶόν τε εἶναι αὐτήν ἀναμνησθῆναι, ἅ γε καὶ πρότερον ἠπίστατο.

17. Sharples (149) calls the proposition Pythagorean, which it is, with reference to transmigration. Here, however, it is applied to all things learned. So it can be reconciled with the doctrines of many pre-Socratics: Parmenides, Heraclitus, Xenophanes, and even perhaps Anaximander.

18. Socrates' statement "I don't wholly remember" in the first exchanges (71c8) is proleptically ironic about *anamnesis*, though of course casually so, as Plato has structured an ordinary flow of conversation. He is answering Meno's question as to whether Socrates thought Gorgias knows what virtue is—a reference to another sort of authority, and one that Socrates will attack more frontally elsewhere, where here he just touches on Gorgias, Meno's mentor, ironically.

19. J. M. E. Moravcsik, "Learning as Recollection," in Gregory Vlastos, ed., *Plato* I (Garden City, N.Y.: Anchor, 1971), 53–69.

20. Konrad Gaiser, *Platons Ungeschriebene Lehre.* See also Marie-Dominique Richard, *L'Enseignement orale de Platon* (Parons: Cerf, 1986).

21.Terence Irwin, *Plato's Moral Theory: The Early and Middle Dialogues* (Oxford: Clarendon Press, 1972), 133–60. Of course the argument from authority (not least from such authority) has no philosophical validity today—a circumstance which has no bearing on the fact that Plato-Socrates used it. For that matter, neither does teaching geometry as a proof for *anamnesis*.

22. R. S. Bluck, *Plato's* Meno, 277–86.

23. R. W. Sharples, *Plato's* Meno, 144.

24. Richard Robinson, *Plato's Earlier Dialectic*, 114–22.

25. "The procedure ... is the same as the procedure which Aristotle in his *Analytics* called 'the syllogism from hypothesis' and held to be importantly different from ordinary syllogism. It is probable that Aristotle had the *Meno* in mind while writing the *Analytics*" (119). Actually it is certain he did, but he does not cite him as a model since his one mention of him there is to criticize his logical procedure. Robinson qualifies the suspension by assigning an important role to hypothesis in the development of Plato's writings (which of course in turn implies that they can be dated with precision—an arguable assumption): "The dialogue begins with refutations

of Meno's definitions about virtue, even if tentative and non-essential, by means of the hypothetical method. It is thus a microcosm of the whole series of Plato's dialogues; for on the whole those previous to the *Meno* are merely destructive and those after it are definitely constructive." Lucid as Robinson's demonstrations are, he would seem here to confuse method with substance. While we see through his demonstrations the power of the method, the assertions it leads to are indeed so "tentative and non-essential" that we are left at the end of the dialogue only with a deference to the religious context in which virtue could flourish—possibly with the aid of *anamnesis*, as well as with the nearly untransmittable political *faute de mieux* of "right opinion," when we had begun with hoping to work out whether or not virtue is teachable, and how. And so, in effect, we are left with the richness and power of the elenchic method itself, which promises what it does not here deliver, the possibility of moving towards further clarity about questions of substance. H.-P. Stahl ("Beginnings of Propositional Logic in Plato," *Plato's* Meno, Malcolm Brown, ed., 180–98) finds crucial discrepancies in this hypothetical method but still sees anamnesis as offering a license to keep inquiring, "it makes sense to go on inquiring (183) ... things known by the soul in Anamnesis are what they are in an *objective* interrelation, which the soul, beginning from individual points already known, tries to get hold of systematically in *anamnesis* (all nature being akin): τῆς φύσεως ἁπάσης συγγενοῦς οὔσης 81c9–d1; 197)." Malcolm Brown ("Plato disapproves of the slave boy's answer," 198–242) finds an implied rejection of the demonstrations made built into the cross-examination through discrepancies in the shifts of terminological definition.

26. ἐνθουσιάζειν, ἐπίπνους ὄντας καὶ κατεχομένους ἐκ τοῦ θεοῦ, ὅταν κατορθῶσι λέγοντες πολλὰ καὶ μεγάλα πράγματα, μηδέν εἰδότες ὧν λέγουσιν.

27. Malcolm Brown, "Plato disapproves," gives the fullest and most severe account of the possible breakdowns in the cross-examination of the slave boy.

Chapter 7

Particles, Qualification, Ordering, Style, Irony and Meaning in Plato's Dialogues

The very conception of the dialogue form, and the variety of the instances of the dialogue that Plato offers us, bring meaning and qualification into a closer rapprochement than they would have in more directly deductive works. One dialogue can often be taken as qualifying another, or as amending and/or amplifying it in ways that amount to a qualification. An entire dialogue, that is, offers a large-scale qualification, both within the dialogue itself, and from this dialogue to other dialogues. On the smallest scale a similar and corresponding function is exercised by the particles, a noteworthy feature not just of Greek expression but of Plato's expression in particular.[1]

There are, then, in general, two registers for the Platonic dialogue. One results from the initial choice of the dialogue form itself among several other possibilities for the philosopher beginning to formulate his ideas between 400 and 380 B.C.E.: the aphorisms of Heraclitus, the prose of Protagoras and Isocrates or the medical writers, the far more developed and extended book-length prose tracts of Herodotus and Thucydides. Aside from prose, Plato would have had available the expressive possibilities of the long philosophical poem; the examples of Empedocles and Parmenides stood within not too distant memory. Or he could also have chosen not to write at all, as Socrates must have chosen to do in the face of so many previous philosophers who chose to express their ideas in writing. Given the preference for the oral in the *Phaedrus* and the *Seventh Letter*, Plato could have confined himself at his most formal to such lectures as the reported "On the Good."

Instead he did take the dramatic form, purging it of verse and also of a determinate structure. This of itself provides him with the first of his two registers. This register does not just derive from the dialogue form but from the carefully maintained discrepancy between a Socrates masked in bewilderment and a speaker or speakers who lay various claims to knowledge. There is an ironically recirculating discrepancy between the assertions of a given speaker at a given moment and the relation of this moment to the topic at hand, as to the dialogue as a whole. Thus, to begin with, the possibility of closure for an explicit doctrine is never abandoned; often it can only actualize itself in the hyperbole of myth which tends, like the passages of *elenchos* themselves, to be progressive.

As for the most puzzling of Plato's kinds of discourse, the myths, they are by definition characterized in Socrates' general description of the Charioteer myth as an approximation ("What it is like," ὧι δὲ ἔοικεν, *Phaedrus*, 246a5). If myths, introduced for explanation, are approximations, then the *elenchos*, too, *a fortiori* bears the character of approximation.

The reminder that the discourse is approximative is scored, and the irony very differently furthered in the second of the registers, that between the constantly mobile particles and the fixity of the deep-structured sentences which they accompany.[2]

Aristotle, by contrast, formulated linguistic and logical traffic rules for the dialectic at the same time that he sheared away from the separate sentence all the flutterings of particle tonality and qualification, many of which amounted to translatable encapsulated predications. He left written down the naked schema of the flat predication, and his bald enchainment of these is so unqualified as to leave it doubtful of some texts whether they are lecture notes or completed utterances.

Plato's particles, of course, go far beyond the necessary presence of such a marker at the beginning of a Greek sentence. Their frequency and range is so remarkable in his work, compared with the use in all other Greek prose and poetry, that more than a quarter of all the references in Denniston's *Greek Particles* (16 index pages out of a total of 57) are from his work. They function as constantly inserted qualifiers. Along with changes of diction they permit, or at least further, such rapid shifts of tone as that noted by Dorothy Tarrant in *Republic* 509b, "the tone of conversation has been effectively lowered from rhapsody to matter of fact." For the mobility of particles, which keeps the two registers in constant relation, heavily assists in conveying a general evenness of tone to the dialogue through all the movement between the serious and the playful, and for all the range through what Thesleff has discriminated as no fewer than ten separate styles.[3]

The particles, in the light of their role as qualifiers, would be unsusceptible of treatment by any of the theories of language addressed in the *Cratylus*, but the Heraclitean theory[4] of absolute flux—to which Cratylus says he inclines in almost his final statement (440e1–2).

Still, this is far from being anything that allows for more than simply the conjectural possibility that Plato took the deep-seated balance of contradiction in Heraclitus' minimalist utterances and maximalized them by putting one speaker on one side of a contradiction, and another or others in some way on the other side or sides. Since one of the speakers, Socrates, contrasted himself, so to speak—as most knowing he claimed to be least knowing—the imbalance between speakers was repeated in the self-dialecticizing posture of just one of the speakers. This made the polyglossic balance (to use a term of Bakhtin's) asymmetrical: only on one side of the dialogic balance was there a managed contradiction implied. The goal to reach clarity—to restore the balance—generates a self-renewing heteroglossia: there is always more to be said on the other scale. Consequently any moment can be declared "the end," as typically some random moment—except in the trial dialogues—can be declared a beginning.

The intrication of logical and pragmatic presuppositions in the linguistic utterance that a dialogue constitutes is highlighted by the unusual range and frequency of the particles. This intrication comes about because the function of the particles as linguistic constituents is limited to stressing features of the relations between sentences, or else the "already existing" semantic and syntactic constituents of an individual sentence. "Logical presupposition is defined on the relation between base (linguistic) structures and the world. Pragmatic presupposition is defined on the relation between utterances and their contexts."[5] The Platonic dialogue sets up a pragmatic context of its own in which it tests logical presupposition, and Socrates typically presses a single lexical item, like *arete* or *techne*. The particles underscore this process by serving to underscore turns of syntax and consequently by reminding the reader of the argument imbedded in a flow of linguistic, fictively oral presentation. The particles, that is, especially insist on connecting the logical and the pragmatic.

Moreover, though we cannot know what the intonational patterns of Plato's Greek were, we can be sure from what is known of linguistic behavior generally that the particles structured the intonational pattern; and thereby they would heighten the fiction that an oral conversation is being reproduced, with all the advantages attributed to oral over written presentation that are propounded in the *Phaedrus*. The particles attached to a single word or phrase, such as *kai*, complicate, as does the English word "even,"[6] the relation to the rest of the sentence of what it modifies, while the majority of the particles, as they underscore the structure of the relation between sentences, provide a condensed and partial phonemic replay of those relations.[7]

As the investigations of generative grammarians have progressively demonstrated, the "deep structure" of a language conforms to, and in a sense creates, complex sets of logical operations. The congruence of these logical operations with "pragmatics," the actual use of a language in utterances, validates the use of dialogue as an instrument in what for Plato is the relatively new area of philosophy. Moreover, the congruence of the logical and the pragmatic further justifies Plato's astonishing valuation of oral over written discourse in the *Phaedrus* and the *Seventh Letter*.

By moving the ironic gestures into a differently calibrated register, wherein they do not simply echo the propositions of their rib sentences or even qualify them in a simple way, the particles provide a partial distortion that prevents the Socratic irony from being an endless regress. Since the main sentences must be in place in the deep structure of the utterance before the qualifying particles are added to it, the particles may be regarded not only as taking it for granted, but as operating in a register secondary to it. Their play works against the assumed fixity of the main sentences and can only do so if that fixity is assumed.[8] They come up against the fixity by a qualification which stays in the second register and so, in its play, mimes but in turn relativizes the larger play of the elenchic conversation. They re-ironize the Socratic irony and arrest it. They, as it were, preempt the irony and limit it at the particular point of utterance where the particle occurs. Otherwise the irony would take a Kierkegaardian form in the interchange.[9] The main register of the dialogue also manages the contextual irony so as to keep all sentence propositions from entering what Jerrold Katz calls the "null context."[10]

However modified the congruence may be between logical propositional structures and the "deep structures" of the sentence, the congruence is one which cannot be "deferred" (to adapt Derrida's term) out of the language.[11] In Katz's "null context," or the uncontextualized bare proposition, an utterance in language retains a logical structure, or at least part of one.

Now Plato never operates in a null environment. The dialogue form heavily contextualizes all his utterances. Correspondingly, if the oral is inescapably contextualized and the written tends to minimalize or even nullify context, then the cuing to contextualization resides in the dialogue form, which applies the written to a representation of the oral. Contextualization also resides in the particles, which are the one element in a sentence not reducible to a component of the deep structure, though the relational particles, those that indicate how one sentence relates to one another, provide a surface link of one deep structure to another, a fictional "oralization" of the discourse which marks it as a discourse. The unusual frequency of Plato's particles, unique in the body of Greek prose, further sustains a busy accompaniment of cuing. The particles call attention to the difference between the tentativeness of (oral) improvisation, while modifying the "written" certainty of the logical congruences coded and largely fixed by the deep structure.

This logical coherence of the sentence, as a communicative and communicable act, preserves it from the radical qualification of describing it as a "trace" just because the inescapable structure of consciousness allows us so to characterize it epistemologically. Some fixity in the sentence meanings is necessary for the modification inherent in the particles to operate upon them. Or, put differently, they move the propositions of the sentences in the "first register" explicitly towards the condition of speech acts and speech events, or rather they keep flagging them as such. Plato's "oralization" also preserves his dialogues from the radical relativization entailed in putting into primary position any metaphoric structures that may be present in the discourse,[12] especially since metaphor itself, in one of its dimensions, can be accorded a logical structure.[13]

In Plato's dialogues the possible closeness of an endless regress is apparent from the simple scheme of falsely echoing negation by which, in short dialogues, an understating "amateur" Socrates faces an overstating, pigheaded professional like Laches, Euthyphro, Ion, or Euthydemus. This scheme is modified and much orchestrated, but not abandoned in the *Protagoras*, the *Gorgias*, and even the *Parmenides*.

Inextricably connected to irony is tone, and tone consequently overlays every word spoken in the dialogues. This tone is uneven at the outset, from the very conception of an initial imbalance between a "know-nothing" Socrates and an interlocutor who is either at odds with him or eager to learn from him. In the *Phaedrus* there is a near balance because of the accord as it develops between Socrates and Phaedrus. This dialogue is preoccupied with the erotic, and it is at the same time ambiguously prefatory to erotic activity. Its playful tone qualifies the dialogue constantly and evenly.

As for the specific conditions governing particles, a transitional particle is almost obligatory in ordinary Greek style. Consequently "*gar*," translated as "for," is more routine than the English word, because it is more necessary. That is the double face of the particle. It is more open to alternatives for the range and subtlety of expression just because it fills an obligatory, given slot in the sentence. But "*gar*" is more subliminal than is English "for," because "*gar*" does not relate to the deep structure of the utterance as proposition. In a given case it happens to be the particular particle chosen as a filler for the blank "particle" space from sentence to sentence, indicating that a new sentence has begun. The necessary particle underscores, and subordinates, each sentence as a parallel proposition. Plato aestheticizes this out of, but not wholly in departure from, a colloquial dialogue. The tautness and flexibility of the very ordering of words is sustained, aided, and itself qualified by particles.

Take a five-word sentence from the *Symposium*, in which two of the words are particles:

λέγω δὲ δὴ τί τοῦτο

And so what do I mean by this?
(Symposium 178d)

We may see several gestures at work in this sentence: 1) The verb, unusually, comes first. 2) This δὲ is unrelated, as a look at the context would make clear. So it is confined to mere emphasis. 3) It points not backward, its usual function, but in this context ahead to δὴ. 4) τί is strangely deferred, displaced from its usual initial position. 5) In this five-word sentence, τοῦτο is split as far as possible from the verb of which it is the object. The reference of τοῦτο itself involves extra emphasis, since Phaedrus, the speaker, has led from declaring Eros to be oldest of the gods to his being more necessary than anything else for one who would live the good life. 6) In this context, δὴ functions somewhat as would italics, covering the whole small metalinguistic declaration, "And so what is this I say?" All of this play is made by the particles to ripple through the simple question of this short sentence.

The beginning of the *Protagoras* exemplifies some of the variety of ways in which particles enter this discourse. It opens with banter about Socrates and Alcibiades:

ΕΤ. Πόθεν, ὦ Σώκρατες, φαίνηι; ἢ δῆλα δὴ ὅτι ἀπὸ κυνηγεσίου τοῦ περὶ τὴν Ἀλκιβιάδου ὥραν; καὶ μὴν μοι καὶ πρώιην ἰδόντι καλός μὲν ἐφαίνετο ἀνήρ ἔτι, ἀνήρ μέντοι, ὦ Σώκρατες, ὡς γ᾽ ἐν αὐτοῖς ἡμῖν εἰρῆσθαι, καὶ πώγωνος ἤδη ὑποπιμπλάμενος.

ΣΩ. Εἶτα τί τοῦτο; οὐ σὺ μέντοι Ὁμήρου ἐπαινέτης
εἶ, ὃς ἔφη χαριεστάτην ἥβην εἶναι τοῦ πρῶτον
ὑπηνήτου, ἣν νῦν Ἀλκιβιάδης ἔχει;
ΕΤ. τί οὖν τὰ νῦν; ἢ παρ' ἐκείνου φαίνῃ; καὶ πῶς
πρός σε ὁ νεανίας διάκειται·

Friend: Where have you appeared from, Socrates? Or is it not clear
that it is from hunting round the youth of Alcibiades? Certainly
when I saw him only a day or two ago, he seemed to be still a
handsome man, but between ourselves, Socrates, "man" is the
word. He's actually growing a beard.
Socrates: What of it? Aren't you a praiser of Homer, who says that
the most charming age is that of the youth with his first beard, just
the age of Alcibiades now?
Friend: Well what now? Were you just with him? and how is the
young man disposed toward you?   (309a–b; Guthrie, revised)

Particles begin (as they must) after the brief first question. The
blunt δή, often connected with δῆλος, points at the particular moment.[14] Still, it "speaks its influence over the whole clause," and
therefore the third sentence uses particles heavily to transpose itself
away from the standard[15] metaphors of the first sentence. Thereby it
points delicately in the direction of another topic. This is the procedure, on a larger scale, of the whole dialogue. As a procedure it raises
the question about how one topic connects to another—perhaps the
most general question we may raise about Plato. Eros is not an explicit
subject here, but it has implicitly to do with the relation of knowledge
and virtue, as becomes clear in Plato's discussion of this topic elsewhere, especially in the *Symposium* and the *Phaedrus*.

Δή may be said to anticipate the ὅτι clause, especially as the copula is omitted, which would tend to fall exactly where the δή does
here. This spread across δή touches in the reminder of an underlying
structure which will become that of the whole dialogue. The *Protagoras*, like this clause, reaches forward through a long *elenchos* as
then it does through the δή, only to state what is "clear" from the
beginning. And δῆλα, "it is clear," as a propositional word, will emphasize the structural interchangeability of verb and adjective.[16]

The next sentence begins with a strong particle run: fewer words,
just four, of which three are particles, καὶ μήν μοι καὶ. The καὶ's
are rhymically correlative, but the first one is more emphatic, in its

linkage with μήν, while the second one is not really correlative with it, since it modifies the immediately following word, πρώτην. It looks simply ahead, while καὶ μήν looks strongly backward as well as strongly ahead. Denniston finds this particular instance combining the adversative and the copulative (357). It is "progressive after strong stops" (352) and characteristically has a strong function of logical sequentiality. Often it serves the minor premise of an enthymeme—only suggested here, because no serious topic has been introduced. It anticipates ἀνήρ μέντοι—a phrase which, again, is also anticipated in the delicate μέν that is *not* called for here and is all the more lightly disjunctive for coming in the middle of the sentence, rather than in the usual position of the second word. It is also more lightly disjunctive because it is matched by no corresponding δέ; hence it is not balanced and enters simply as a further mild emphasis in the train of progressive particles, straining forward to the serious topic of the dialogue while bantering the here irrelevant topic of erotic attraction.

Μέντοι, in so far as it pauses to repeat μέν, in the combination μεν plus τοι, is a longer word, but in fact a shade weaker here, all the more that it is repeated almost at once in Socrates' answering speech. Its weakness is that of an unnecessary superadded emphasis, "really." The next μέντοι is stronger, since it accompanies the question that expects an affirmative answer, and also italicizing the σύ, which is itself emphatic. In the sentence before, the one with the first μέντοι, there is another italicization, the γε in ὡς γ'. Since the "Friend" emphasizes "we" and Socrates emphasizes "you"—the same person, but this time singled out in the singular—the two forms of italicization have logically the same ultimate reference. Immediately, however, μέντοι emphasizes the person, as the first μέντοι had emphasized the man Alcibiades. And this dialogue, too, will have much play about persons. The γε is fairly unusual here as an emphasis for the ὡς that introduces the parenthetical relative clause—as though there were a contagion of particles.[17]

Switching the emphasis, the next clause, the longest so far, has no particles at all. But then there is a strong particle, οὖν, "therefore," in the Friend's replying question. Questions themselves in this run stand as the big signature of heightened dialogue; six of the first seven sentences are questions. There is all the more reason, then, for us to expect the logical connective "therefore" to go with an affirmation, but we know that it will not, because it follows τἰ, "What?" "And what, therefore, about things at the moment?" The rephrasing of this question begins with another light particle, one we have not had in the run yet, ἤ. It rarely appears by itself in prose (Denniston, 282), as it does here. Especially since Homer has just been quoted, it may be taken perhaps, in this passage, as in others where Plato uses it by itself, as a faintly heightening poeticism.[18]

The play throughout this opening has been unusually playful, and unusually digressive. To these features the riot of particles has cued us, and has provided a constantly varied, constantly qualifying accompaniment, as though to say, "Yes, with so much qualification we cannot have an urgent argument under way; otherwise the attention to the main clauses in the interchange would be more exclusive, and the qualifications would be more pointedly structured."

Another manner for this process of modification appears in the particle placements of the *Symposium*. In that dialogue the balance keeps shifting and so does the tone. The *Symposium* is certainly serious because of the topic. It is certainly comic because of the context delineated in the fiction and because of its persistent playfulness. Therefore the strategy of interpreting its presentation of Eros must hang on ascertaining how the particular mix of serious and comic is sustained in the unfolding sequence of the series, and how it functions. This question comes up particularly in the speech of Aristophanes, who is said at the beginning (177e2) to know about *ta erotika* because of his devotion to Dionysus and Aphrodite—a statement that could seriously mean that he has won competitions at the festivals of Dionysus, and his comedies deal with sex. Playfully, it would be a way of saying that he is absorbed in wine, women, and song. Aristophanes can be seen as resembling a character in one of his own plays or as functioning philosophically like the author of them in his composition of the fable and myth about the original androgynes.

Now the small details of the particles, as generally in Plato, keep alive this balance between the serious and the playful in special ways. An orchestration of particles accompanies Aristophanes' speech, a speech that is itself richly modified by its formal and propositional similarities and differences to the array of other speeches brought forward here as encomia on love. When Aristophanes gets into the thick of his playful-serious anthropological-allegorical fable about the origin of sexed human beings, he creates a double attitude in the gods, who out of defensiveness have cut the original beings in two but have reshaped them out of pity for their haplessness before the idea of separation. The gods' mediating solution is to readjust the position of the genitals. As Aristophanes moves to this presentation, he keys up his discourse, and in doing so he further modulates its qualifications. This we can trace in the special manipulation accorded to the particles at this point:

τέως γὰρ καὶ ταῦτα ἐκτὸς εἶχον, καὶ ἐγέννων καὶ ἔτικτον οὐκ εἰς ἀλλήλους αλλ᾽ εἰς γῆν, ὥσπερ οἱ τέττιγες—μετέθηκέ τε οὖν οὕτω αὐτῶν εἰς τὸ πρόσθεν καὶ διὰ τούτων τὴν γένεσιν ἐν ἀλλήλοις ἐποίησεν, διὰ τοῦ ἄρρενος ἐν τῶι θήλει, τῶνδε ἕνεκα, ἵνα ἐν τῆι συμπλοκῆι ἅμα μὲν εἰ ἀνὴρ γυναικί ἐντύχοι, γεννῶιεν καὶ γίγνοιτο τὸ γένος, ἅμα δ᾽ εἰ καὶ ἄρρην ἄρρενι, πλησμονή γοῦν γίγνοιτο τῆς συνουσίας καὶ διαπαύοιντο καὶ ἐπὶ τὰ ἔργα τρέ᾽ ποιντο καὶ τοῦ ἄλλου βίου ἐπιμελοῖντο.

For of course they had originally been on the outside—which was now the back—and they had begotten and conceived not upon each other, but, like the grasshoppers, upon the earth. So now, as I say, he moved their members round to the front and made them propagate among themselves, the male begetting upon the female—the idea being that if, in all interweavings, a man should chance upon a woman, conception would take place and the race would be continued, while if man should conjugate with man, he might at least obtain such satisfaction as would allow him to turn his attention and his energies to the everyday affairs of life.   (191b-d)

Since γὰρ clearly indicates a causal connection, especially after the emphatically placed adverb τέως, καὶ is somewhat supernumerary and so touches on the note of pity. Aristophanes modulates his voice so as to mime dramatically the attitude of the gods that he is describing. Behind that, he touches on the note of the speaker's fantasy in which the pity is included, since by intensifying his seriousness Aristophanes is stepping up his play. In the continuation after the parenthesis, begun by the particle group τε οὖν, the τε is again supernumerary and adds a feigned gentleness. Denniston notes the rarity of the collocation of prospective τε with connective οὖν and indicates Plato's fondness for it.[19] Εἰ καὶ effectively conjoins the condition to the full connection (Denniston 301), while γοῦν flatly indicates the full effectuation of Zeus's change.[20]

The run of οὖν's is unusually rich throughout this whole passage, as though to insist that the causal pattern holds with special force; and this, again, amounts to an assertion by Aristophanes that his fantasy corresponds to reality, which in turn ironically implies the opposite, with a lightness that is almost wholly invested in these particles, as they continue.[21]

There are, by contrast, few particles in Socrates' later dialogue here with Alcibiades, where for the emotional-intellectual nuances we might have expected them. Alcibiades' later encomia are spare of particles, except towards the end, but full of false starts and overqualifications, and full as well of the repetitions and provocations of the drunk. They violate unknowingly (because they were set before he arrived) the special condition of sobriety for this banquet, which is declared at the outset when the guests voluntarily dispense with the usual continuation of drinking in order precisely to keep their heads clear for such discussion. The relative absence of particles in some places, and their relatively random abundance in others, by comparison with all the foregoing speech, helps to underscore the crudity of Alcibiades here, and hence the oversimplicity of a position that the main propositions of his speech would present forcefully, rather than as here in the distortion of contrast.[22] He ends asserting that he will take care and not be "like the ninny, to learn by suffering," as a sort of anti-Aeschylus, quoting a proverb, as though to touch base on a popular wisdom for confirmation. Socrates's answer restores rhetorical balance and indicates the fact by once more proceeding to touch in particles, where the twists of Alcibiades' utterance, in its drunken career, has momentarily displaced them: we measure his wildness, and the increase in comic exhibition, both by the paucity of particles and by the exaggeratedness of what seems idle rhetoric. Alcibiades in both the negative sense (use of particles) and the positive (wild speech) proves himself unable to walk the chalk line of the sober man's speech.

The particles cue us further that this speech of Alcibiades is not the culmination of a crescendo, even though (as nearly always with Plato) astute and condensed arguments may be deduced from what he says. Rather, it is a decrescendo, and the absence of particles underscores the bluntness and exaggeration of what is said, full of repetitions as it is, and without any of the "stretto" that the paucity of particles gives to the crescendo of Diotima. The verbal reeling of Alcibiades, and his dexterity as he reels, emblematize his overall career, and at this moment they usher in the controlled comic patter of the very last sections of the dialogue.

Very different, as the particles help us to see, is the run of Diotima's intricate layering of clauses at the crest of her speech (210–11d), with its many rises of contrasted pairings, and with offered sequences in the "stepladder" of perception.[23] In this peak passage among the high level of Plato's stylistic triumphs, the particles have been relegated, suddenly, to a use far less pronounced and prominent. Here also the rhetoric takes over in a different way, as the paucity of particles helps us to see. They are touched in lightly and schematically, as distinct from their play variously in earlier parts of this dialogue, and also as distinct from the later bluntness of Alcibiades. The system of qualification has been subordinated to the indirections of the quasi-mythic existence of Diotima, who is virtually unique as a speaker in Plato's dialogues, even if a speaker distanced by quotation.

Particles are at once the sign and the celebration of all these processes. Riding along on the subtle syntax of Plato's sentences, they signify their quasiorality while conforming in their own nested or embedded structure to the logic of the discourse they accompany and ornament.

Notes

1. J. D. Denniston, *The Greek Particles* (Oxford: The Clarendon Press, 1954 [1934]), 441. I indicate here by parenthesized numerals in the text the page on which Denniston's particular definition appears.

2. As an example of flexibility in the same particle complex, J. Riddell, *A Digest of Platonic Idioms* in *The Apology of Plato* (New York: Arno Press, 1973 [1867]), 118–251 (Para 147), remarks of *alla gar:* "Here we must

observe that there is no Ellipse ... The sense forbids such a supposition: for the *alla* sits much closer to the clause immediately subjoined than the *gar* does. *Alla gar* has two meanings: one when it introduces an objection, and is therefore ironical; the other, which alone needs illustration, when it has the force of 'be that as it may,' or 'but the truth is.'"

3. Dorothy Tarrant, "Style and Thought in Plato's Dialogues," in *Classical Quarterly*, LXII, 1948, 28–34. Holger Thesleff, *Studies in the Styles of Plato, Acta Philosophica Fennica*, Fascicle XX, 1967.

4. For a brief summary of Cratylus' possible positions as a Heraclitean, see Paul Friedländer, *Platon* (Berlin: de Gruyter, 1957 [1930]), II, 82–83.

5. Edward R. Keenan, "Two Kinds of Presupposition in Natural Language," in Charles J. Fillmore and W. Terence Langendoen, eds., *Studies in Linguistic Semantics* (New York: Holt, Rinehart, and Winston, 1971), 45–53.

6. See Bruce Fraser, "An Analysis of 'Even' in English," in Fillmore and Langendoen, 151–80.

7. Even more than their analogues in English, the particular fusion of semantic and phonetic elements in the Greek particles would render quite complicated any discrimination of deep structures from surface structures. Such analysis many times would have to involve a repetition of a whole tree diagram for a single particle.

8. In this process, again, the particles still further assume a correct "uptake" on the part of a competent auditor or reader, and assume he will register the fixity in their performance-assistance to the main sentences, whatever general philosophical qualifications may be brought to bear on that fixity. As J. Riddell says (*A Digest of Platonic Idioms*, Paragraph 144, p. 182) "In order to understand and to interpret certain combinations of Particles, regard must be had to the fact, that they enter *simultaneously* into the sentence, as it were speaking at once rather than in succession."

9. These ironies are elaborate and to a certain extent self-generating, as discussed in Gary Handwerk, *Irony and the Ethics of Narrative* (New Haven: Yale University Press, 1985). The interchange in Plato's dialogues, however, resists the possible endless regress of a Gricean implicature, A's speaking in the knowledge that B will be speaking in the knowledge that A ... except, perhaps for Socrates. Even in that case the series stops with the author, Plato himself, and with his presentation of the suppositions that Socrates "holds in reserve" for much or even all of a dialogue.

10. Jerrold Katz, *Propositional Structure and Illocutionary Force* (Cambridge: Harvard University Press, 1980), 21, "Our conception of semantics and pragmatics finds these two accounts of meaning to be reconcilable on the thesis that *meaning is the information that determines use in the null context*" (italics Katz's).

11. Of course this is a large subject on which I intend my observations

about Plato to bear as a challenging case that may be taken to call herme-neutically not only for the current tradition of deductive exposition but at once for Wittgenstein's qualifications, Derrida's *différance*, and the range of relations offered by the generative grammarians. The deconstructionist and skeptical readings would not be dropped, but rather demoted to the status of interpretational qualifications in relation to other readings of propositions; and the notion that there is some logical contradiction between the two would disappear, once the propositional implications of such skeptical read-ings were reduced. As a variant on a common contradiction to deconstructionist readings in general, it can be pointed out that just the na-tive speaker's demonstrable capacity in competence and performance to handle the deep structure of utterances (and therefore their propositional logicality) will make that deep structure impervious to radical deconstruc-tion. Chomsky himself posits a congruence between deep structure and the propositional meaning of a given sentence, but his views have been much qualified by discussants like Willard Quine ("Methodological Reflections on Current Linguistic Theory," 104–17); Gilbert Harman ("Review of *Language and Mind*, 201–18); both from Gilbert Harman, ed., *On Noam Chomsky* (New York: Anchor, 1974); and Jerrold Katz, among others.

12. These two arguments, and combinations of them inform the work of Jacques Derrida and Paul de Man, where however it is deliberately on prin-ciple left unclear how far logically their radical qualification of the logic underlying discourse is to be taken. Among many discussions of this ques-tion, a particularly full one is Charles Altieri, *Act and Quality* (Northampton: University of Massachusetts Press, 1981). For the many communicational nuances of an oral context, only some of which are expressible in such forms of inscription as Plato's particles, see Erving Goffman, *Forms of Talk* (Philadelphia: University of Pennsylvania Press, 1983). A different typology for context-pragmatics is offered by M. A. K. Halliday, *Language as Social Semantics* (Baltimore: University Park Press, 1978), discussed in Altieri, 78ff. This comprises "field" (shared expectations), "tenor" (role relations) and "mode" (metalinguistic category frames).

13. See Samuel R. Levin, *The Semantics of Metaphor* (Baltimore: The Johns Hopkins University Press, 1977), and *Metaphoric Worlds* (New Ha-ven: Yale University Press, 1988). For other dimensions of metaphor, see Albert Cook, "Aspects of Image: Some Problems," *Journal of Aesthetics and Art Criticism*, Spring, 1979; incorporated, with considerable further discus-sion, into *Figural Choice in Poetry and Art* (Hanover, N.H.: University Presses of New England, 1985). See also "Metaphor: Literature's Access to Myth," *Myth and Language*, 248–59.

14. Denniston, 204–05.

15. J. Adam and A. M. Adam in *Platonis Protagoras* (Cambridge: Cam-bridge University Press, 1953 [1905]), ad loc, adduce parallels to "hunting"

as a metaphor for pursuit in love. ὥραν is a dead metaphor … it equals "blooming moment in youth."

16. On the deep-structural similarity of verb and adjective, see George Lakoff, *Irregularity in Syntax* (New York: Holt, Rinehart, and Winston, 1970). On the copula, which would have to be ἔστιν, see Charles Kahn, *The Verb "Be" in Ancient Greek* (Dordrecht: Reidel, 1973).

17. Still, in use with the same verb, ὥς γε is repeated in the dialogue at 339e3.

18. In Socrates' next answer, not quoted above, a δέ, again moved to the middle of the sentence from its more normal position, is both tentative and adversative. It more strongly exhibits both these senses for being too far from the μέν four speeches back, and with too much syntax intervening, to balance it. It acts strongly by itself, and it provides a stepping stone for the καὶ γάρ, and then the καὶ οὖν καὶ in the sentence's two concluding clauses. Γάρ, as Denniston says (108), is usually the connective, and the καί adds to it "also," "even," or "this fact." If "both," then it is answered by another καί. Here the combination means all three, and the answer is correspondingly fuller, καὶ οὖν καὶ. Even the γάρ is repeated in the counterthrusting syntax of a genitive absolute, παρόντος γὰρ ἐκείνου. Καὶ οὖν is itself a strong counterthrust of forward and backward, "a very rare combination," as Denniston says (445), who cites this passage. All this tones down somewhat in the third μέντοι which underscores the adjective ἄτοπον, rather than a noun, as the first two μέντοι's had.

19. Denniston, *The Greek Particles*, 441.

20. Denniston notes that γοῦν has two senses, "part proof" and "ironical connection" (449). Both these senses are strongly present here, the first especially so since we are near the beginning of Aristophanes' presentation of the motive for the particular shaping of the new creatures. And Denniston notes, further, of γοῦν, that it tends to appear in apodosis (453), and so to have an air of capping proof. Δὴ οὖν in the next sentence points ahead as well as backward (469), picking up another οὖν in the very next sentence and another δὴ in its final clause.

21. The next μὲν οὖν is anticipatory (470), and it picks up another δὴ almost at once. There are two μὲν οὖν's later on (192b5–6), cumulative but differentiated. In the middle, parenthetically but emphatically, comes the great proof, the μέγα τεκμήριον (192a5–6). This, while applied to just one aspect of a sexual alternative, constitutes a bolder causal assertion in the primary register, and so in the deep structure of the utterances. This phrase picks up and leads at once to a καὶ γάρ. This καὶ γάρ, reverses— but as it were echoes—the γάρ καὶ in τέως γὰρ καὶ at the beginning of the run I have been discussing. Denniston (109) notes the explanatory emphasis in this very passage, as connected to τεκμήριον. Still later the touch becomes lighter—an ἄρα (Denniston, 39), an ἄρα γε to introduce a

pretendedly emphatic question (50), and an εἰ γάρ addressed to the inter-locutory possible question of the silent, attentive audience (d8;61). Earlier, in δή οὖν, both the δή and the οὖν indicate both connection and emphasis (469), and therefore they may be said strongly to reinforce each other—and in this context to reinforce the lightness in exaggeration of the irony.

What Denniston says of ἄρα is apposite here, "ἄρα denotes the appre-hension of an idea not before envisaged. Usually ἄρα conveys either, at the most, actual scepticism, or at the least, the disclaiming of responsibility for the accuracy of the statement." (39). And he cites this very passage: Ἄρα γε he says, "adds liveliness and emphasis"—which goes without saying here (50), though he remarks on the special force of γε in connection with a conjunction of questioning. He reads this particular γάρ as suggesting "I mention these facts because they are particularly deserving of mention" (61).

22. Martha Nussbaum, stressing a more positive reading of this speech, traces the contour of Alcibiades' career as it matches his role in the *Sympo-sium* (*The Fragility of Goodness*, 165–99).

23. Thesleff, 137–38. "Diotima passes from a fairly simple [semi-liter-ary conversational style modified by an intellectual style] over more and more solemn styles and shades of [a rhetorical style], to the great climax of the mystic passage 209a–12a [which fuses the first two of these with the pathetic style, the ceremonious style, and the Onkos style]." We may note in passing that Thesleff's discriminations are wonderfully apt; and still they can be felt as secondary to the remarkable evenness in the ascending progression of Diotima's speech.

Chapter 8

Some Statements in Plato's Dialogues Bearing on the Validity and Ontological Range of Language

1.

Aristotle has settled for a language that has become the ordinary language of philosophy, a prose discourse that has freed itself of the aphorisms of Heraclitus, the verse of Parmenides and Empedocles, and the dialogic presentation of Plato. This language follows the same direction taken by the historians and medical writers among his predecessors. In his own discussions of language, Aristotle focuses on the proposition, not only in the elaborate definitions of the *Organon* but even in the *Rhetoric,* where he might have confined himself to presentational effect but constantly reverts to analysis of what amounts to propositional substructure, at times overlapping into the topics of the *Organon.*[1]

Plato, on the other hand, remarkably develops a propositional logic, as Robinson and others have demonstrated.[2] But his discussions of propositional structure are always incidental to other questions. The dialogue form itself encapsulates a presentational paradox, since it is a written simulation of the free interactive oral inquiry that Plato in the *Phaedrus* and the *Seventh Letter* claims is preferable to writing. In addition to such references, Plato's actual presentation plays across the discrepancy between speech and writing. The *Phaedrus* sets off its discussion by quoting an entire speech of Lysias, the text of which Phaedrus is carrying. Euclides in the *Theaetetus* (143) gives an account of writing down what he had assembled from one of Socrates' inquiries, after himself choosing the dialogue form over narrative. But this introductory dialogue encapsulates the written dialogue that is said to be handed over to Terpsion. "Well, boy, take the book and read it," he reportedly said, and the body of the dialogue follows.

By this act of self-referentiality the dialogue form, the writing down of an oral discussion, tries to escape the paradox inherent in a written praise of oral discussion, but Plato never tells us so, nor does he discuss the dialogue form as writing. Plato does, however, in various contexts, discuss language, and he also varies his use of it, especially when he moves away from elenchic presentation into myths. For both of these kinds of discourse (or three kinds, if we allow mathematics to be a separate kind), he propounds constraints as well as analyses.[3]

The *Phaedrus,* while expounding a quite positive view about poetry, embeds a notion of limits to human language. There, when Socrates is about to introduce the myth of the soul as a winged chariot, he feels he must abjure the thesis that one who does not love ought to be preferred as a lover to one who loves. I should like to reexamine this passage for its bearing on the conception of the nature and limits of language.

Socrates is going to tell a fairly long story (which he characterizes as "smaller"), the story of the soul as a winged chariot. First, however, he begins with a passage that contains an astonishing definition of poetic expression, and of the reach of language generally. He does not explicitly deal with poetry in hexameters and in strophes, just with the poetic madness, under the influence of which he claims to be speaking:

Περὶ μὲν οὖν ἀθανασίας αὐτῆς [τῆς ψυχῆς] ἱκανῶς·
περὶ δὲ τῆς ἰδέας αὐτῆς ὧδε λεκτέον. οἷον μέν ἐστι,
πάντηι πάντως θείας εἶναι καὶ μακρᾶς διηγήσεως,
ὧι δὲ ἔοικεν, ἀνθρωπίνης τε καὶ ἐλάττονος· ταύτηι
οὖν λέγωμεν. ἐοικέτω δὴ συμφύτωι δυνάμει ὑπο᾽
πτέρου ζεύγους τε καὶ ἡνιόχου.   (246a2–7)

As to the soul's immortality then we have said enough, but as to its
formal idea there is this that must be said. What manner of thing it
is would be a long tale to tell, and in all ways a god alone could
tell it, but what it resembles, that a man could tell in briefer compass. Let this therefore be our manner of discourse. Let it be likened
to the union of powers in a team of winged steeds and their winged
charioteer.   (tr. R. Hackforth, slightly revised)

As an implied view of language, this passage sets out some important principles under the aegis of three differential signs. These
signs let us associate, and also distinguish, the connected utterances,
the *diegeses* of a god from those of a man. But to be able even to approach such an approximation of divine language a man must speak
under the influence of a beneficent poetic madness. The key word
here is *idea,* a variant of *eidos,* and it can be affirmed that Socrates-
Plato here gives a narrative corollary, or what could be called a
diegetic one, for the Theory of Forms: *eidos,* in any case, plays a
fairly complicated role as a term in the *Phaedrus,* as I have indicated
above.

First—and it is indeed the image of a speaking god, rare in Plato,
that authorizes a strong reading of *idea* as "Form" in the technical
sense—the god deals with the subject πάντηι πάντως, "entirely,
absolutely"; while man, even if he is inspired, can do so only in the
way Socrates will be conducting his discourse. In the *Timaeus* (29b-d)
the same expression is repeated, πάντηι πάντως, and in a context
of the discussion about constraints on discourse with relation to repre-
senting the gods: "If therefore, Socrates, for many things about many
things, the gods and the genesis of the all, if we are not able wholly
and in every way (πάντηι πάντως) to give out accounts (or words,
λόγους) for them that correspond and have been rendered accurate,
do not wonder." This is so even when "words are akin to that of

which they are expounders" (ἐξηγῆται, a term often used of religious oracles) and when "being is to becoming as truth is to belief," to
guarantee the likeness—but only the likeness—of human words to
what they describe, image (εἰκών) to pattern (παραδείγμα).

Second, in this passage from the *Phaedrus* the god concerns himself with the sort of thing the object "is itself," οἷον μέν ἐστι,
while man is obliged to limit himself to resemblances, very much like
the painter and the poet of *The Republic*—yet still with the gamut of
positive possibilities indicated in the passage from the *Timaeus* just
cited. It should be noted that here, as distinct from the better-known
version of Plato's views in the *Republic* about the distance from its
object of poetic representation, it is assumed that the poet's capacity
to carry through a representation in words is not questioned, though it
would be limited by the impossibility that a man could take up the full
expressive powers of divine speech.

Third, the narrative of a god is long and that of a man is lesser or
shorter, ἐλάττονος. That the relative length of the diegesis is indeed
a differential sign is indicated by a strong condition, "What it resembles a man could tell, and in briefer compass." Even then human
language cannot be more than an approximation. It can be said that
the common Platonic phrase "so to speak," "ὡς ἔπος εἰπεῖν"
names the notion of such an approximation.[4]

This view of man's language as limited by the notion of his hu-
manity as seen in light of the language of the gods finds echoes
throughout Plato's work.[5] In the *Cratylus* (391d–393), Homer is seen
as preferable to Protagoras on the basis of his access to the true names
used by gods, as opposed to those used by men. Because they are derived from the gods the folk etymologies Plato expounds at length are
taken as givens. "The best principle (κάλλιστον τρόπον) is that
we know nothing about the language of the gods, either themselves or
the names they use. First it is apparent that the ones they name are
true. The second principle of rightness is the law for us to pray in
prayers, that the names whatever and whence they enjoy being named,
for us to call them by these, since we know nothing else" (400d–
401). So (405b–f) the name of Apollo is derived from fumigatory
practices and the purifications of body and soul, linked in turn to music, poetry, religion, myth, and the *elenchos,* but always for humans

without convincing accuracy. And in the *Cratylus* it is reiterated of the gods (425c) that men are actually ignorant: "Knowing nothing of the truth [about the gods] we conjecture/picture our opinions about them."[6] The *Seventh Letter* (341c–43c) declares limits not only to written discussions but to any language at all that might be used for philosophical purposes.[7] In the *Critias* (107d6–8) it is said that "we love statements about heavenly and godly things even when they have little resemblance, but we inspect statements about mortal and human things for accuracy."[8] In the *Laws* (803b–d) man is the plaything of God and should shape himself accordingly.[9] The playful ripples of the dialogue form conform to this interpretation of human activity, as they conform to the priority of orality. In the *Republic* (582c–e) λόγος is the instrument (ὄργανον) by which the philosopher obtains pleasure.[10] This activity of logos is then coupled with experience (ἐμπειρία), and intelligence (φρόνησις), and the "philosopher and the lover of words" (φιλόσοφος καὶ φιλόλογος) are linked as one person in one function.

2.

In Plato's act of modeling the dialogue form on the flow of oral debate, he has taken a crucial step towards the whole development of modern philosophy, which in its informal manifestations conducts itself orally. Where Plato's predecessors had either closed themselves in prose or verse into set positions, or like Socrates confined themselves to free oral discourse, he bases himself, as modern philosophy characteristically and often does still, on settling some questions while leaving aspects of them open.[11]

Plato himself, however, does not discuss discourse as such. Even though he calls names "acts" or "events" (πράξεις, *Cratylus* 387b), and even though a name in his handling is so complex that in itself it nests a proposition (421), his discussion in the *Cratylus* focuses almost wholly on names, rather than on propositions or on dialectic—and even though a dialectician is said to provide the names (390c). The same emphasis on separate names is found in the *Euthydemus* (277e–78e) where Socrates uses metaphors about wrestling and about a Corybantic initiation to characterize the *elenchos,* but then switches instantly to "proper nomenclature," quoting Prodicus on "the necessity of learning the right use of names."[12] Here he refers playfully to his "extemporizing" (αὐτοσχεδιάζω), an activity in which he does not engage, according to Hermogenes in the *Cratylus* (413d). In the *Charmides* (163e4–5) Prodicus is said to have given countless definitions of names.

The folk etymologies of the *Cratylus* are meant to illustrate the full congruence of word and a composite object that combines one datum and another, since the appropriateness of the etymologies is based on the associability, for example, of gods (θεούς) to running (θέοντα), and so on. The barbarians named gods as heavenly bodies, which were then seen to move, so the gods were named from the verb "to run" (397). In the extended etymologies offered here, this sort of fit embraces many large areas treated in fuller accounts by philosophy.[13] A little later in the *Charmides* (164e–65) Socrates discusses alternate expressions for some meanings. On the one hand, different letters and sounds are mentioned. On the other, under the aegis of an oracle of Apollo, "Know thyself" is read different ways, one of which is "Be prudent," thus tying in with the central puzzling question of the relation of prudence to knowledge, especially in the light of the deeper question of the possibility of a knowledge of knowledge. The terms "prophet" (μάντις) and "more riddling" (αἰνιγματω-δέστερον) come up here. The origin of words may get lost or twisted, but if correctly etymologized remains a trustworthy guide to their meaning (421c–21d). And one can lead confidently from simpler to more complex words (425de–26). At the end of the *Cratylus* the rug seems to be pulled out from under this whole long discussion in the suggestion that "things may be known without names" (438e),[14] though the immediately appended phrase "if these [names] are thus"[15] produces a perfect equivocation. Yet this question, still confined to names, provides a principle for the functional, provisional use of words in *elenchos*.

The range of senses in the word "logos" itself constitutes a ground for the potential theory of language, but Plato uses these various senses rather than investigating them. "A name [ὄνομα]," he says, "is an instrument of teaching and of distinguishing being as the shuttle is of distinguishing webs" (388a–c), attributing to the name what one would expect him to attribute to the *elenchos*. He also employs, according to David Wiggins, the display function of names.[16]

In the *Sophist* (233–48), "being" (τὸ ὄν) is tied up with language, and specifically with its name. "Distinction" (διάκρισις) is linked to "purification" (καθαρμός) (226d10). And the discussion involves many "forms" (εἴδη) for one ὄνομα. Then the dialogue reverses this situation, giving many names for one form (249d–e).[17]

These theories in the *Cratylus,* as they attend mostly to diction, mount at least three versions of the relation between word and object, suggestively enough to allow for many complexities of adjustment and justification.[18] We may leave aside the possibility raised at the very end (439a) that the direct learning of truth is a better method, especially since the question of how this could at all come about is left hanging. On the words themselves Rudolph Weingartner finds three theories there: Hermogenes' "unconventional conventionalism" *(nomos);* Cratylus' own view of "metrical signs" (in Weingartner's sense rather than the later one of the Stoics) in which the name in both sense and word reflects its referent *(physis);* and a third doctrine towards which Socrates is tending, not fully formulated.[19] In fact it can be said that the whole discussion crosses over and overrides the key Platonic distinction between *nomos* and *physis*. This is especially clear at 389b and 390e. Now in the final relation between knowledge *(gnosis)* and flux that the *Cratylus* envisages, Brian Calvert finds Plato to be in a "genuine ontological perplexity."[20]

Socrates early on broaches a "firmer" principle for language (386a) and quickly moves past the thorough *ad hominem* relations of Protagoras by introducing the distinction between those with intelligence and those without. Nevertheless he would seem to vacillate among various principles, including the theory of natural signs, the somewhat contradictory thesis that a skilled practitioner is a natural establisher of norms *(nomothetes)* [21] for terminology[22] in his own field, and a principle that actions *(praxeis)* are free of our opinions *(doxai)* and so are not "dragged up and down by imaginings" *(phantasmata,* 386e).

Naming itself, then, is part, but only "part of speaking" (387c).[23] Without attaining the schematic sharpness of Heraclitus on this question, Plato has carried the issues further. In the reported words of

Heraclitus, "The lord, he whose oracle is the one in Delphi, does not speak or conceal but gives a sign" (Heraclitus, B93). In the explorations and equivocations governing his discussion of language, Plato touches base on notions implied by all three of Heraclitus's verbs here, and since Heraclitus is the governing presence in the *Cratylus,* it would be an engaging exercise to line its doctrines up not under the flux fragments, as the dialogue does (whatever the flux doctrine really came to), but under λέγει, κρύπτει, and σημαίνει. But if we did so we could line all of what Plato says on this question under "gives a sign"; "speak" would then be superfluous and "hide" wholly implicit. To do this would give us a cue that he has produced many fruitful reflections without carrying the discussion further than Heraclitus does—in his theory. In Plato's practice, however, he simply accords with the aphorism. By choosing the dialogue form, Plato neither speaks nor hides but gives a composite sign that cannot be reduced to its constituent signs of words and sentences.

Now in using words, in combining them into sentences, and in intertwining sentences dialogically, language must enlist redundancies, or it would be unintelligible. It must also enlist differences of sound and meaning, or it would be tautologous—or even, so to speak, pretautologous. Rhetoric resembles language in its deployment of redundancies and differences. To that degree, then, language is rhetorical; there is no language whose patterns cannot be assimilated to those of a describable rhetoric.

Just because of the similarity between language and rhetoric, it solves no problems about either one to insist on the rhetorical cast to dialogic communications. Comments about rhetoric are comments about structure; nothing more, nothing less. For content, we must raise other questions, and Plato does.

If dialectic is comparable to piloting in admitting authority to its practitioners (390c), we cannot be sure how far this principle could extend, perhaps far enough to constitute another theory. The notions that words themselves are elaborate composites, as are the medicines put together by druggists (394a), might furnish still another, reminiscent for complexity (if not in its structure) to the sign-system of Peirce. "Looking forward and backward" through an argument as Cratylus does, takes a prominent part in the dialogue (428c). Socrates comes to the belated conclusion that "it is possible to learn reality [τὰ ὄντα] without names [ὀνομάτων], if necessary" (438e), and it is even better to do so (439b). This proposition would cancel the dialogue and abolish the puzzles about the relation of word and theory—unless Heraclitus' theory, rejected by Socrates but accepted by Cratylus, were not introduced.

At the end of this dialogue extremes of possibility are brought up that would close it out.[24] The extreme application of Heraclitus' flux theory would result, Socrates urges, in no communication taking place at all; and yet Cratylus insists on adhering to it. Indeed, the notion that names are stable seems suddenly to be abandoned, as has the implicitly related possibility that if the name "gods" comes from a kind of flux, the running motion in the heavens, then flux cannot be fully rejected. Socrates asks what we are to make of it if the establishers of names, praised earlier in the dialogue, were "as though falling into a whirlpool and stirred round,[25] and push to drag us in too" (439c). But then he goes to the opposite extreme and praises a beauty immune to flux, a beauty reminiscent of the high point in Diotima's ladder in the *Symposium*. He goes on to the corollary (440b) that knowledge *(gnosis)* cannot change and remain *gnosis*. This position, again, would seem to be firmly anti-Heraclitean, but it precedes Cratylus' final assertion in praise of Heraclitus.

Heraclitus serves at the end a function similar to that of Protagoras at the beginning, to set the limits of an erroneous view to the discourse. Chosing out false alleys may point to true.[26] In understanding the use of Heraclitus in this dialogue, it will help to see how complex Plato's presentation of him is at another point, notably when Heraclitus is quoted, and slightly but revealingly misquoted, in the *Symposium*.

Heraclitus refined the conditions of utterance by taking the underlying binary assumptions of Homeric expression and re-rendering them in logical form as aphorisms that are turned so as to reveal their own implications. While it is true that Plato's references to Heraclitus center on content and not on form, he addresses the notion of flux (whatever it may have been) and possibily also fire and logos (whatever they may have been).[27] Yet interestingly his approach to Heraclitus involves a more than usual qualification of the circumstances. Are we to take as Plato's the overconfident Erixymachus's claim in the *Symposium* that Heraclitus statement (B51) "They do not know the one, differing, agrees with itself, a stretched-back harmony, as of a bow or a lyre," is absurd or inconsistent?[28] This doctor in the *Symposium* does cure Aristophanes' hiccups, but he somewhat fumbles the concept of *harmonia*, which elsewhere Plato has developed at great and subtle length; and also in telling summarizes. Moreover, B51 is one of Heraclitus' expressive triumphs. Socrates, to be sure, presses always for clarity, as Erixymachus seems to be doing here. But such a self-confident exposition goes against the more normal posture of questioning in the dialogues. While Plato often does not quote accurately, the discrepancies, or errors, in Erixymachus' quotation, by comparison with the statement as we have it, are all revelatory, and they are consonant with the view that Heraclitus escapes Erixymachus's strictures rather than being subject to them. First, Erixymachus leaves off the introductory phrase "they do not know"—a telling omission for one who does not know he does not know—and this is the standard posture for those in other dialogues, the one who will receive instruction from a Socrates who is wisest, according to the *Apology,* because he does know he does not know. The form of the *Symposium* does not admit of having Erixymachus undergo an *elenchos.* But he can undergo ironic presentation, and this is part of it.

Second, in accusing Heraclitus of *alogia,* absurdity or inconsistency, he is stating the obvious in the form of a simple disclaimer. Heraclitus' *logos* would be *alogos* if it were not founded on setting contraditions into play, just as in this aphorism. Erixymachus' second mistake is to leave out the key word *palintonos,* "backbending"—or in another reading *palintropos* "back turning." (The very existence of alternate readings for this word would substantiate its presence in the aphorism.)

Omitting "palintonos" leads to Erixymachus' other large mistake. For Heraclitus harmony is coordinate, not a subordinated comparison. Erixymachus has the comparison between the coordination of opposites and harmony, "like a harmony." But in the aphorism "the one" is not "like a harmony"; it *is* harmony. Then the harmony—or else its character of being "bent back"—is "of a bow or a lyre."

Comparably, there is no simple solution to the use of Heraclitus in the *Cratylus* either. The relation between some version of Heraclitean flux and the validity of verbal use has not been fully expanded or refuted, and we are left with Cratylus' statement that he still inclines towards Heraclitus' view.

Socrates asserts here that consistency is no guarantee of truth, or even the correct application of names. If there is a "small and imperceptible fault" in the outline or proposition *(diagramma),* then the *whole* rest is forced to follow suit:

> He may have forced the rest into agreement with the original error and with himself; there would be nothing strange in this, as sometimes in diagrams which have a slight and invisible flaw but agree [ὁμολογεῖν] with one another in all the other entities [τὰ ὄντα] that follow.   (436c–d)

This assertion answers a question about the total correspondence of name and object. As a principle of full correspondence, it is the other side of the approximation theory given in the *Phaedrus.* From the beginning a full correspondence (ὁμολογεῖν) is both necessary and impossible to achieve. Heraclitus' doctrine of flux is called in and applied to words, and as is also asserted in the *Phaedo* (83b) there is no truth in fluctuating objects.[29] But dialogue manages skillfully as it handles the technique of counterstatements, the ἀντιλογικὴ τέχνη (454a–b).

The two theories taken together, though if forced together they stand in contradiction, will well characterize the Platonic enterprise, true in the expressive completion of the given dialogue while tentative in its launching of propositions. Plato can be approached either from the side of his propositions or that of his tentativeness and his notions about language reflect the possibility of either—the exact fit of word to object buttressing the former and the bewilderment about the limits to language evoking the latter.

3.

In *Cratylus* 439a, Socrates, having just checked for assent on the large proposition of the dialogue, that names are "images of things" (ὀνόματα ... εἶναι εἰκόνας τῶν πραγμάτων), goes on to a condensed series of partially overlapping and nesting pairs:

Εἰ οὖν ἔστι μὲν ὅτι μάλιστα δι' ὀνομάτων τὰ πράγματα μανθάνειν, ἔστι δὲ καὶ δι' αὐτῶν, ποτέρα ἂν εἴη καλλίων καὶ σαφεστέρα ἡ μάθησις; ἐκ τῆς εἰκόνος μανθάνειν αὐτήν τε αὐτὴν εἰ καλῶς εἴκασ' ται, καὶ τὴν ἀλήθειαν ἧς ἦν εἰκών, ἢ ἐκ τῆς ἀληθείας αὐτήν τε αὐτὴν καὶ τὴν εἰκόνα αὐτῆς πρεπόντως εἴργασται;

If, then, it is really possible to learn things through names, and suppose also that you can learn them from the things themselves. Which is likely to be the more beautiful and clearer way—to learn of the image, whether the image and the truth of which the image is the expression have been rightly pictured/conjectured, or to learn of the truth whether the truth and the image of it have been fittingly executed? (Jowett, slightly revised)

Καλλίων has to mean "more beautiful" or "more felicitous," and would apply both to names and πράγματα, a term which can be taken as meaning either "things" or "events." It would be "more beautiful" because going directly to the thing is a possible epistemological move; and it would have the elegance and simplicity of one less step, as well as an avoidance of all the problems of mediation. The mediation of language offers solutions also, however, and a type of flexibility that would make it too, alternatively, καλλίων. Names also would, arguably, be clearer, σαφεστέρα, since they would frame the object, and the more especially because of the principle, just adduced, of the homology between name and image of thing—the thesis (weak in the modern conception) most often associated with the *Cratylus* that dominates most of the dialogue. Yet a greater clarity would come into force in a direct approach to "things" or "events" (πράγματα) when all the confusions of language were dispensed with.

All that is one large set of questions. It leads to another more elaborate set that uses language in a way not allowed for by these assertions and perhaps, therefore, expanding them. Here the learning involves matching the name to the thing of which it is an image, while the image involves only one of these four terms. Image is, as it were, forced into the sort of strength-by-comparison reserved for the term which elsewhere in Plato takes on such heavy functions, through its more honorific synonym εἶδος. This is already more explicit when the image is an image not of things or events but of truth, which could be their higher aspect. This gives us a second pair, "image" and "truth," which can be made partially to match the first pair, "image" equaling "name" and "truth" equaling "things" (or "events" or "what has been actualized as the case").

But this momentary congruence generates a number of problems that are not dealt with here—and need not be, if language is entrusted, in spite of all the flux which is precisely under discussion, to carry through the matching of truth and image. There is a condition on imaging. It must, to effectuate μάθησις, be "beautifully pictured/ conjectured," καλῶς εἴκασται. As the tense of the verb also tells us, the process must already have taken place. Καλῶς, "beautifully," is the same word in the positive that was given above as one of the criteria in the question about names and things, but given in a comparative. This suggests that both alternatives would work καλῶς, but that one would be "more beautiful," καλλίων, than the other. The condition fulfilled, the process can continue to its terminus, "truth," and instantaneously, as a corollary of the learning's having taken place. All this, however, still adds up to a question involving only one side of an alternative. The verb μανθάνειν carries powerfully through the whole series.

4.

Eidos, of course means both "image" and "idea" if one were to translate it, but it is a powerful word at the intersection of much of Platonic thinking. The term covers, on occasions in the *Republic* and elsewhere, a final crux of Platonic thinking about perceiving and conceiving. It also, in the *Parmenides* and elsewhere, serves as the key term in his most intricate thinking on such matters as the general and the particular, the experiential and the summary, the visible and the invisible, and the object and its referent(s). In this last area it engages, and complicates, linguistic theory, notably in the handling of such notions as the "weaving of ideas," which is also the "weaving of images," and can be said to have as a central reference the syntactic combination of names. The phrase itself, συμπλοκή εἰδῶν occurs in the *Sophist* (259e4–6) and requires considerable exposition to be understood. The presentation there intersects with the presentation in the *Cratylus*. The proposition itself, as it is inspected by J. L. Ackrill, is powerful enough to encapsulate both Forms and concepts, and if it is confined just to Forms (or for that matter, if it were confined just to concepts), would result in the contradictions that the interpretations of the phrase by Cornford and Ross would lead to.[30] "It is because of the interweaving of Forms with one another that we come to have discourse."[31] Cornford and Ross connect this proposition too explicitly to the Theory of Forms, but Ackrill demonstrates the necessity of going from Forms to concepts for it to make sense, as it connects also to other passages. He reads "ideas" here as "fixed things to guarantee the meaningfulness of talk," and his demonstration can also be extended to the use of the phrase in a similar context of the *Theaetetus* (202b), "The weaving of names is the essence of language."[32]

In the question of the preferability of the invisible to the visible, Plato, as not infrequently, can be found working both sides of the street. Is the Form par excellence mainly invisible? The answer is mainly "yes" to this question, but even at its most rarified the notion of an "image" and the connection of εἶδος with the root *vid,* to see, hangs over the question. It seems to dominate the question when the final Form of the beautiful in the *Symposium* (211a–b) is at once visible and at the same time "both without language and without knowledge."[33] It is, besides, changeless in this passage, even given its connection with the "wide sea of beauty." And so it crosses another set of categories, the distinction between the changeless and the changeable, often connected by Plato with the distinction between body and soul. Now when the heading "changeless" usually implies "invisible" and "soul," here in the *Symposium* it implies the opposite of both, "visible" and (wholly undifferentiated and unparticularized) body.

In the *Cratylus,* too, these categories undergo a permutation that is hard, if not impossible, to analyze fully. But two seemingly contradictory activities are envisaged: the necessity of language to any thinking and perception, and the possibility of both thinking and perception wholly "without language" (the οὐδέ τις λόγος of the *Symposium*). Moreover, another contradiction is envisaged when Cratylus and his interlocutor Socrates insist, especially towards the end of their presentation, in pressing to the ultimate the "whirl" of the Heraclitean flux in its application to language, in the face of both the necessity and the fact of an etymologically validated stability of the connection between name, the letter-constituted reference, and its object.[34]

Socrates speaks in the *Republic* (488a), of "straining after images," ὡς γλισχρῶς εἰκάζω. There is the subsidiary case, too, which Socrates' statement would include, of the persistence of nonce metaphors in Plato's text.[35] Producing syllables to form a word is likened to producing a good image (431d). Also in the *Theaetetus* (163b) distinguishing letters is itself used as a metaphor for thinking, just as it is in a key transition of the *Republic*.

5.

In the *Cratylus* the divine origin of speech and the gods' perfect use of speech recede before the onslaught of Socrates on tangential questions. But the task remains of measuring all the other doctrines examined, underlying the etymologies that dominate the dialogue.[36] As the *Cratylus* moves toward the end, language is declared to be perhaps the greatest of all subjects (427). Plato also sometimes offers a sense of completion, as in the *Philebus* (14a), where the possibility is broached of "saving ourselves from unreason" by "bringing our discussion to an end like a tale."[37] Now there are inclusive doctrines, or a notion of such, suggested in Plato, as when in the *Republic* (432) it is said to be possible to speak of something without knowing it, a notion explored also in the *Charmides*. In the *Theaetetus* a sort of basic knowledge is perceived but cannot be retrieved (201e). This notion is arrived at when one interlocutor matches his dream with another's. The elements they discuss are said to be like the formation of a letter. This thread is picked up again (208b10) when in speaking of "the dream that we were rich in, thinking that we had the truest account of knowledge."[38]

In the *Republic* (497d) it is said as an aside that all fine things are difficult. Indeed occasionally the asides in Plato curiously represent doctrines that are among his fullest because they are unqualified in the particular context or by reason-series in other dialogues. So "philosophy is the highest music" *(Phaedo, 61a)*, an expression put into a subordinate, passing absolute construction that can be taken as governing everything else that is said in the *Phaedo*. Similarly in an absolute expression, also given in passing *(Meno,* 81d1), is arguably of a higher order of generality than anything else in that dialogue, "All nature being akin." Yet in the *Phaedo,* (88c–91c) for all the difficulties in discourse, a warning is issued against hatred of words, misology, a negative counterpart to music of the soul. In the *Laws* (832b) discourse is presented as involving a lifelong quest.[39]

Notes

1. "Rhetoric is the counterpart of dialectic," Aristotle says at the very beginning of the *Rhetoric* to distinguish himself from the writers of previous treatises on the subject. He brings up the enthymeme early in the First Book (1355a), returning to it and the syllogism, notably at the end of the Second Book (1395b–1403b).

2. Richard Robinson, *Plato's Earlier Dialectic.*

3. One gets, of course, various complications of discourse, as the mathematical speech of the Muses about generation *(Republic,* 545–6).

4. Perhaps it is possible to discern an echo here, feeble but distinct, of the Indo-European tradition, above all in Sanskrit literature, which often speaks of the originals of epic poems written by the gods and possessed by them, in versions many times longer than their human copies. (It could even be that the Platonic notion of earthly copies of heavenly originals is also an echo, more distant still, of this Indo-European tradition.)

5. Yet in the *Republic* (473a) in a passing remark the verbal delineation of an action is said to correspond exactly to the conceived event, "Is it possible for anything to be realized in deed as it is spoken in word, or is it the nature of things that action should take hold of truth (ἀληθείας ἐφάπτεσθαι) less than speech?"

6. οὐδὲν εἰδότες τῆς ἀληθείας τὰ τῶν ἀνθρώπων δόγματα, περὶ αὐτῶν εἰκάζομεν.

7. This view is argued by Kenneth M. Sayre, "Plato's Dialogues in the light of the *Seventh Letter,"* in Charles L. Griswold, Jr., *Platonic Writings, Platonic Readings,* 93–109. Sayre stresses that the limitation applies to oral expression as well, "Far from extolling vocal over written speech, the primary burden of these passages in the *Phaedrus,* like those of the *Seventh Letter* ... is to draw attention to a kind of intellectual awareness that eludes expression in speech and writing" (98). As Konrad Gaiser says, however, "And in particular the boundary between exoteric or open actuality and esoteric teaching activity inside the school does not simply coincide with the

difference between literary writing and oral lectures" *(Platons ungeschriebene Lehre* 5).

8. τὰ μὲν οὐράνια καὶ θεῖα ἀγαπῶμεν καὶ σμικρῶς εἰκότα λεγόμενα, τὰ δέ θνῆτα καὶ ἀνθρώπινα ἀκριβῶς ἐξετάζομεν.

9. Thomas McFarland discusses this aspect of Plato in *Shapes of Culture* (Iowa City: University of Iowa Press, 1987), 83.

10. The connection between language and intimate involvement is an understood premise when Pausanias in the *Symposium* (182b) offers an explanation for the curious situation of Elis and Boeotia where a people who are "not wise at speaking" μὴ σοφοί λέγειν and "unable to speak" ἀδύνατοι λέγειν hold a simple and permissive attitude that unqualifiedly allows homosexuality so as to spare the lover the arduous task of persuasion.

11. As Gadamer says, "It was a new question Socrates asked, what a thing was. It rested on the intimation and the experience that he who said something did not always know what he said, and straightway the art of speaking, the common fluency of representations, conjured up the danger. A new art was needed to promise salvation against the danger. That was the art of conducting a discussion and thereby to ban a propensity for confusion of knowledge, the never-changing happenstance of speech." H. G. Gadamer, *Dialektik und Sophistik im siebensten platonischen Brief* (Heidelberg: Karl Winter, 1964), 34.

And again, as Guthrie says (V, 208) of language in the *Philebus,* "The enquiry, it says, must start from the admission that one and many become the same *through discourse* (ὑπὸ λόγων). Their identity pervades *everything that is said,* is a permanent feature of speech and thought and something inherent in our own nature, and a young man's first awareness of it is an intoxicating experience. From this point the argument goes on to show, first, that our understanding must be disciplined by dialectic; and second, that, so disciplined, the form of our sentences and thoughts does reflect the structure of reality and is not *only* something 'in us', i.e. subjective."

12. περὶ ὀνομάτων ὀρθότητος μαθεῖν δεῖ.

13. Timothy M. S. Baxter in *The* Cratylus, *Plato's Critique of Naming* (Leiden: Brill, 1992) distinguishes two etymological methods in the *Cratylus,* the semantic of arbitrary deictic association and the mimetic of the sound symbolism somewhat supported by modern linguistic research. Both are lumped together by Plato. R. Brumbaugh (*Review of Metaphysics* 11, 1957–8, 502–10) links the etymologies in the *Cratylus* to cosmology, anthropology, psychology, and ethics.

14. δυνατόν μαθεῖν ἄνευ ὀνομάτων τὰ ὄντα.

15. εἴπερ ταῦτα οὕτως ἔχει.

16. David Wiggins, "Sentence Meaning, Negation, and Plato's Problem of

Non-Being, in Gregory Vlastos, editor, *Plato I* (New York: Anchor, 1971), 268–313. Wiggins emphasizes "the *display* function for names" resting on *Cratylus* 411d1, "to show what sort each thing among existents is." "A sentence may be seen as showing ... the hearer ... or *displaying* for him ... some situation in Reality" (278). Of course in the passage Wiggins is discussing, as generally in the *Cratylus*, Plato is speaking not of sentences but of words.

17.   Even if, as Richard Sorabji argues *(Time, Creation and Continuum*, London: Duckworth, 1983, 142–44) the knowledge of the Forms is reached by a propositional process, the final result would not have to be propositional. The "ladder of thought" *could* dispense with proposition, as Diotima is made to allege in the "no language and no thought" at the top of her ladder *(Symposium,* 211a), especially if one accepts what Sorabji refers to, its incommensurability in writing *(Protagoras* 329a, 347c; *Phaedrus* 274b–77a; *Seventh Letter* 341c–44d).

18.   The large bibliography on the *Cratylus* is summarized, title by title, in Josef Derbolav, *Platons Sprachphilosophie im Kratylus und in den Späteren Schriften* (Darmstadt: Wissenschaftliche Buchgesellschaft, 1972), 221–308.

19.   Rudolph Weingartner, "Making Sense of the *Cratylus,"* *Phronesis,* XV, 1970, 5–24. However, Weingartner argues that Socrates holds the relativism of Protagoras in view as a sort of control over the "natural sign" theory and he claims that Socrates considers it false; as we certainly would. This is hard to believe when more than three-quarters of the dialogue is devoted to expounding it, and I at least do not see irony as vitiating the assertions here.

20.   Brian Calvert, "Form and Flux in Plato's *Cratylus,"* in ibid., 26–47.

21.   The qualification is made, however, that some *nomothetai* are better, some worse, 429.

22.   As Richard Robinson summarizes in "The Theory of Names in Plato's *Cratylus,"* *Essays in Greek Philosophy* (Oxford: Clarendon Press, 1969), 101, "In his conception of an *onoma* there lay undistinguished at least five notions that are distinct now: the proper name, the name, the word, the noun, and the subject of predication."

23.   τοῦ λέγειν μόριον τε ὀνομάζειν.

24.   Derbelav (52) claims that Plato deliberately has Cratylus described as going to extremes about the names used by slaves (383a4–b2) and other extremes come up, such as the "private speech" of Hermogenes.

25.   εἴς τινα δίνην ἐμπεσόντες κυκῶνται.

26.   The principle of "testing truth" (ἐλέγχειν ἀλήθειαν) so that truth is what is left unrefuted, was explained by David Furley, at a Brown University conference on truth. The notion finds a strong early expression in Parmenides:

κρῖναι δέ λόγωι πολύδηριν ἔλεγχον
ἐξ ἐμέθεν ῥηθεντα. μόνος δ' ἔτι μῦθος ὁδοῖο
λεῖπεται ὡς ἔστιν.

Judge by logos the hard-hitting refutation
that I have uttered. Only one single account of a way
is left: that it is. (Diels-Kranz, B7–8)

27. Albert Cook, *Myth and Language,* 290–91, "Heraclitus: the Conditions of Utterance." "Almost all [previous commentators] attempt in some way to connect *logos* and flux or *logos* and fire. We may remain convinced that such a connection obtains, and yet we cannot define it in the face of such small overlap between any pair of these terms in the statements of Heraclitus we do have. Of some one hundred and forty-seven B fragments in Diels, only ten at most mention fire, and only five mention it outright … Of all those there is only one that mentions *logos,* B31, and the connection is by no means firmly deducible in its exact effects there. There are at least eleven fragments where *logos* or its verb occurs, and another twenty-four mention such arguably related notions as *hen, noos, onoma, gignosko,* and *eidenai.* There is next to no mention, direct or indirect, of fire in all these thirty-five statements nor does any one of them mention the three flux fragments, nor is there any overlap at all between 'flux' fragments and 'fire' fragments. To use the terminology of modern information theory, this lack of overlap offers far too much 'noise' and far too little 'redundancy' to offer a message: a ratio of 50 percent would usually be needed for defensible decoding, and the language here—though the ratios could be variously tabulated—offers on any tabulation only a minute fraction of that requisite ratio. This verbal-phenomenological fact should stand as a massive caveat against those who would construct some specific physiological doctrine for Heraclitus."

28. In Hippolytus's version of Heraclitus' words, as I have translated them here, the text reads "οὐ ξυνιᾶσιν ὅκως διαφερόμενον ἑωυτῶι ὁμολογεῖ. παλίντονος ἁρμονίη ὅκωσπερ τόξου καί λύρης." The version given by Erixymachus reads "τό ἕν γάρ φησι διαφερόμενον αὐτό αὑτῶι συμφέρεσθαι ὥσπερ ἁρμονίαν τόξου τε καί λύρας" *(Symposium,* 187a5–6).

29. This is a frequent assertion in Plato's work. It can be found in the *Parmenides* (506d–9c; 611b); the *Phaedrus* (246a, 274a); the *Sophist* (254c); the *Statesman* (262c, 263b, 284d); and the *Timaeus* (28c, 48c, 53d).

30. J. L. Ackrill. "ΣΥΜΠΛΟΚΗ ΕΙΔΩΝ," in Vlastos, ed., *Plato I,* 201–9.

31. διά τήν ἀλλήλων τῶν εἰδῶν συμπλοκήν ὁ λόγος γέγονεν ἡμῖν.

32. ὀνομάτων γάρ συμπλοκήν εἶναι λόγου οὐσίαν.

33. οὐδέ τις λόγος οὐδέ τις ἐπιστήμη.

34. But the Heraclitean doctrines offer a "hive of wisdom" (401e5), and Heraclitus' river is brought in here where Rea and Kronos are being discussed. Rea has her name derived from ρεῖν, "flow," and Kronos from κορέω, "to sweep clean."

35. Pierre Louis catalogues the richness and frequency of Plato's metaphors in *Les Métaphores de Platon* (Paris: Belles Lettres, 1945). Among those Louis lists as recurrent, many relate to language: multiplicity is a hive (32); "classify" equals "assign place in chorus," *(Euthydemus,* 63) or in a contest *(Republic* 413d, etc., 35); πλανεῖν "to wander" is used for dialogue; speak is "weave": πλέκειν, *Hippias Minor* 369b, and included in the use of συμπλοκή in the passage from the *Sophist* quoted above; an ἀπορία is compared to being stung by a rayfish *(Meno,* 80a–c; *Republic,* 503d; 84); the verb "become dizzy" is used of thought (ἰλιγγιάω, *Lysis,* 216e; 92).

36. On aspects of the divine language in the etymologies, see J. C. Rülarsdaam, *Platon über die Sprache* (Utrecht: Bohn, Scheltema & Holkema, 1978), 183–88.

37. κἄπειθ ἡμῖν οὕτως ὁ λόγος ὥσπερ μῦθος ἀπολόμενος οἴχοιτο, αὐτοὶ δὲ σωιζοίμεθα ἐπί τινος ἀλογίας.

38. Ὄναρ δή, ὡς ἔοικεν, ἐπλουτήσαμεν οἰηθέντες ἔχειν τὸν ἀληθέστατον ἐπιστήμης λόγον.

39. As Gérard Bucher well observes in *Le Testament poétique* (Paris: Belin, 1994), 63, "And so it is precisely because it exploits *and* obscures the revelatory power of language that metaphysics, derived from Plato, remains locked up in the enclosure of a conception that is essentially aporetic."

Chapter 9

The Black Eyes of the White Horse: Love in Plato's Dialogues

> Why after all must ethical theorists always return to the enigmatic
> problem of the relation between pleasure and the final good, in what
> directs human action so far as it is moral? Why always return to
> this same theme of pleasure?[1]   Jacques Lacan

Pausanias (1.30.1) records that "before the entrance to the Academy
there is an altar of Love." The worship was placed outside, the discussion inside. This discussion included an inquiry about how to
understand love. In the form we have, such dialogues as the *Phaedrus*
and the *Symposium*, were carried on in a language that exuded something like the exaltation of worship.

For sexuality itself, how to rule sexual desires is a persistent question in Plato, and sexuality is presented as an overpowering
physiological force in the *Timaeus* (91). There are positive and negative poles to Plato's discussion of love, just as with his discussions of
poetry. The negative pole is, again, notably predominant in the

Republic, with its strict control of emotion and its severe censure of unregulated erotic activity.[2] In Book Three limits are placed on even the most harmonious love relationship (402d1–3), where "a beautiful disposition residing in the soul and in the [bodily] form concur and share in the same type."[3] First the object is just something to look at (θέαμα), then it is "most lovable" (κάλλιστον ἐρασμιώτατον). A person attuned to harmony through having had the musical education discussed in the context (a μουσικός) would even love if there were something discordant (ἀσύμφωνος) in the body of the beloved, though not if in the soul. Socrates goes on here to ask if this excessive pleasure (ἡδονή ὑπερβαλλούσῃ) can have any community (κοινωνία) with prudence, and Adimantus replies in the negative, since love puts a man out of his mind (ἔκφρονα). The pleasure of love also drives him away from any other virtue, since it is the greatest but also the most affiliated with madness (μανικωτέραν). Socrates then proposes a limited father-son relationship between lover and boy-beloved for his projected Kallipolis, all in the context of the youth's musical education. He may just "kiss him and be with him and touch him,"[4] but otherwise he must act "so as never to be seen connected in any other way."

In Book Five the lover is said to misdescribe the physical defects of the beloved (474d–e). And much later, in Book Nine, love is associated with the decline from the democratic to the tyrannical man whose overall activities resemble love (573a–b); and Love is called a "Tyrant" for that reason. Here throughout, along the lines of his usual de-emphasis, Plato is silent on the nuances and transports of love for heterosexual partners. Marriage is earlier described in terms of its breeding arrangements (459d–61e), and a man who has a union outside certain age limits or without prior approval of the ruler is seen also from the point of view of his offspring as "imposing on the state a child who is a bastard, unaccredited and unholy" (401b6–8).[5]

All this armature of strictures, and more, is emphasized in the *Laws* (636e; 838–41), and without any of even the modified play of qualification found in the *Republic*.

In the aspectual handling of this topic, it should not be left out of the reckoning that there is also a neutral focus presented by the late *Philebus*, which makes only passing reference to love as the highest pleasure (63c). This particular notion is implicitly echoed elsewhere in Plato's work—in the *Symposium* and in the *Republic* at 403a, where the term for love is in this instance a heavy reference to physical pleasure, τὰ ἀφροδίσια. The *Philebus* in its intricate discussions of pleasure does not at all address the relations between love and pleasure, or between pleasure and desire, or between love and intelligence. One could construct a congruence between the balance of pleasure and intelligence that is its final solution and the revelation of the emergence of love into a perception of the form of the good at the top of Diotima's ascending staircase of love, but Plato does not do so here, any more than love enters the picture in the presentation of the Line that introduces the deductions from the discourse about the Cave in the *Republic*. We would expect him to do so, of course, only if we were to hold him to an ideal of consistency and overall topical coherence to which modern philosophy conforms—as do most or all of his predecessors, except probably Socrates—but to which his own dialogues do not, while within the individual dialogues he consistently holds such consistency of definition forth in an ideal that gets articulated in the close and powerful reasonings modern commentators have concentrated on discerning.[6]

Direct questions about pleasure (*hedone*) do not come up in the *Phaedrus* and the *Symposium*, though the word does occur there. Still less do they come up in the less intense investigation of the *Lysis*, where the friendship of a more ordinary *amour* is in question, even though, as in the *Phaedrus*, poetry is connected to love; in the *Lysis* that connection takes the correspondingly weaker form of the use of poems for purposes of courtship (204d–e).[7] Beauty too, a key term for Plato, is characteristically limited and even fused with the good (*kaloskagathos*). In the *Symposium*, however, "kalos" or *to kalon* comes into play expectedly and almost automatically at such moments of hyperbole as those of Diotima's peroration—or indeed in Alcibiades' subsequent byplay. Beauty serves as the point of entry in the *Protagoras* between Alcibiades and the as yet unnamed new arrival from Abdera, the Sophist himself (309a–e). Still, beauty is not always brought into conjunction with love; and love, beauty, and pleasure nowhere undergo the arguments-by-division to which virtue, knowledge, temperance, wisdom, courage, and justice are elaborately subjected. Most of those desirable qualities are connected to love throughout the *Symposium*, summarily by Agathon in his speech (196d) and at other points by the other eulogists of love there. In a sort of neutrality about love and desire, pleasure undergoes a separate examination in the *Philebus*, as it had in the *Gorgias*, the *Protagoras*, and Book Nine of the *Republic*. In the *Philebus*, this is an intricate examination but one that is neutralized and, as it were, purged by the absence of the myths which flocked around the discussion of love (except for a brief one 16c–d; 18b); as though to differentiate love from the topic of the pleasure with which it is associated so often, and in our post-Freudian world so comprehensively.

Aphrodite is referred to early in the *Philebus* (12c) as a synonym, the "truest name," for pleasure, but this abstraction is kept severely free of illustration, exuberancy, or even elenchic qualification. Rather, the very synonymity allows the discussion to continue with pleasure (*hedone*) as the center, leaving Aphrodite aside. An argument about desire is repeated in outline form (35–36) and in its physiological implications (47a–c).[8] Anger, suddenly, is accorded the vividness of poetic characterization. Homer compares it to honey oozing from the comb—by way of investigating the puzzling cases, of which pleasure at a tragedy is one (47–48), in which pleasure seems to be mixed with its opposite.

The psychological question here leads to logical questions of limit (*peras*) and the unlimited, sign, opinion, and causality. Indeed a whole battery of logical distinctions come up concerning like and unlike, the one and the many, etc.—discussions so closely and intricately reasoned that this particular dialogue has drawn the prolonged attention of modern philosophical analysts. Without summarizing their discussions and without trying to refine them, we may note again that the effect of Plato's discussion in this dialogue is not to explore the multiplicities of pleasure, any more than it is to expore the multiplicities of color, with which they are compared (12e2–5).[9] Rather it is precisely to define general and particular, like and unlike, one and many, with respect to pleasure.

Seen thus, the dialogue solves in action its initial question—shall intelligence (*phronesis*) be preferred, or pleasure (*hedoné*)?[10] It solves the question by enacting considerable feats of definition over pleasure. This dialogue is noteworthy, too, for registering its intellectual gains and not closing them off, as in comparable dialogues where these questions are discussed, especially the *Gorgias*, and indeed, the dialogues where love is not neutralized but enters its gamut of Platonic possibilities, in the *Symposium* and the *Phaedrus*. The *Philebus* is noteworthy for elaborating its elenchic distinctions so extensively that some commentators have puzzled over whether the main subject is indeed pleasure, when this dialogue confines itself as exclusively as any to just this main subject. It can be said to have its cake and to eat it too by exhibiting intelligence *about* pleasure, rather than offering results on the question of the role of pleasure or its qualities, as the more mythical *Phaedrus* and *Symposium* do. The mixture of intelligence and pleasure is the result attained (59d–66a), and the tonal range is comparable to that of philosophers engaged in the hedonistic calculus, like John Stuart Mill and John Rawls.

Those more mythicizing dialogues take their intelligence for granted, except at the high point of Diotima's ladder, and except in the implied comparison between Socrates and Lysias in the *Phaedrus*, Socrates' superior adaptability and vision indicates greater intelligence. The *Philebus* takes the qualities of pleasure for granted by treating it globally and going through the process of using it to refine the ontological questions which offer pleasure to the intelligence of the philosopher; at the same time, finally, the soul takes the good, courage, mind, prudence, and, in short, the usual Platonic virtues as both pleasure and the good—and then the various métiers are examined (55–56), reducing finally to mind, pleasure, and truth (65c). At the same time, too, this dialogue offers the ideal of a life without excitement either good or bad, "neither rejoicing nor suffering grief" (33b1)—a life Socrates here, astonishingly, calls "most godlike" (b7).[11]

At the positive pole of his discussion about love, in the *Phaedrus* and the *Symposium*, Plato unfolds a universe of delicate perceptions about erotic psychology, expansively enough to give *eros* the eschatological dimensions that indicate his most comprehensive sense of human activity and existence. In one allegation he all but reverses the love of the *Republic* when he has Agathon in the *Symposium* allege that love is the very cement of the social fabric: "It empties us of estrangement and fills us with intimate connection" (197d1).[12]

As usual, the delicacy of his exploration is built into the form as well as into the arguments carried by his presentation. The myths in the *Phaedrus*, just by themselves, imply by qualification and "poetic" exaltation a vision and a fictiveness inseparable from the topic itself. In the *Symposium* the mixture of earnest and play intersects with the double function of the sequenced, contrasted, and partially hierarchized speeches. These speeches are alike in conforming to the assignment that Eros should be praised (so that in that sense they equal one another) but differ in that each is profoundly characteristic of the speaker (so that in that sense they are deeply *ad hominem* and cannot escape their situational siting). All this makes them neither relativistic nor absolute; these implicit self-qualifications remove them from either fixed viewpoint and orient their view of love in each case in such a way that no one aspect can wholly take over any other— Vlastos' impersonality, for example, or Nussbaum's reading of an insistence on the personal attraction of individual to individual. The drama of Alcibiades' attachment to Socrates certainly does make the personal attachment an inescapable factor (except at the top of Diotima's ladder), even if it were not echoed throughout in the attachment of Pausanias to Agathon and Socrates' old flirtation with Phaedrus, and even if the substructure of the argument that Nussbaum spells out were not woven into the dialogue.[13] If the top of Diotima's ladder presents an overarching impersonality, the attention of the participants and the reader are brought back to earth (and to the puzzling implications of the sequence of events) in the subsequent insistences but also in the further subsequent disappearances of Alcibiades.

The careful, focused investigations of Dover, Vlastos, and others have cleared the way for further discussion by determining and describing the homoerotic center of Plato's *eros* in its Greek social context.[14] As often and characteristically in the realm of sexuality, there are many crosscurrents. While Vlastos demonstrates the distinct *physical* base for Platonic love, as indicated even in the *Republic*, it retains its great sublimative and idealizing force. Still, there is evidently some opprobrium attached to homosexual activity, or parents would not have discouraged their sons from listening to an *erastes*

(*Symposium* 182–83; this is also the assumption in Book III of the *Republic*). This sense of impropriety held even in Athens, with no laws or customs (*nomoi*) against homosexuality, and where the situation, as in Sparta, is variegated (*poikilos*). Elis and Boetia accept homosexual love entirely, while the *nomos* in Ionia and other places makes it shameful, and it is also forbidden wherever there are barbarians and tyrants (*Symposium* 182b6–c4).

Indeed, the Athenian opprobium cannot be confined just to the *kinaidos*, the passive partner scorned not because he is homosexual but because he is unmanly. While epithets in Aristophanes—nowhere touched on in Aristophanes' presentation here—do emphasize this feature, his play *Thesmophoriazusae* makes much of the effeminacy of Agathon (without the specific confinement to the *kinaidos* role), an echo we can allow to hover over the dialogue of about 415 here for this play of 411, if we can allow the dialogue to be hinting at Alcibiades' career after this dialogue's earlier dramatic date. Here Agathon and Aristophanes are persons on a mutually convivial par, as well as stand-in representatives of the comedy and tragedy that are referred to at the end of the dialogue. Aristophanes allows in his speech for a heterosexual love that is more than just physical (191d1–e5). These heterosexuals are included in the general "name for love, the desire and pursuit of the whole" (192e10).[15] And his earlier discussion (191c–d) puts homosexuality and heterosexuality on a par.

The Greek tradition in poetry about love melds the bitter and the sweet, as Anne Carson has shown,[16] and the bitter operates in this dialogue through the pathos of Aristophanes' creatures, as well as through the dejected state of the mythical mother Poverty (Πενία) assigned by Diotima to Eros. Taking such elements, Plato—who is said to have begun as a writer of tragedy, and whose surviving poems are erotic ones (if indeed they are his)—detaches them from plot and modulates them into interesting myths, with a subtlety and penetration that brings him into the orbit, and the ken, of Freud.

In the *Phaedrus*, the meaning of ἔρως is bound up with the gods, and with myth, as Gerhard Krüger has shown.[17] It is the musically adept, the μουσικός, who is most open to ideal love (*Republic*, 402). "Philosophy is the greatest music." Closing this particular circle of music, love, and philosophy, is Diotima's highest form of love, itself a kind of philosophy. The connection is also made by Agathon (196e; 197e), and by Eryximachus (187a–b). The *Symposium* saves its unfolding eulogies of love in a play of circumstances, each a strain of possible modification for the light and seemingly associative "melodies" of eulogy it counterpoints.

All the speakers here tend to globalize love, and for all the distinctive character of the individual speeches, there are still many echoes from one to another. Agathon (197b8) speaks of Eros as one with all kinds of desire for the beautiful (τὰ καλά), and this notion is easily reconcilable to Aristophanes' "desire and pursuit of the whole." He also includes in his description the courage that Phaedrus had stressed in his speech. Aristophanes' distribution of his three sexes to sun, earth, and moon (190b) picks up the cosmological perspective of Eryximachus. At 193b–d he compares his own speech to those of other speakers, and his summary can be correlated to all the others, even Socrates and Agathon, by anticipation. Agathon's reference to necessity (197b) echoes Pausanias (whom he is set by the love connection to echo anyway), just as his role of tragedian sets him into a pair with the comedian Aristophanes and as a lover with the youth Phaedrus, and also when he refers to Aphrodite as stronger than Ares (196d), recalling Phaedrus's army of lovers. His reference to the skill of the wise man, the *sophos*, aligns him to the *techne* of Eryximachus. His *logos* (198b) is various (*pantodapon*) in its inclusions. In asserting Eros as the prime cause of all good things (197c), Agathon is also echoing Pausanias and expanding on Eryximachus. He is echoed by Socrates (198e, 205d) in agreement with Aristophanes. Diotima's praise of the more beautiful and permanent (209) echoes the vision of Pausanias. All are following Phaedrus in trying to account for the genealogy and hence provenance of Love.

All these partial harmonies produce an unusual banquet. The normal celebration would have been to drink more, to listen to the music of the flute girls, and then to go to bed with them; the speeches exist also as a substitute for these abrogated activities and are thereby accompanied by overtones of self-restraint (these eager philosophers are utterly down on drink and the casual sex of the banquet, and they do not invoke music and sex). Yet they are also self-indulgent (they are captured by the sound of their own voices, though not so much as will be the famously self-indulgent Alcibiades of the last speech, who has also not restrained himself from drink).

In sparring with Agathon, Socrates starts out an *elenchos* and is told if he is allowed to continue, they will never get back on track in praising Eros. Persiflage is a natural accompaniment of gratuitous eulogy, and Eryximachus (189a7) characterizes Aristophanes as "causing laughter when he just starts speaking" (γελωτοποιεῖς μέλλων λέγειν). Ironically Socrates says he won't compete or hear laughter but will tell the truth. Typically, and in this context with a dramatic irony, he sets up the elenchic series barred earlier (194d), and he submits to an *elenchos* by Diotima. In a metalinguistic twist of irony, the speakers "correct" the myths of other speakers, themselves playfully invented, as though correcting fact.

There is an interaction between the speeches, which are assembled in a series ambiguously ascending and just shifting, and the ongoing image of Socrates, a figure who is here shown all at once as impervious to love in Alcibiades' presentation, heedless of full conclusions, available for summary, and tireless in participation.[18] One point of playfulness is reached in the unveiling, and then the handling, of Diotima, and another in the abrupt and drunken interruption of Alcibiades, but Socrates lasts through it all.

The effect of the intermittent mythologizing of the speeches is to keep the presence of all these factors open and fluid. In the absence of any full elenchic demonstration, the conditions setting the stage are not superseded, as the dialectic supersedes the comparably rich conditions at the outset of the *Republic*. In that dialogue, once they are inside the house of Polemarchus, the festival of Bendis is behind them, whereas in the *Symposium* the air of celebration, and therefore the air of nostalgia, contributes to the tone of the ongoing, alternate discourses. Consequently the discourses come through as flashes of imagined striving for integration—a desire and pursuit of the whole—rather than arguments, tentative or otherwise. It is in banter that the eulogies about love begin, banter in which Eryximachus and Phaedrus exchange pleasantries. When the former says, "The beginning of my speech will be according to the *Melanippe* of Euripides," he is directly passing the mythos to Phaedrus via an implied quotation from that play. But the form of his words is susceptible to an interpretation that would tangentially bring that play into view. Whatever the *Melanippe* was about, exactly, has been lost, yet it is clear that it involved an intense erotic enterprise between Melanippe and some god, followed by distress over her children, and perhaps by metamorphosis. The auditor can passingly and reassuredly hope that in the sense that love is in question, "the *logos* will be according to the *Melanippe* of Euripides," but not so harrowingly as in that play; this celebration in honor of a tragedian will view tragedy at moments but not itself be tragic.

What they will produce, Phaedrus goes on to say, is a substitute for the hymns to Eros which do not exist—thus aligning their discourse with poetic discourse in advance—but also with prose, the discourse of the Sophist Prodicus about Heracles. The speeches—in a way that sustains the atmospheric qualifying of the whole dialogue—are explicitly said to be twice sifted to incompleteness; they are said not to have been remembered fully by Aristodemus, and his report is also not completely remembered by Apollodorus (178a1–5). He will report what is "most worthy of recall" (ἀξιομνημόνευτον). First, all elements are held in the distances of the narrator's recall, from the distancing of another narrator's recall. Second, all the conversations are modally defined as contributions to the celebration of Agathon's victory at the Dionysiac contest for tragedy, in the company of his own beloved, Pausanias.

Phaedrus, in his speech, characterizes Eros as the oldest of the gods, and he at once translates genesis into quasi allegory by quoting Hesiod's *Theogony*—just a line and a half of it, enough to launch a triad of gods: Chaos, Earth, and Eros. The further citation of Parmenides is enough to broach a governing principle of order among the three, and the omission of Hesiod's Tartarus from the list—he puts him just before Eros—raises the contingency of an initial smoothing on either Phaedrus' part or Plato's. Taken for their orbits of reference, Chaos is undifferentiated, Earth is an enabling location, and only Eros connects to, and inspires, an activity. But Eros is further singled out (178b) in the line of Parmenides quoted because Plato has chosen to omit the subject;

πρώτιστον μὲν῎Ερωτα θεῶν μητίσατο πάντων

First Eros did [it] devise of all the gods.

What is "it"? "Necessity" has been suggested, and "Aphrodite." In Empedocles, as perhaps in his predecessor Parmenides, the two are one. In any case, Phaedrus has brought a wide range of literary sources into view —the poetry and sophistry (which does not treat of Eros), the epic, the philosophical poetry, and the prose logographer Acusilaus (which do).

As the most ancient, Eros "is the cause of the greater goods" (μεγίστων ἀγαθῶν αἴτιος, 178c), an inference which is feeble in its logical connection but strong in its psychological suggestiveness. If this proposition is admitted, then indeed it is the case, as he goes on, that there is no greater good for either lover or beloved. It follows that one should take Eros as a guide for living well through one's whole life—an implied extrapolation from the brief, intense affair an adolescent would have before his adulthood into the principle of an entire lifetime. The same point will be made later by Aristophanes when the proof that boy-beloveds are not effeminate is provided by the fact that "such men alone go on to subsequent political careers" (192a6–7).

Shifting ground from love to honor, Phaedrus in his presentation does not really shift ground because "all great and beautiful works," public and private, are achieved through love. The psychological cause for this has a negative sanction: the lover, or the beloved, were he to act shamefully rather than honorably, would be more ashamed before the beloved than before "father, companions, or anyone else" (178d–e).

From this psychological state of affairs Phaedrus derives a fantasy that draws on and combines two main spheres of Greek life: the personal life as intensified in love and for which Homer stands (and Homer is now cited, 179b) and warfare, which for Plato, as for traditional Greek society, is the major organizing force over the entire polis. Phaedrus imagines a whole city or an army of lovers, whose resistance to shame, for the reason given, would make them both the best managers of their city and invincible in war (179a–b).

The most extreme test case here—loosely connected to the military situation under discussion—is the willingness to die for another person. "Only lovers are willing to do this, not only men but also women" (179b4–5). Three legendary instances are examined, two heterosexual and one homosexual: Alcestis, Orpheus, and Achilles.

Alcestis did this so "beautifully" (*kalon*) that even the gods took notice and brought her back from Hades; "so do the gods honor zeal [*spoude*] and excellence in the matter of love" (179d). The perilous situation in Hades, this extreme measure, is then taken as the hinge of the next case, that of Orpheus, who "gave the impression of going soft," since he was a lyre player, and of "not daring to die for his love, as Alcestis was, but to contrive to get into Hades alive" (179d–e). In this account it was for this wavering that the gods gave him the punishment of being put to death by women. This is a notable divergence from other accounts, in which he is punished for scorning women and turning homosexual, or, according to Aeschylus, for scorning Dionysus, but out of grief over Eurydice (not mentioned by Phaedrus as an alternative). In Hades the gods gave him a mere phantom (*phasma*), not the real Eurydice, as in later legend.

Noteworthy here is the tone of correction; Phaedrus has the air of revising other explanations about the death of Orpheus, though we cannot assess them since the versions are mostly considerably later than Plato's. Yet even more noteworthy, in view of the vast presence of Orphism in Plato's time, and in Plato's own work according to one modern view, is the absence of any cultic or doctrinal material on Orpheus here. In this heavily mythologizing account, Orpheus is as though demythologized, as an adjunct to his being an inadequate lover. Phaedrus' severe, if self-exalting, coherence allows him to be seen only from the angle of willingness to die as a proof of love. This failure, which entails and amounts to a failure of courage, is savagely punished—and, here in accord with later legend, by women who are not described as bacchantes or in any other way, so totally are they confined to this instrumentality. To interpret them we are forced back to the criteria of Phaedrus' account—to love, and hence a heterosexual and marital love that is exemplified in both the adequate Alcestis and the inadequate Orpheus.

The next case is once again a case of adequate love and, perhaps in a traditionally ascending rhetorical series, it is a homosexual one, that of Achilles and Patroclus. Achilles is contrasted in the same sentence with Orpheus; he was sent to the Isles of the Blest; he knew he would die after he killed Hector but kills him anyway to avenge Patroclus; and so Achilles was not only willing to die in place of his beloved, like Alcestis, but to die after Patroclus had been killed. He is willing to do this even though he was not the older *erastes* (Phaedrus corrects Aeschylus' "nonsense" on this) but the more youthful beloved—when it is the *erastes* who is the "more godly" (*theioteron*) (180a–b). Achilles, therefore, is the climactic third among the cases. The gods "honored him more than Alcestis."

Leaving aside speeches he has forgotten (180c)—a way of saying that the topic is even wider and more various than this wide and various series—the narrator then has Pausanias challenge Phaedrus, perhaps jealously. He offers a counterargument but not a real *elenchos*, and the argument somewhat misfires. Supplementing Eros with Aphrodite, Pausanias introduces the distinction between physical and spiritual love, or more exactly between common love (Eros Pandemos) and heavenly love (Eros Urania). According to this account, the descent of Eros is from Aphrodite, daughter of Zeus and Dione, in the first case, and from the "motherless" Aphrodite, daughter of Uranus, in the second. Now the fact that Aphrodite Urania is motherless may be taken to allegorize her near exclusion from the physical in love. It is obvious that introducing Aphrodite this way does not refute Phaedrus, who has consistently emphasized the honor and devotion in love and who has concluded with the word "in-godded." Consequently Pausanias, again in the spirit of this festive occasion, should be taken just rhetorically rather than logically. A further tinge of *ad hominem* byplay governs his self-presentation; he is guarding the shrine of love by the right of being the beloved of Agathon, who is at once host and guest of honor.

The hypersensitivity of Pausanias is betrayed by his insistence on excluding heterosexual love from heavenly Eros, as the preceding speakers had not done. This mere assertion raises no points to refute Phaedrus' presentation of a love, in which heterosexuality as well has a strong spiritual component. Pausanias' hypersensitivity is further indicated by his anxious sense of psychological threats to a love affair, a deducible motive behind his lengthy consideration of the status of homosexuality in law and custom (*nomos*) of various Greek states, the more civilized the more tolerant. But there is a quality to this defect in Pausanias; his sensitivity opens him to a fundamental and comprehensive distinction about the erotic life, one that is still with us, the Freudian distinction between direct expression and sublimation. The opposition between Eros Pandemos and Eros Urania clarifies these elements in relation to each other and allegorizes them into a pair whose interdependence is actively cooperative, "the one co-active with the other" (180e2).[19] The distinctiveness between these kinds of Eros is still unmodifiable, though merely physical relations are stated as a constant threat by Pausanias (183b–84).

Aristophanes' hiccups defer his speech, which was to have been next. The reference to such impediments—when so much else has been forgotten in the slips of transmission as they are fictionalized in the dialogue—firmly re-limits the sequence of eulogies into the circumstantial.

His overemphasis on how to conduct a homosexual affair has drawn Pausanias away from his central exposition, and he has left hanging, as it were, the possibility of reconciling physical and spiritual love. He "didn't finish off sufficiently" (185e6–7). The physician Eryximachus comes in to take up this topic with gusto. Medicine is a *techne*,[20] one often adduced by Plato elsewhere as an example of the proper competence with a sphere of skilled activity. While Eryximachus' remarks bear very much the stamp of his *métier*, the topic of love inspires him, as it were, to expand well beyond his sphere into the realm of universalizing speculation, along the lines of the pre-Socratic philosophers to whom he intermittently refers. What he says is especially consonant with the visionary system of Empedocles, who also furnishes mythological material of a different sort for Aristophanes—in place of whom Eryximachus, who has cured the playwright's hiccups, is now speaking, (185d).

Music, astronomy, and poetry are realms that come into convergence elsewhere in Plato, usually at the point of pure revelation, as they do in the myth of Er at the end of the *Republic*. In this dialogue their concordance is assigned not to some special phase of existence; rather it is derived from the permeating influence of love, and so Eryximachus, for all his limitations, by not taking up the antinomian side of Empedocles and neglecting the counterbalance of "strife," echoes Plato's concern in his emphasis on harmony, love, and the beautiful. In this emphasis he anticipates Diotima's highest phase of love.

Eryximachus' discourse is so general that it does not broach the question of heterosexuality versus homosexuality one way or the other. If anything, his emphasis on the process of generation favors the former, even though Greek custom and some (but by no means all) of the speakers in the *Symposium* actually or implicitly favor the latter. The good physician knows how to encourage the good love and discourage the shameful. Also as a good demiurge ("workman," but perhaps with a hint of godlike creativity) his knowledge (*epistemé*; a term now broader than "skill") allows him to bring love into being "for those in whom it is not." He does not dwell on this astonishing claim, which perhaps finds no parallel, except among quacks, until millennia later in the institution of psychoanalysis. All this, however, he bases on the notion, at once Platonic and pre-Socratic, of the reconciliation of physical opposites, touching base again (186d–e) on the psychological basis which is the justification of his *techne*.

He goes from the obvious to the inobvious subjects of medicine, from bodily training to even farming (the god of medicine, Asklepios, would "pilot" farming, perhaps, because health bears on both the farmer and his crops). Finally he brings up "music," a term that, as Dover points out, could cover the whole of culture, or at least poetry, in addition to music.[21] As Eryximachus explains it, however, he means both music in the stricter senses and the larger *harmonia* of attunement that the *Phaedo* discusses at length (85e–86b; 91c–95a).

Both of these meanings are clear from the aphorism of Heraclitus, which Eryximachus brings in to substantiate his points, while at the same time criticizing it.[22] There is a passing oversimplicity here, where Eryximachus sees that the contradiction set up by Heraclitus is " a great contradiction" (πολλὴ ἀλογία, 187a7), which it is Heraclitus' whole intent to pose. Eryximachus also is certainly off the mark, because whatever Heraclitus "wanted to say," he was probably not subsuming music under medicine, as Eryximachus says perhaps he means. Without knowing it Eryximachus is moving under the influence of his topic for asserting some equivalent for the Heraclitean "One" (187a5), in which medicine, like love and music and cults and

the gods and thought and much else somehow partake. Music extends
to the erotic through harmony and rhythm, wherein love may be
"recognized."[23]

He goes on to give Eros Ouranios the lead as a muse, but he also
fancifully gives the name of a muse, Polyhymnia, to Eros Pandemos;
Polyhymnia is a name resonant with suggestiveness for physical love,
whose "pleasure" should be "reaped," in a managed moderation,[24]
which under the physician's care, including diet-management, will
bring about "having the pleasure without sickness." The last expression seems almost exclusively physical, but the doctor at once speaks
of watching after "each kind of love," which, he repeats, resides in
"music and madness." The seasons, meteorological phenomena, epi-
demics, if love is mismanaged, "all sorts of sacrifices and that over
which the seer's art holds sway" (188b6) are under the guardianship
of Love. Impiety (*asebeia*, the charge under which Socrates is to be
prosecuted) "tends to come about from not honoring the ordering
Eros, which, again, the seer's art also manages ... and heals"(!)
(188c7). By the time he finishes, the speaker is speaking of "all love"
and listing a number of virtues in it, ascribing to it "power"
(*dunamis*) over men and gods.

At the next turn of the series, in broaching his own quasi-Empedoclean myth that explains love by the "biology" of human origins,
Aristophanes abandons the terrain of abstraction and definition held
by his two predecessors. ("I have it in mind to speak in a different
fashion than you and Pausanias spoke," 189c2–3). He will act in
character, as the poet of the *Wasps* and the *Clouds* (though not quite
yet, except by anticipation, of the *Birds*). In lightening the tone of
"seriousness" still further, he will at the same time be sharpening the
suggestibility and, by a large measure, the poignancy inherent to this
vision. In his account, it is only after struggles—only after clumsiness,
ineffectiveness, total distractedness, and mortal yearning—that the
twice-remanipulated bodies of human beings come to "the desire and
pursuit of the whole" (192e). These protohumans are finally differentiated by sex into male and female, the ordinary distinction. This
differentiation between male and female is put strangely on a par with
an extraordinary distinction—the principle of classifying a given individual among the types of origin he has had with respect to the initial

four-legged being from which he has been split off. Here equating common biology with outlandish fantasy has the effect of casting a fantasy over the biological facts, while at the same time giving an air of playful but ultimately persuasive solidity to the quasi-mythical human attributes. Aristophanes' three classes of humans, by being referred to their fancied biological originals (male-female, female-female, and male-male), remove all human beings to the same plane, creatures dependent on a desire they cannot shape or manage. In so far as that is the case, the physical component in love is intensified, while the spiritual component variously emphasized by the three previous speakers is virtually ignored—except that the myth spiritualizes the whole situation. In a comic-celebratory acceptation, the myth implicitly embraces everyone, including the female homosexual to which this is one of the few if not the only distinct reference in classical literature.[25]

Origin has been a question haunting all the speakers, who have referred the question to traditional mythology for solution. Aristophanes treats the question at once radically and capriciously, according to what humankind has suffered (παθήματα, 189d6). Indeed, the bunching of the belly and the navel after the first reshaping are fancied to be a "reminder of the ancient suffering" (191a5).[26]

Only at the second reshaping of these proto-humans do the genitals come into play (191b5–6); so that desire for union, a desire desperate enough to make the divided halves cling together and die of hunger and inactivity (191a5–b4), precedes the known human use of the genitals. (Previously men are said to have "put it into the earth like grasshoppers.") This change from the first reshaping to the second reassigns the priority of spiritual over physical, but at the same time the genital-less yearning is a nearly physical one, with disastrous physical effects.

Agathon characterizes his own discourse as combining the serious and the playful. "having a share in sport and also in moderate seriousness" (197a).[27] Still, he is agreeable, but the least playful so far. The host has shown, perhaps, that his role gives him less latitude than his guests. Picking up with a playful contradiction of his guests—Love is not the oldest but the youngest of gods—he returns to the earlier abstractions, "proving" Eros soft and beautiful, good, and consequently full of blessings for men. This is the very point with which Aristophanes had finished: Eros is the god "who most benefits us now, leading us to what is close to the intimate (οἶκειον), and he provides the greatest hopes of the future for those of us who provide piety to the gods, having established us in our ancient nature and, healing us, he makes us blest and felicitous" (193d).

Agathon only echoes Aristophanes. Even this evocation of the softness and tenderness of love and the parts of the body that Eros inhabits adds touches of poetry to the vision of Aristophanes, while simplifying it in a delicate optimism. Socrates, before launching on his own discourse, pays Agathon the compliment of a brief *elenchos*, testing in the host a notion that was more forcefully argued by Aristophanes: that one has to desire only what one lacks. Having rapidly brought Agathon to agree that if love desires the beautiful, love cannot be beautiful, Socrates begins a discourse that will rise to a paean supremely asserting the beauty of love. Putting a speech in the mouth of a semidivine prophetess, Diotima, endows it with awe, with make-believe, and also with the kind of finality it is accorded just because it comes arguably last.

Alcibiades' subsequent remarks both count in the ascending series and do not count. Some of what Alcibiades says fleshes out and vivifies the contrast between physical and spiritual love, through anecdote rather than through either *mythos* or *logos*. Some of his speech heightens and centers Socrates' speech, and this central figure will reexhibit the stamina Alcibiades praises by outstaying nearly everybody. In this connection what Alcibiades says throws a spotlight on Socrates, and therefore back on Diotima, as Nussbaum well urges. By coming in drunk, Alcibiades not only condemns himself to partial incapacity, he also points up his violation of the dialogue's condition, that speeches will substitute for drinking, not cap it.[28] He is drunk himself when he says no man ever made Socrates drunk (220c).

Before this, the stage having been cleared by the *elenchos* and the obligatory ironic self-deprecation, Socrates will have a speech that reviews and exalts what has been said already; love is endlessly various and endlessly repetitious. The Sufficiency (*Poros*) and Want (*Penia*) of Diotima's fable echoes the "surplus" (*plesmone*) and "emptiness" (*kenosis*) that Eryximachus speaks of (186a7), as well as the lack in desire of Aristophanes' fable and of Socrates' *elenchos.*[29]

Diotima's pair of allegorical figures, while abstract, has considerable resonance and associative power, easily subsuming as well as matching these oppositions through their flexibility in the permutation of the myth or fable about them. They are introduced (201) to settle the "desire what you lack" puzzle over Agathon's Eros. At the beginning Socrates has "her" use abstractions to mount the fable: just as right opinion is midway (she is said to teach him) between knowledge and ignorance, so Eros is midway between good and shameful or ugly (*aischron*). This set of definitions already revises the *elenchos* with Agathon and transposes the earlier discussions about shame. The further paradox, that though all call love a great god, there are some who effectively do not, may be resolved if it is remembered that he lacked the good and beautiful for desire of them (202a–d). Leaving this question unresolved, she calls Eros also intermediate in status with respect to desire, being neither god nor mortal but a "great daimon." The middle ground in fact is that on which exchanges of sacrifices and benefits take place between men and gods (203)—both when men are awake and when they are asleep (!)—an appended assertion (203a3–4) which bids fair to wrap up the whole human psyche under the dominance of Eros (and to be easily reconcilable with Freud's discovery of the libido-shaping in dreams).

Then, in response to Socrates, she tells the fable (202b–204), limiting its inception on a feast at the birth of Aphrodite attended by Sufficiency son of Craft (Metis). Drunk on nectar, Sufficiency is seduced while lying down by Want, who is desirous of bearing his child. Eros, born of this union, becomes a servant of Aphrodite. The presence of these five allegorized or allegorizable figures complicates and attenuates the psychological symbioses the fable is designed to suggest, in accordance with Eros's traits of softness, harshness, neediness, courage, compactedness (*suntenos*), skill at hunting, restlessness, and bent for philosophizing—and the other traits that, once the matrix of the fable has been set up, Diotima can quickly list as derivatives of it. Other traits could be listed too; the variable nature of the elements entering into this "birth" render it susceptible to quick hermeneutic manipulation. Moreover Diotima has been, just in this regard, considerably more rapid in her characterization than have the other speakers.

Philosophers, too, it turns out—once it is clear that Eros loves to philosophize—exist in an intermediate state between wisdom and ignorance (204). This state is derived, again, from Sufficiency on the one hand and Want on the other. After directing Socrates' attention to the *eidos* of love and the "name of the whole" rather than "variable names" (205b4–5), Diotima goes on to talk of creation (*poiesis*)— which is defined ontologically as "the cause for anything at all in getting from not-being to being," with the corollary that all skills are "*poiesis*." This, with its plural *technai*, sounds very much like the affirmations of Eryximachus, generalized still further and freed of their specific medical emphasis. All, therefore, who carry out "poiesis" should be called "poet" but only one branch of creation is so defined, the part dealing with music and meter. Similarly with Eros, the term is confined to desires for the good and to "the greatest and treacherous love of being happy" (205d), but love of business, athletics, and philosophy should also be included.

These abstractions continue to lead back to and out from further versions of what others said. So, Diotima goes on, her "*logos* does not say love is of the half or of the whole" (205e). Rather, it is a desire for the good in any form, which is also the beautiful.

These general principles stated, Diotima now applies them to heterosexual reproduction (206c–d), which shares in the connection of physical to spiritual (206b8 and 207e1–4). "This is a godly thing, something immortal in a mortal." The connection is emphasized by the vivid details of bodily response, which can be taken to supplement the varied details of the psychological response given by Aristophanes. His desire-smitten and bewildered humans are seen through the mist of the bantering atmosphere of his myths, whereas here the *logos* of Diotima has shifted into an earnestness tinged with indulgence for the "learning" Socrates (μαθησόμενος, 206b6). Her continuing speech echoes Eryximachus again in extending this activity of love to the intercourse and care of offspring in all creatures. She touches at Phaedrus' key criterion of willingness to "die for" a beloved by repeating the rare verb he employs, ὑπεραποθνήσκειν (again 208b2); but she tones it down and spreads it out by including it in a series of abstractions. For men, body and soul, this includes all attributes that, as in the process of generation, come to be and pass away—"ways, customs, opinions, desires, griefs, fears" (207e2–4). Already more comprehensive than Eryximachus' universalization, the principle of coming-to-be-and-passing-away also embraces the (forms of) knowledge itself (*episteme*, 208a5–10). Knowledge, however, through the interaction of memory and forgetfulness, *seems* the same; "in this fashion all of the mortal is saved, not wholly the same as the godly ... but in the new thing leaving something similar" (208a7–b2). "By this means," she goes on, "the mortal shares in immortality ... This zeal and eros follows for everyone for the sake of immortality." Diotima has now entered, via love, the apocalyptic climax familiar from other dialogues—the *Phaedo*, the *Republic*, the *Phaedrus*, the *Timaeus*. She is speaking "like the complete Sophists," and the word *teleios* itself carries connotations of perfection, authenticity, and immaculateness, as well as of accomplishment and full growth.

She then applies this still more developed idea of love back again to human actions, and reintroduces Phaedrus' notion of dying for others. In the process she employs his two "good" examples, Alcestis and Achilles, substituting for his cowardly Orpheus the selfless Attic king Codrus, who put himself in the front line of battle to be killed so that the terms of an oracle for Attic victory could be met.

One can, she goes on, be pregnant in soul as well as body, so as to generate intelligence (*phronesis*) and virtue (*arete*; 209a3–4). The best intelligence is, she declares, civic; it leads to an ordering of the public and private "for which the names are prudence and justice" (209a7–8). Already Diotima has derived from love the main portion of the entire Platonic program, as Agathon had begun to do; and in so doing she at once invokes the highest Platonic ideals and soars beyond the puzzling connection of the physical and the spiritual in erotic love.[30] This speech goes on to embrace an educational succession, in which here Hesiod and Homer figure, as well as "the other good poets." Lawgivers too, like Lycurgus and Solon, are to be honored, "and any other, Greek or barbarian, who have revealed numerous beautiful deeds and given birth to excellence of all sorts" (209e1–3).

Having established all of this, she goes on now to praise beauty of soul over beauty of body—in agreement, as it were, with Pausanias, but dropping his negative tone. Her conclusion intensifies the permutations of all the *logoi* she has been building on. It is through *logoi* that the lover has been able to move from body to soul in his relations with a single beloved (210a7–8;c1–3), and when he turns to the "multiple sea of beauty" he will give birth to "multiple beautiful *logoi*" (210d3–4).

As the lover moves to the top of the staircase, the beauty he perceives will be deprived not only of face and other features, but of the very *logos* and knowledge that had been a bridge to it (211a). Thus the perception unveiled by Diotima is paradoxically unnamable (because she names it), "without any *logos* and without any knowledge."[31] This is a startling assertion to find in Plato, first because understanding is stated to move beyond its two interdependent vehicles and contexts, *logos* and *episteme*. Next, the assertion is remarkable because here the final understanding is firmly attached to what is visible, whereas almost always in Plato such final knowledge is attained only when the visible has been left behind; it is invisible.[32] The passage continues in a run of superlatives fortified by excluding negatives. This next-to-final perception is not only not attached to a body or any part of one, but "not ever in any other thing, such as in a living creature or in earth or in heaven or anything else, but is itself by itself with itself, a one-formed being always,"[33] and the passage continues in a riot of further superlatives. The top of Diotima's staircase allows a vision of the beautiful to equal even the top of the quadripartite presentation of the Line in the *Republic*, since the highest realization lies beyond the lessons (μαθήματα) that in other contexts are coordinate with the highest intuitions. Just as a progress had earlier been made from "knowledges" in the plural to "knowledge" in the singular, so here, finally, the lover goes from the plural "beautiful *mathemata*" to a lesson in the singular, "to end at that *mathema* which is a *mathema* of nothing else than that beautiful itself, so that he ends by knowing it as what the beautiful is." And he knows (γνῶι) directly, without the intermediation of the *logos* and the knowledge (ἐπιστήμη) that had already been detached from beauty at the prior stage.[34]

Yet back earlier in her speech, when she was speaking of the detachment of Eros from a single body, and then from bodies in general, she lingered over the metaphors of being pregnant and giving birth, for soul as well as for body, as though to insist on a community of qualities in all forms of Eros. This is especially the case with her unusual use of the term "immortal" to describe a physical generation, where a desire for offspring is curiously stretched to imply a desire for immortality. The very uncertainty of this application assists the spread, because it cannot be delimited, or at least the terms are not provided for limiting it, even though in the speech Diotima adduces a hierarchy of immortalities where on one construction we would think that immortality did not admit of degrees: something would be either immortal or not. Yet in her presentation when an understanding of the beautiful comes to be born, "such persons ... have a stronger friendship, a greater community, in more beautiful and more immortal children."[35] The movement from immortal and mortal to body and soul involves a logical shift, since it is not really prepared for by Diotima, and yet through association the shift seems obvious and effortless. The whole emphasis had been the desire for immortality, and the examples of Achilles and Codrus illustrated this (with Codrus easily subsumable under a fellow-feeling, a φιλία, but not under Eros). The distinction between beauty and ugliness, too, falls away (210a4–5), which had been a hinge for the *elenchos* between Socrates and Agathon, and will later become transposed in Alcibiades' praise for the outwardly ugly and inwardly beautiful Socrates. In general, Alcibiades (215a) will try to praise Socrates through *image (eikon)* instead of moving him through reason.

There are, indeed, in Diotima's account, at least four stages beyond the stage of begetting bodies (210c–e).[36] In the first body-liberated stage, the lovers will "give birth to such logoi" (τίκτειν λόγους τοιούτους) and be forced to see "with respect to a Form of beauty" (τὸ ἐπ' εἴδει καλόν, 210b2) behind the beauty of this or that body. Then the lover will seek to improve so that, at a second stage, he is brought to realize the superiority of beauty of soul to that of body, and will be "forced to contemplate the beautiful in pursuits and instituted laws" (ἐν τοῖς ἐπιτηδεύμασι καὶ τοῖς νόμοις). "Thus he will see that all this is congenital with itself" (πᾶν αὐτὸ αὐτῶι συγγενές), and the word "congenital" picks up the birth-template, which is something more than a metaphor, running through much of Diotima's discourse. At the next stage, which is at least a third, the lover will make the transition from pursuits to "knowledges" (ἐπιστήμας), and so he will be "turned" to "the multiple sea of the beautiful," (τὸ πολὺ πέλαγος ... τοῦ καλοῦ). He will see the "beauty of the knowledges," will "contemplate many beautiful logoi and give birth to lofty ones, and to thoughts (διανοήματα) in an abundant philosophy." Then, at a fourth level, "so strengthened," he will "suddenly see beautiful things rightly" and will "see some single knowledge of this sort" (τινὰ ἐπιστήμην μίαν τοιαύτην). At that point the distinction between beautiful and ugly is declared to be inapplicable because it is accidental; the particular bodies have disappeared. Diotima runs through the high points of these stages (211c1–9), repeating such key terms as "end" or "goal" (τέλος, τελευτῆσαι), and using the word elsewhere applied to mathematics in both the singular and the plural, stretching it to "an [abstract] lesson learned." In Socrates' own final summary of this account he himself stretches its general philosophical sense by allowing that some other term than "Eros" might perhaps be applied to the whole gamut of such wisdom, "Consider this encomium, Phaedrus, to have been spoken towards Eros, or if you please to give it any other name, call it that" (212c). Socrates is as though taking the wordless and knowledgeless indivisible insight of Diotima's final stage and bringing it back round as a rudimentary and quickly vanishing beginning for an entirely new *elenchos*—which is passed by immediately because Alcibiades bursts in, offering his own psychodramatic antitheses to this speech, and to all.

Alcibiades' strong personal presence, and the pungency of his confession, can be taken as an antithesis to the depersonalized ideal that Socrates has just praised. But the evidence of Socrates' resistance to Alcibiades' blandishments can also be taken as a fulfillment of that ideal, especially as the beauty of soul that Socrates contains inside the ugliness of his Silenus exterior seems strongly to accord with the highest beauty that Diotima defines. Yet again, the attractiveness of Socrates' "music" (215b) is like the pipes played by another satyr,

Marsyas, and that music is compared to the song of the Sirens (216a). Thus the music praised earlier by Agathon (197b) for being one with philosophy and with love is now seen, even if comically, in a sinister light. So, indeed, is philosophy itself; it is compared to the bite of a serpent by Alcibiades (217e–18a), a comparison fiercer and more negative in cast than the "stingray" to whom Socrates is compared in the *Meno*. In this way an intense set of qualifications, easily formulable as paradoxes, plays across Alcibiades' speech, all the more because of the contradictions and unreliabilities built into his later career and exemplified in his present heavy drunkenness, made the heavier by his quaffing off an astounding half gallon of wine during his speech (214a). He praises Socrates for the courage that earlier Phaedrus and Agathon had adduced as attributes of the lover, and he also praises him for prudence (*sophrosune*). It can be said that he himself exemplifies courage without exemplifying prudence. Indeed, reversing the usual courtship pattern between lover and the beloved, making the advances as a boy-beloved that normally an *erastes* would make, his account leaves open how one might judge the other possibility—since even Diotima allows a physical love affair to be the first approach to a perception of beauty, to be left behind (but not rejected at the outset) as the lover becomes worthy of beginning the ascent up her staircase. In that sense the chaste Socrates depicted by Alcibiades goes her one better—or else illustrates the simplification of his own idealization.

The dialogue throughout declares love to be rich and various not by any presentational arguments, but indirectly, and dramatically, through the encapsulation of each speaker into his own conspectus. That love tends to expand under discussion is indirectly demonstrated by the very echoes of one conspectus with another; they are not globally closed off and exclusive. It also shows in the celebratory and festive spirit of an occasion permeated by the effects of love through the act of agreeing to talk about it when they have abjured erotic activity with the flute girls and, so far as they are engaging in discourse, with each other. They are carrying out a more civilized version of what Alcibiades finally half-jokingly complains about, Socrates' preference for spiritual contact over the physical acting out of erotic attraction. In their delicacy, especially as it contrasts with his drunken hyperbole, they are also quasi Anacreontic. That poet's civilized fusion of wine and love is echoed, as well as the more primordial connection in Dionysus.

Diotima is said at one point to have told Socrates he has "perhaps undergone a mystic initation into matters of Eros."[37] The soul, in Aristophanes fable, at a crucial point of love cannot speak but must "prophesy and riddle" (μαντεύεται καὶ αἰνίττεται, 192d1–2). In moving beyond these forms of utterance, Plato also incorporates them, and even in this one dialogue he does not offer (nor does he deny) final propositions. Rather he sets out explorations, imitations, and the formulations whose appropriateness, rightness, and comprehensiveness are carried by glorying in an unchallenged air of the tentative.

The long myth of the Charioteer in the *Phaedrus* is almost wholly reconcilable with the speech of Diotima in its assertion, but the modality of myth, and the particular myth here invented, endows it with a different range of psychological aperçus about spiritual experiences that are fundamentally erotic and confined more to that domain than are Diotima's universalizations.

The circuit, wide as the heavens, around which the Charioteer conducts the chariot of the soul, automatically provides a largeness and openness to the perception. Where Diotima rises to delicately modulated intensification of the already inclusive terms that she brings into still more heightened convergence in her climactic words, the form of the myth in the *Phaedrus*, and its relative freedom from specific tradition,[38] effectuates at once a convergence to which such arguments as Diotima's may be conceived of as preliminary. Erotic energy as well as spiritual force spurs the white horse, and the black one can be kept in tandem, contributing powerfully if subliminally to the whole. What else is broached by the black eyes of the white horse, that can look out powerfully and seriously on a universe while embodying and locating at the point of visual perception the very color—and since color is here quality, the quality—of its counterpart, the black horse?[39] The access to both the beautiful and the love from which it springs comes centrally through the eyes (250b, 251a, 255c).

The other horse, differently formed, is not an exact match; *his* eyes are neither white nor black, but grey (*glaukommatos*, 253e3).

This color is puzzling; visually it is a self-effacing, nondescript blur; but traditionally it must suggest the color of Athena's eyes; she is *glaukops* in Homer. Perhaps the point is that it *can't* bridge the association.

A flight in the heavens replaces Diotima's guided steps. In the myth that Socrates now tells here, all factors bear simultaneously on the mounting charioteer. This in itself, as an imaged perception, deeply nuances this myth's large areas of congruence with the presentation of Diotima, the doctrines of body and soul balanced out in both accounts.[40] The topmost vision of the truth here, easy for gods but very difficult for humans, consists in a truth in a knowledge of what is, unvarying through time, "a knowledge essentially in that which really is" (247e).[41] The inextricability of the rhetorical situation from this presentation further seals them. Love and rhetoric are put here through a dance of which the point is not just to plot out the separate steps but to observe the conjunctions.

As is true of this dialogue generally, the myth of the Charioteer of the human soul who drives his black and white horses is qualified by many modalities. First, as Martha Nussbaum points out, the whole presentation is governed by being cast as a "recantation" (243b).[42] The recantation is not simple, but rather is caught in the paradox of the Cretan liar. For if the first speech, like the speech of Lysias, could be characterized as the sort of speech that was designed to trick a courted boy by pretending an objective altruism while actually making a play for him, the substitution of this idealized account could be reckoned to be aimed at the same goal, especially if at no point in the dialogue is love wholly disentangled from rhetoric. To say "I deceived you the first time but now I am telling the truth" can serve as another turn of deceit. At a division of his presentation, beginning to wind down, Socrates addresses Phaedrus as "beautiful boy" (ὦ παῖ καλέ, 252b2). The connection between rhetoric and love, to be sure, will persistently go both ways: not only is the communication between persons attracted to one another tinged with courtship, but the technique of managing communication, rhetoric, may have its highest function in that seemingly "mad" activity. The speech, too, is characterized as akin to one of the kinds of good madness, a poetic madness, when it praises another kind, love madness. As Nussbaum says, that very praise revises the basing of love on any form of reason and knowledge, as in the *Symposium*. But it also carries the qualification further, as does the fact that it is cast inextricably in a mythical form that allows the features of body and soul to interact tempestuously, where Plato usually sets them in a hierarchy. The whole account begins with an address to the implications of immortality (rather than directly of love), and it is characterized as imperfect from the outset by being a briefer and less precise version of what only a god could tell (246a). And of the peak of this vision there are no human poetic versions available, "Of this super-celestial place no poet of those here ever duly sang or ever will sing" (247c2–3).[43] The human charioteer is further qualified (247–248) by being contrasted with the wholly good charioteering of the gods—a limit that also implies a likeness, since man resembles the gods in this activity as well as differing from the conditions under which he carries it out. Some hint of the Phaethon myth plays over this moment of the presentation, but an analogy to Phaethon cannot be applied fully: unlike Phaethon, the human charioteer can succeed if he keeps the black horse managed.

This vision fairly quickly broadens to encompass not only love but all of truth, coming from the soul's remembrance of its visit to the gods before returning after a transmigration to the body (250). Falling in love unveils a resemblance between the beloved and the gods (251). It is, curiously and for Plato uniquely, the *bodily* responses of the lover that allow him to grow wings (in the alternate version of the winged person, rather than of the Charioteer with white and black horses). He links up the features and psycho-spiritual dispositions of the beloved to the particular gods, to Zeus or Hera or Apollo or others (253a–c). At the "ordinance of Nemesis," under the name of Adrasteia or "she who does not run away," the soul finds its disposition towards one of a series of nine human professions, only the first of which involves a lover. At the same time he may attain to a vision of the usual list of Platonic virtues and capacities, justice, knowledge, and prudence (247d, *sophrosune*), even though elsewhere *sophrosune* is the contrary of the *mania*, one of whose forms, that of love, is here being praised. The myth allows Socrates to shade over into these other areas and past intermediate contradictions.

Why does the white horse have black eyes? The presentation is so
intense that it glories in forbidding us a full answer to this question.
This myth is cast in allegorical form, which means that the details call
out for interpretation and also surpass it. The black eyes of the white
horse both contain their opposite (the blackness of the black horse)
and control it by harnessing it using it to see rather than blindly hur-
tling downward through the sky. But how do they contain their
opposite while at the same time managing it? To see and to rein in are
two incommensurable activities. Love carries out everything, but it can
only flash in such an intense detail. The staircase of Diotima and the
wordless intuition are neither contradicted nor supplemented in the
play of this allegory and all the modalizations that bear upon it. While
playing with directness, the myth here indirectly testifies to the triumphant variegations that Plato presents about love.

Notes

1.   Jacques Lacan, *Le Séminaire Livre VII* (Paris: Seuil, 1986), 46.
2.   Eros remains steadily a high value for Plato, however, and Stanley
Rosen finds traces of that high value even in the language of the
interchanges in the middle books of the *Republic*. See Stanley Rosen, "The
Role of Eros in Plato's *Republic*," *The Quarrel Between Philosophy and
Poetry* (New York: Routledge, 1988, 102–18. Rosen makes a case for the
general pervasiveness and finality of Eros in all of Plato.
3.   ὅτου ἂν συμπίπτηι ἔν τε τῆι ψυχῆι κακά ἤθη ἐνόντα
καὶ ἐν τῶι εἴδει ὁμολογοῦντα ἐκείνοις καὶ συμφονοῦντα,
τοῦ αὐτοῦ μετέχοντα τύπου.
4.   φιλεῖν μὲν καὶ ξυνεῖναι καὶ ἅπτεσθαι.
5.   νόθον γὰρ καὶ ἀνέγγυον καὶ ἀνίερον ... παῖδα τῆι
πόλει καθιστάναι.
6.   Indeed, this propensity to shift emphasis to a degree where
seemingly relevant topics are obscured, even if it is not erected into a
principle—and if it were not one, why would so powerful a philosopher have
so regularly shifted?—is a more defensible explanation than are the
ultimately indirect inferences about "development," to account for the
absence of any discussion of Forms in the *Philebus* when Forms are
connected to the good elsewhere in Plato, and to love in the *Symposium* by
Diotima. For that matter, if the lateness of the *Philebus* were the
explanation, how would we explain the continued attention to Forms in the
Parmenides, and in the *Seventh Letter*?

7. Even in that small compass doubt intrudes. The *Lysis* achieves some definitions of friendship, but Socrates declares in its last sentence that "we have not yet become able to find out what the friend is" (223b).

8. For a full discussion of this and related questions see J. C. B. Gosling and C. C. W. Taylor, *The Greeks on Pleasure* (Oxford: Clarendon Press, 1982).

9. Color is returned to briefly as a topic in 53a; this time purity, and degrees of whiteness are the questions at issue.

10. The question of mixing intelligence and pleasure in life is also introduced 22a–b.

11. These propositions are dropped and a simple piety substituted for pleasure by the intelligent man, according to the *Eighth Letter*: "God is the ruling principle for prudent men, pleasure for the senseless" (354e6), "θεὸς δὲ ἀνθρώποις σώφροσιν νόμος, ἄφροσιν δὲ ἡδονή."

12. "οὗτος δὲ ἡμᾶς ἀλλοτριότητος μὲν κενοῖ, οἰκειότητος δὲ πληροῖ."

13. Martha C. Nussbaum, "The Speech of Alcibiades: A Reading of the *Symposium*," *The Fragility of Goodness*, 165–99, especially 176–78.

14. Kenneth J. Dover, *Greek Homosexuality* (Cambridge: Harvard University Press, 1978), 4–5, summarizes the patterns of homosexual response in Plato, and of course for Greece generally. See also Gregory Vlastos, "The Individual as Object of Love in Plato," *Platonic Studies*, 3–42.

15. τοῦ ὅλου οὖν τῆι ἐπιθυμίαι καὶ διώξει ἔρως ὄνομα. The particle οὖν is made the more emphatic by the unusually pronounced and summary ordonnance here, and its role as a roundup of conclusion becomes stronger. Greek is a verbal language, and the thrust onto nouns is striking here, especially as they are verbal nouns. One might, in any case, more colloquially expect the genitive, and the double activity, well sequenced (first desire, then pursuit), links through language, the "name," for an ἔρως which takes on comprehensiveness as the last and culminating word of a sentence where its position immediately after ὄνομα has the force of a colon. The expansiveness in this terminal word is perhaps further suggested by the fact that just one of the defining terms, put colloquially into the dative, is a synonym for ἔρως, which does mean ἐπιθυμία. That it means διώξις is rather slipped in. It might not occur to anyone that this term could be included as a lexical entry for it. The effect, then, is to emphasize the pursuit, which is the common denominator of the various phases Aristophanes has delineated.

16. Anne Carson, *Eros the Bittersweet* (Princeton: Princeton University Press, 1986).

17. Gerhard Krüger, *Einsicht und Leidenschaft* (Frankfurt: Klostermann, 1973), "So with special force does the derivation of philosophy from Eros present us with the general problem of the relation between *philosophy* and

religion (6). The spiritual self freed straightway in the mania of love (12) ... The exaltation of Eros is new, and it is decisive for the spiritual atmosphere in which *philosophy* grows" (20). As Margot Fleischer well says in *Hermeneutische Anthropologie* (Berlin and New York: de Gruyter, 1976), 131, "Eros on its highest plane is philosophy. So philosophy is Eros. It is madness as a transport to the true in the act of recall."

18. For the implications of Socrates' posture here, see Steven Lowenstam, "Paradoxes in Plato's *Symposium*," *Ramus*, 14 (1985), 85–104. Lowenstam sees a scene-setting congruence in Socrates's statements to Aristodemus on the way to the banquet (174a3–75d7), "I've beautified myself so I may go beautiful to someone beautiful" (ταῦτα δὴ ἐκαλλωπισάμην ἵνα καλὸς παρὰ καλὸν ἴω), which he corrects to "The good go to the feasts of the good." Socrates in this passing conversation may be said to assume a view which is directly the opposite of the one he will expand in his main speech, where one seeks the good and beautiful if he lacks it (204a8–b5).

19. τὸν μὴν τῆι ἑτέραι συνεργὸν.

20. Eryximachus refers to his *techne* 186b1–5; 186e3; 187e5; 187e6.

21. Dover, ad loc.

22. Eryximachus once again resolves a puzzle by a reference to "musical *techne*" (187b1–2). Dover expounds the aphorism of Heraclitus here (B51), "They do not understand how what differs agrees with itself; a bent-back harmony, as of a bow or a lyre." For an interpretation from a somewhat different angle, see Albert Cook, *Myth and Language*, 105.

23. Or "diagnosed." Eryximachus had used the same verb, *diagignosko*, in that technical sense above, 186c7, "nor is the love a double one here" (187c7–8). By its not being double, Eryximachus surely cannot mean that the physical is excluded. Double must mean in its absence that the physical and spiritual in harmony become one—a large theory just suggested here. This is a position developed later by Aristoxenus, Plato's successor; and so Plato's own position on this question, if it was really fixed, cannot be divorced from Eryximachus'.

24. This short passage gives two of the dialogue's few uses of the word ἡδονή.

25. So Dover characterizes it (118), glossing ἑταιρίστριαι (192e5). But there is at least one place in the *Lysistrata* (78–84) where Lesbian overtures seem to appear in the action.

26. μνημεῖον εἶναι τοῦ παλαιοῦ πάθους.

27. τὰ μὲν παιδίας τὰ δὲ σπουδῆς μετρίας ... μετέχων.

28. *The Fragility of Goodness*, 165–99. Nussbaum emphasizes the contribution of some elements in Alcibiades' speech to the question—not directly decided in the dialogue, I find—as to whether love is to be understood as love for a unique individual in what may be deduced from all

these speeches, or is effectually just for a collocation of desirable attributes in one person that could theoretically be collocated in another person. She also stresses the congruence between Alcibiades' assertions and the events of his own life, "A man who died shot by an arrow will speak of the words of love as arrows or bolts wounding the soul (219b). A man who influentially denounced the flute as an instrument unworthy of a free man's dignity will describe himself as a slave to the enchanting flute-playing of a certain satyr (215b–d, 213c, 219c). A man who will deface holy statues compares the soul of Socrates to a set of god-statues and to the injustice of rubbing out, or defacing, Socratic virtues (213e, 215b, 216d, 217e, 222a). A man who will profane the mysteries puts on trial the initiate of the mystery-religion of *erôs*" (166).

29.   Steven Lowenstam ("Paradoxes in Plato's *Symposium*) underscores the paradox involved in this passage. This view could be elaborately correlated with Lacan's metaphysics of desire, except that in Plato here it is aspectualized by the very variety of the speeches.

30.   Martha Nussbaum's chapter, "The Speech of Alcibiades" well elaborates this climax of Diotima's speech (*The Fragility of Goodness*, 176–84). Yet stressing its opposition to some of what may be derived from Alcibiades' speech runs the risk of modifying the play of variety through the dialogue—a variety that is "philosophical" as well as "literary." The term "parergon" or "gratuitous addition" is used by Socrates to define the speech of Alcibiades (222c5).

31.   οὐδέ τις λόγος οὐδέ τις ἐπιστήμη. The particulars have been left well behind here, and this is a unitary beauty. The Loeb translator, however, tries to sidestep the force of this assertion by rendering οὐδέ τις as "no particular," and he is silently followed by others who pass over the challenge this statement offers to interpretation. But τις with a negative attached, and especially in an adjectival use, means always or virtually always "not any," rather than "no particular." This distinction is clear from the Οὖτις of Homer on, when Odysseus is not saying to Polyphemus "No one in particular," but "Nobody [at all]."

32.   In this passage, contra Dover, φαντασθήσεται is grounded in a steady visual emphasis and cannot have, as Dover alleges, "a suggestion of illusion, appropriate to the particulars (a6–b1) with which abstract beauty is contrasted." Of the word φανεῖται, which appears shortly, Dover concedes that "it is more appropriate to understand that 'it will clearly be'." And actual vision is clearly stated both before the passage in question and after, in κατίδηι τινὰ ἐπιστήμην, "see some knowledge" (210d7), and θεωμένωι αὐτὸ τὸ καλόν, "seeing the beautiful itself" (211d1–2). The presence of the visible here is the more remarkable if we bring to bear on it the extent and power of the dimensionality of the *invisible* in Plato, as Otto Apelt sketches it in *Platonische Aufsätze* (Berlin: Teubner, 1912), 7, "to win

an exact overview over the ways by which Plato attained to his supersensual world. If we may connect the teaching of Aristotle with what we can derive from Plato's own writings on the question, then four viewpoints come into consideration: 1. the ontological, 2. the logical, 3. the psychological, and 4. the ethical."

33. αὐτὸ καθ᾿ αὑτὸ μεθ᾿ αὑτοῦ μονοειδὲς ἀεί.

34. It was then still communicated through the vision (φαντασθήσεται) that drops away at an earlier stage of the Line, even though that presentation supplements the visual construct around the Sun.

35. φιλίαν βεβαιοτέραν ἅτε καλλιόνων καὶ ἀθανατω-τέρων παίδων κεκοινωνηκότες.

36. For one account of these stages, see F.M. Cornford, "The Dialectic of Eros in Plato's *Symposium*," in Gregory Vlastos, ed., *Plato II* (Notre Dame, Ind.: University of Notre Dame Press, 1978 [1971]), 119–31. A more precise and detailed account is given in Anthony Price, *Love and Friendship in Plato and Aristotle*, (Oxford: Clarendon Press, 1989).

37. ταῦτα μὲν οὖν τὰ ἐρωτικὰ ἴσως, ὦ Σώκρατες, κἂν σὺ μυηθείης.

38. Wings are traditional, even though "no poets have yet sung" (247c), and so are horses—and, in Indo-European tradition, horses that move in the heavens with the sun. Even a winged horse is traditional: Pegasuses are spoken of early and in the plural. What is not traditional is this story, with its opposite-colored horses, and its allegory.

39. In the *Republic* (474e) darkness and whiteness are connected to love as both attractive.

40. The substitution of perception of unity for the perception of pluralities here in the *Phaedrus* also echoes a stage in Diotima's account of the ascent to knowledge (249b6–c1), "a man ... going from many perceptions to a unity brought together by a reasoning," (ἄνθρωπον ... ἐκ πολλῶν ἰὸν αἰσθήσεων εἰς ἓν λοιγισμῶι συναιρούμενον).

41. τὴν ἐν τῶι ὅ ἐστιν ὂν ὄντως ἐπιστήμην οὖσαν

42. Martha Nussbaum, "'This story isn't true,': madness, reason, and recantation in *Phaedrus*," *The Fragility of Goodness*, 200–34.

43. Τὸν δὲ ὑπερουράνιον τόπον οὔτε τις ὕμνησέ πω τῶν τῆιδε ποιητής οὔτε ποτέ ὑμνήσει κατ᾿ ἀξίαν.

Chapter 10

Plato and the Historical Consciousness

1.

Plato situates his dialogues uniquely and originally at the intersection of an actual set of events, often precisely datable, and one or a group of encounters at least partly fictional. Thus they are not exactly historical, but they are angled so as to mime, and qualifiedly to recall, a historical situation. The situations they depict cover at least a fifty-year span, from the *Parmenides* which features a youthful Socrates at about 450 B.C.E., through the *Protagoras* of about 433 and the *Symposium* of about 416, down to the four dialogues set in 399 at his trial and death. They often keep in view a consciousness of a historical bearing on the questions they raise, while exhibiting in the range of their modes of address what can be ascertained of Plato's own historical consciousness.

Their set of determinants, indeed, is fairly expandable; the combination Plato carries off is only conceivable on the assumption of his expanded historical consciousness. There is Plato's sense of himself with relation to public action, which plays a large role in his letters, particularly the *Seventh Letter*. Plato refers in his letters to his own earlier political ambitions, and he summarizes his advice at moments of the smaller-scale political situation in Sicily. Then there is the effacement of his person and its displacement throughout the dialogues, as these permute with his sense of events present to himself. Such events permute also with the past events of Athens, back to the Homeric world and before, and to other city-states like Crete and Sparta, pointedly in the summaries in Book Three of the *Laws*, but intermittently elsewhere. That present and that past, public and personal, permute with the patterns of political process, both actual happenings and idealized ones, the projections ahead of how the systems might work in the *Sophist*, the *Republic*, the *Statesman*, the *Laws*, and elsewhere. Finally, impinging on these and related to all these, Plato's view of history involves millennial series, especially in the *Timaeus* and the *Critias*, which themselves have some relationship both to the ideal systems and to the proximate histories, public and personal, present and past. The interaction of these coordinated interpretive matrices toward the historical-social process provides an implied locally organized dialectic, questioned by Plato only in the *Republic*, and then obliquely.

The death of Socrates comes at the end of Plato's youth, which is also the end of the hegemony of Athens. So that the representation of a continuing near present—the very sort of present faced by Thucydides and Herodotus before him—is occluded, restructured as philosophy, or else displaced at a distance and into action, the space of Sicily where he is an advisor, as Solon was to Cyrus, a comparison he makes himself (assuming the letter to be genuine) in a letter to the tyrant Dionysius:

> As for you and me and our mutual relations ... it is a natural law [πέφυκε] that wisdom and great power converge. They are always pursuing and seeking after each other and coming together. Furthermore, this is a subject that people always find interesting whether they are themselves discussing it in a private gathering, or are listening to the treatment of it by others in poems. For example, when people are talking of Hieron or the Spartan Pausanias, they like to introduce their association with Simonides and recount his conduct and remarks to them. Again, they are wont to celebrate to-

gether Periander of Corinth and Thales of Miletus or Pericles and Anaxagoras, or again, Croesus and Solon as wise men and Cyrus as a man in power. Moreover, the poets copy these examples and bring together Creon and Tiresias, Polyidus and Minos, Agamemnon and Nestor, and Odysseus and Palamedes. With much the same idea, I believe, the first men brought together Prometheus and Zeus. The poets also show how in some cases the two characters became enemies—in others, friends—how in some cases they were first friends and then enemies, and how in others they agreed in some things but differed on other points.

(*Letter Two*, 310e–11d, tr. L. A. Post, revised)

This not only blends actual into legendary relationships but presents them all as generating an attention to history through what amounts to dialogue. Many of these persons are from another place than Athens, and Plato also displaces his considerations into historical time, to the time of Solon or old Crete or old Sparta. In the comparative perspective that the letters easily manage, Plato gives a public dimension to his reflections as he compares Dionysius' relations with the Carthaginians to the policies of Darius and to those of the Athenians in the seventy years after the Persian Wars (*Letter Seven*, 332–33). Yet in the light of the events discussed that involve the Persians by way of Herodotus, Thucydides, and Xenophon, Plato is implicitly archaizing and ethnocentric. The Persians, still prominently active on the horizon of his time, are scarcely less prominent in his writings than the Egyptians, though neither gets anything like Herodotus' prolonged attention to their historical development.

Book Three of the *Laws* is framed along the lines of a conjectural reconstruction of human history: the recovery from an original earthquake or flood; the gradual establishment of the three city-states Argos, Messene, and Lacedemon; their subsequent rivalries; the course of the Trojan and the Persian Wars; the rise of Darius and Xerxes; and the development of Athens.

Mathematics, strangely to the modern reader, stands as a further dimension, or else as a limit, to the historical situations that themselves Plato so boldly permutes. The four or fivefold recursive series of historical successions in the small, and also such vast successions as the Great Year in the large, verge on the mathematical mystique that, in the *Republic* Plato has Socrates apply expansively to a large-scale social-spiritual process. A mathematical correlation to history may come at any time in his work, as in the exact calculation "squaring and cubing" the tyrant's removal from "true pleasure" (587b–d). Measure and number are associated to the twelve proportionate divisions in an ideal society (*Laws*, 746–47). An elaborately calculated geometric number governs "better and worse births," and the guardians must take care not to "miss" this number in mating prospective parents (*Republic*, 546c–d).[1]

In Plato's extant writings Number does not attain a Pythagorean purity of application to history. Still, in the associability of society and number it cannot be asserted confidently that Plato has divorced himself from the rigorous connection that obtains for Pythagoras between mathematics and a synchronic social order. He has loosened that connection, and at the same time he has historicized it, moving it onto a sequential generational pattern away from the eternal present of the closed Pythagorean society (which in that feature repeated the ideal imagined present of Greek society on the Homeric pattern). This is true notably for the Pythagoreanism of the *Republic*, which, however much it be operative in the numerology to which that work recurs, does subscribe to the Pythagorean notion that society should be conceived on an ideal plan, while at once rendering that plan contingent and deploying it back to an imagined unchanging present in the future from a time line of past, present, and future. The Aristotle of the *Politics* and *The Constitution of Athens* shrinks all these procedures, as well as removing them from any numerological mystique. Plato, it can be said, is a giant sport in the Greek development, more combinatory in his historicizing than Aristotle, but also more primitive, while at the same time more fully divorced from the Homeric pattern, to which he also variously does homage.

The "big book" project of Herodotus and Thucydides was completely new in Plato's youth, as was the long private meditation, accumulated in solitude and presumably unaccompanied by the social *situs* of a teaching such as a Protagoras or a Hippocrates exercised. Plato combines and transforms these modes. It is surely all the more remarkable that of all his great contemporaries of the previous century, Herodotus and Thucydides are virtually alone in never once being named by Plato. Aristotle, by contrast, mentions Herodotus in a variety of contexts, but interestingly not Thucydides. Nor is the word *historia* much used by Plato.[2] It is as though Plato wanted to give himself immense elbow room for dealing with events in the remote past or structures in the comparatively recent past. That at least might explain why he has kept a blank space for himself to fill by not mentioning these historians who bulk large as prose writers on his horizon. It can be felt that Plato means some historiographic validity to accompany these historiographic speculations. It is indeed a desperate expedient to ignore one's greatest predecessors. Plato does not so severely limit himself in any domain of philosophy. But he seems to be doing it here with history.

While Plato studiously ignores Herodotus and Thucydides, he does raise in various forms versions of the questions about history that lie behind their practice. Furthermore, in the centuries preceding, from Hecataeus and Anaximander on, the historiographic inquiry had impinged on the philosophical enterprise. But until Plato it had not been transmuted. Plato's philosophical predecessors, with the possible exception of Heraclitus, do not include or modulate human history at all. By comparison with Plato, Herodotus is able to go far just by taking the geo-historical template of Hecataeus and filling it out, while Anaximander provides a principle too abstract even for the macro-analysis of history. Indeed, Anaximander's summary, as we have it in his first fragment, would not be hard to coordinate with Plato's *Republic* in its connection of time with justice, "To give recompense to one another for injustice according to the arrangement of time."[3] Another route than Plato's can be seen in the one Xenophon took, who was also a pupil of Socrates and wrote about him. Plato breaks so radically with the historiographers who immediately preceded him that he does not mention them at all, while Xenophon in the *Hellenica* continues Thucydides' work where it left off.

Moreover, if one looks for an analogue in the prose writing of the generation before Plato to antithetical speeches on given topics, the sort of presentation that attains a colloquial fluidity in the dialogues, the closest approximation, leaving aside Antiphon, would be the speeches of Thucydides, where speakers and groups of speakers take opposing positions and bring them to bear on a single question of policy. Such discourse, even for modified proponents of oligarchy like Thucydides and Plato, derived from the fairly new democratic freedom of discourse, the ἐλευθερία that so uniquely characterized society at this time and had taken on a thick and tensile activity in the years of Plato's youth.[4]

Xenophon's statement at the very end of the *Hellenica* that somebody else in turn can take over implies a team or assignment approach to history, de-individualized, in a way that would have seemed foreign to all his predecessors. It is "professional" in a median sense, operating midway between the problem-oriented Plato and the task-oriented Aristotle.

Plato, instead, modulated this set of inquiry, still following the spirit of factual accuracy that cannot be found firmly before Herodotus and Thucydides. In the *Laws* (680–83), again like the Archaeology of Thucydides, data and quotations from Homer are cited with the same sense of their validity as witnesses, τεκμήρια. The technique is described in 683c8, "Let us put ourselves in our thoughts [ταῖς διανοίαις] at the time when Lacedemon, Argos, Messene and those with them were effectually subject to your ancestors." One passage (685c–d) sees Trojan time in the light of large Empires, standing towards the Assyrians as those of the present stand towards the Persians.[5] In connection with the Cretan criticism of the myth of Ganymede (636c), he introduces the utility of drunkenness, a rapid Herodotus-like comparison of customs, though he does reject cultural relativism (637c–d).

He constantly exercises a historical consciousness that could be defined as an internalization of the principles deducible from Thucydides, as is the case, for example, in the assertions of the Athenian in the *Laws:* "They say the laws must look neither to war nor to the whole of virtue, but, whatever the established constitution may be, to look to the advantage (τὸ συμφέρον) for it, so as to rule ever and not be dissolved, and the best definition of justice in nature to call it ... the advantage of what is in power" (714b–c). A little later, discussing the "axioms of rule" (ἀξιώματα ἀρχῆς), he singles out what is essentially the same principle, and he cites Pindar for calling it "according to nature the most powerful control in judging" (715a).[6] He might well, indeed, have cited Thucydides, and all the more because he does not quote Pindar's actual words, but rather summarizes him, when Pindar, unlike Thucydides, does not comment on such political power struggles. The summary that follows of how dominant groups contrive to stay in power is, again, Thucydidean in its emphases: "When rule gets fought over, the victors so dominate affairs in the city that they give no share in rule at all to the vanquished, to themselves or to their descendants, and they live on guard against one another, lest ever someone come to rule mindful of the wrongs that transpired previously."

Now Thucydides would serve as a close analogue or illustration for this formulation, but Plato does not mention him, when he will draw on both Gorgias and Protagoras at length and will refer by name to political figures like Pericles and Alcibiades, who are at the center of the events Thucydides discusses. Further traces of Thucydides' historicism can be found in many places, as at *Laws* 634c, where a general principle is applied to a hypothetical man who is inspecting the laws in detail, "wishing to see at the same time the truth and what is best."[7] Plato does let Gorgias take the stage in showing how rhetoric exercises what amounts to a political domination over other professions (*Gorgias*, 452–56). But when he expounds the effect of airs and waters in specific locales on their inhabitants (*Laws*, 747d), he is grazing the theories in "Airs, Waters, Places" of the Hippocrates whom he does not cite, though he does mention his theories in the *Phaedrus* (270c)[8] and refers to his person once elsewhere (*Protagoras*, 311b). Of course, analogies to the practice and presuppositions of medicine are a standard resource for Plato.

2.

Plato's constant awareness of a military dimension to his political speculations shows in the conservative, nearly Homeric focus of his assumptions, while his reconstitution of the military element and his subjection of it to recombination appears in the obliquity with which he characteristically introduces the subject.

In the *Republic*, when Socrates proposes to "make in theory [or "in speech"] a city from the beginning" (369c),[9] the military is introduced very soon, at a third stage (373e), after the production of sustenance and the provision for trade. He is inventing his society from scratch, and while his originality, once again, shows in the fact that he does start from scratch, his conservatism, a corollary of his attention to history, shows in this military provision. The very name for his philosopher rulers, the "guardians" (φύλακες), retains the motive of the military element, and these are said to combine philosophical and military characteristics, "philosophical and spirited and quick and strong by nature for us would be the prospective beautiful-and-good guardian of the city" (376c).[10]

Glaucon here has been praised for his courage at the battle of Megara (368a). It is proposed that it is permissible to lie to enemies in war (382c). The *Charmides* opens with Socrates' friends surprised to see him returning from the battle of Potidaea "where others of our friends had died" (153c). The *Theaetetus* is framed by Theaetetus' being a promising young philosopher-mathematician who fell in battle. Associations among philosophy, virtue, and love of battle, play through the dialogue. Alcibiades praises Socrates as a fellow soldier in the *Symposium*. Phaedrus in his discourse there adduces an army of lovers as invincible and measures the strength of love in Achilles, Patroclos, Orpheus, and Alcestis by whether they are cowards or not. Calling Orpheus a coward is unconventional in fact and procedure, but using a conventional—indeed, a Homeric—standard of measure. This army of lovers throws into relief Plato's more puzzling combinations of love and war. Politics enters the combination too when he has Phaedrus assert that it is *paidika*, youths in a protégé love relationship, who later develop into politicians.

The military comes up persistently in Plato's work, an undercurrent-substitution for the preoccupation of Herodotus and Thucydides with military history. At the same time it never rises to a theory of the dominance of conflict, such as may be deduced from Thucydides or is stated by Heraclitus: "War, the father of all and of all the king, shows some gods and others men, makes some slaves and others free" (B53).

Er at the end of the *Republic* lies on the funeral pyre from battle, but the concerns he communicates in his reported discourse leave warfare far behind. While Plato is Homeric in the centralization of war, he expands Homer's psychology away from war. The friend-foe opposition is not accepted from Thrasymachus, who as a Sophist rationalize∶

the Homeric assumptions, but the dialogue moves powerfully beyond this stage. So there is the puzzle of gentleness and fierceness in some souls (*Republic* 375c). Harshness and gentleness are in an instability for Plato in ways that would have been inconceivable for Homer. As he says in the *Laws*, (766a1–4) "Man, as we say, is gentle; nevertheless, if he happens to have a correct education and a fortunate nature, he will usually be the most godlike and gentle creature, but if not sufficiently and well raised, he can be more savage than anything that ever was on earth."[11]

Now when Socrates evolves his "city from scratch" in the *Republic*, his set of classes already differs from the social-contract formulation of the earlier argument with Thrasymachus. He goes from providers of food clothing and shelter, to providers of tools for these, to importers and merchant traders; and then, through a sketched development, to providers of luxury. Luxury then entails a necessity (paradoxically, as it were) for the soldiers who will be necessary to defend the borders because luxury causes an expansion to the edge where defense is necessary. This *Lebensraum* concept, a specifically Greek geopolitics, then mounts a whole puritanically controlled group of guardians. At this point the sharp division between necessity and luxury may be said to be a new puritanism in Greece, a distinction found only in the Spartan society Plato admired and in the vague parameters of such maxims as "nothing to excess."

There is the general Greek assumption of the citizen soldier, which is passed over for Kallipolis when Plato has Socrates make the agreed point that there must be professional soldiers rather than the citizen-soldiers of the Athenian democracy. A luxury defined by a military-oriented puritanism evidences a new Greek self-consciousness. Luxury is to be protected by those who are confined by discipline to necessity, the military. Necessity defends luxury.[12] This process, a scheme for history though not a history in itself, sets into place something like Herodotus' contrast between Greeks and Persians and also posits a war-ready society like Homer's on grounds quite different from Homer's conception of a harmonious agricultural society, in which the very notion (but not the fact) of luxury would be foreign.

3.

In his handling of religion Plato's expansiveness of an approach towards history allows him completely to incorporate the range of existing Greek practice, as he notably does in the *Laws* and elsewhere, while at the same time mutating his attention toward ideal forms for theological notions about evil, the soul, and the demiurge.[13] The whole of Plato's enterprise gives every evidence of having been conceived so as to stay open to the religious in the full social process he draws on, and also in the unitary vision he aims at for the soul and the Forms. As Dover delineates the "accepted" morality of Greece in Plato's time,[14] the vocabulary and even the oppositions it offers are inescapably that from which Plato begins. Yet he borrowed deeply from esoteric traditions as well, as he performed transmutations on all these in the process of elaborating his broad, detailed, and repeated expositions of eschatological views about the soul and the afterlife.

Plato's acceptance of the layered historical gamut of Greek religion shows itself all but inertly, as though providing a base to which the reaches of speculation may return in triumphant orthodoxy. However complex the incorporation of Orphic and Pythagorean elements in Plato is argued to be, it does not involve the social correlative of splitting off into an esoteric social group: a sect. To that degree the Academy is "professional" and its historical syncretism, which amounts to a historical consciousness, allows for it the continuity with the mainstream of Greek society that can manifest itself as an acceptance of such systems and obligations as the military, as well as of the standard religious festivals. When in the *Sophist* he describes the elenchic process as a laying bare, learning is connected to purity, and this system is praised as "best and most prudent" (βελτίστη καὶ σωφρονέστατη). Further connected to this is the strange notion of a blessedness, an εὐδαιμονία to be measured by the standard of purification even for the [Persian] Great King (230d).

Plato is so full of data about religious practices that his work can be used, as Detienne and others use it, for a quarry to document practices anthropologically. As Detienne says in this connection, however, "Paradoxically it fell to a philosopher, more lucid than others, to let it be known that the world of illusion was inhabited by memory and by tradition."[15] And Plato's manipulations, added to the obscure differences of the place of religion in Greek society from our own, might tempt a Paul Veyne to read a Roman skepticism or indifference about religion back into Plato, all the more because Plato revises so deeply, starting with the posture of a Socrates who combines piety with radical questioning.[16] And how thoroughly Socrates breaks the mould is thrown into stark relief by Marina Barabas.[17] At the same time the conservative religious practices will stay full-blown in all their force and nuance for the Kallipolis, while the whole society that includes them is changed from the ground up—an implausible proposition, of course, but the only one that makes sense to Plato. A kind of stereoscopic vision of wholly new and wholly old governs his conception of ideal polity, and this bears on, limits, and confuses his sense of how an art in obligatory attunement with religion functions in the city.

Xenophon (*Memorabilia* 1.1.6–8; 4.7.10) says that Socrates advised his friends to consult oracles on various occasions. "The gods reserved to themselves what was not clear to men." In his religious practice, Socrates was attentive to sacrifice, sought responses from Delphi, and said prayers (*Memorabilia*, 1.3,1–4). He was fond of quoting Hesiod's "As far as you are able sacrifice to the eternal gods."[18] Of "oracles, statues, altars, and shrines," it says in the *Laws* (738c) "A legislator should avoid the slightest interference with all such matters."

Religion interweaves through the discussion about laws controlling access to wine (*Laws*, 645–61). This discussion a) shuts out absolutes, b) connects (as it says) the public and the private (647b1), c) raises the question of the unity of the virtues, d) ties in with Dionysian religion, e) relates concretely the laws of the state both actual and proposed. Book Two of the *Laws* continues the discussion from the angle of regulating symposia; it refers to many gods, to the Muses, and Apollo and Dionysus together (653).

Plato's manipulation, within his acceptance, of religious practice is well exemplified by the presentation of the festival of Bendis at the beginning of the *Republic*, as it continues in overtone accompaniment of the *elenchos*. "Let us carry out this feast" |εἰστιάσθω| (354). It is Thrasymachus who says this, and he may be mildly ironic, but still it is said and the metaphor-reminiscence is continued. In this brief return to the religious festival the term "feasting" is first introduced by

Socrates himself, who gives the word to "fill out for me the rest of the festival."[19] Speaking with metaphorical overtones in the last of his agreement-replies, Thrasymachus is cutting off discourse by not offending the others (as he earlier said), but at the same time he is working to complete the standard responses. So that religion sets the stage for his here fully denying, or refraining from affirming, the large final Socratic proposition, "Virtue is the justice of the soul" (ἀρετή ψυχῆς δικαιοσύνη). Consequently his metaphor about celebrating the festival is not only metaphoric, since the festivals often included feasts, and Socrates' complete satisfaction would make him a happier participant in the religious festival. There is also the secular sharing in food, and his verb here points to the secular good feeling evidenced in this very visit to the home of Cephalus and Polemarchus.

The term "gluttons" (λίχμοι) continues the metaphor, since the phrase "eagerness for the next course" means moving ahead to the "banquet" of discussion. Religion and the elenchos are thus coupled in the figure of speech. This eagerness, too, is ironic. In that sense the discussants have not cleared things up, and Socrates "doesn't know," as he is about to say. But he also does know, and in the ironic sense he is not a glutton, but rather proceeding measuredly as he broaches the still unfilled (hence denying the earlier "fill out"). Questions are indeed left, as he thinks, and Thrasymachus does too. The irony points one way to completion and a closing out in "ignorance"; it points the other way toward actualizing the gains of the discussion so far—and in the interplay of religious, social, and philosophical contexts that is coded through the "let the feast be carried forth" of Thrasymachus; he is thus an unwittingly "just" contributor to the cooperative discussion which his participation in the *elenchos* exemplifies and this interplay designates. Hence, in an unironic as well as an ironic sense, Thrasymachus is "blest," "*makarios*," and the religious tinge of that word embraces him too.

4.

The expansive flexibility of Plato's access to a historical consciousness is deployed through his foregrounding of such persons in the dialogue, a startling fusion of the practises of drama with those of ordinary prose discourse. The historicity of the persons themselves is not especially foregrounded, but it is present in compacted form just from the mention of the person's name. Characteristically a wealth of persons gather for the dialogue. Parmenides, Protagoras, Agathon, Nicias, Euthydemus, Adeimantus, Glaucon, Cephalus, Prodicus, Gorgias, Meno, Hermocrates, Aristophanes, Socrates himself and notably Alcibiades, stand at a point in time that a given dialogue indicates. Brought to bear on that moment of time is the elaborate sequence in time of the political and characterological actions of such a person as the Alcibiades of the *Symposium*, behind whom lies much of the action Thucydides recounts, as well as his actions after the time that Thucydides breaks off. There is still more in the private life of Alcibiades—especially his connection with Socrates—that lies outside of Thucydides' presentation but that is felt as bearing on the presence of the figure in the dialogue. These persons connect in a society, as Field has reconstructed their connections.[20] But the connections do not end there. The density of these unmentioned associations permit the philosophical concerns of the dialogue to range through historical assocation, now and then touching base on some specific event. The historical dimension stands, having been imported through the person-orientation of the dialogue form, but it exercises control only when it is invoked.

This act of fictionalizing actual people from the recent past and setting them into situations that lightly reflect the concerns they are set to discuss is something completely new in Greece. It can only derive from an expansive security in Plato's historical consciousness. The correspondence of a moment in the dialogues to historical actuality can attain complexity, and it always has a shadow of development as well as a temporal locus, as when the very aged Parmenides, with all his doctrine behind him, is imagined to confront the very young Socrates with all his philosophical activity before him. History is strongly in the picture when the exhibitionistic, jaded, gifted, wily Alcibiades is imagined in the *Symposium* on the eve of his destruction of the herms and before the first of the long exiles that will lead him to death. The casting of these persons into fictiveness opens up the dialogue into the multiple possibilities that it is implicitly declaring it has mastered and will master. It can control the actuality of interpreting history not by analyzing actual events, the manner of Thucydides or Herodotus, but by projecting persons into actual situations so as to cast the sort of solution-puzzles that the Greek tragedians present, while remaining free of the tragedians' subjection to legend.

The historical and the dramatic setting interweave with the theoretical questions that the dialogue mounts. As the giant discussion about justice gets under way in the *Republic*, we are presented with Cephalus, the good man in ordinary life. He is old, but youths are present; so both youth and old age are compassed. Very soon Cephalus leaves for the festival from which the others have just come. But his dodging the *elenchos* does not subject him to it, as it does the Sophist Thrasymachus. This historicized and dramatized counterpart of Gorgias, Protagoras, and Isocrates is not singled out exclusively when he engages the *elenchos*. The dramatization brings it about that Cephalus' middle-of-the-road situation is accepted as a possibility, implicitly qualifying the maxim of the *Apology*, "The unexamined life is not worth living." Cephalus, as an ordinary life counterpart to the vast theory, matches the *elenchos* about justice undertaken by Polemarchus, Thrasymachus, Glaucon, and Adeimantus—the last two hinting that Plato's concerns are not far off, since they are Plato's brothers.[21]

In the *Meno* the conclusion trails out on a sort of truncated historical vision. Virtuous men of the recent past, Themistocles and Pericles, are matched to their sons, who puzzlingly do not follow their virtues; this puzzle is solved in the *Republic*, Book Eight, when the reaction of sons to the ethos of fathers forms the basis for the complete fourfold cyclic development of society.

Change is built into Plato's political scheme itself. He is often concerned with principles of social change. One general principle for it is enunciated in the *Laws* (641c2–3), "Culture brings also victory, but victory sometimes brings lack of culture."[22]

In the *Statesman* (269–70), all human useful human occupations are figured as those of herdsmen and statesmen. The progressive division of "flocks" goes back to the beginning (*arché*), and the speaker moves at this point to a *mythos*. The first one offered is a quarrel between Atreus and Thyestes about astronomy. Then the demiurge momentarily reverses the course of the stars, which has the the startling effect of also reversing the life course: grown men get younger, grow backwards into infancy, and disappear. Here is offered not a cycle but an entire reversal of time, an index of Plato's free play with temporalities. This engages briefly but totally still another dimension of time than the opening on the past or the millennial enlargement of the scale.

As it says in the *Laws* (636a4–5), "It would seem to be hard for that which concerns polities to come about unambiguously in act and in theory equally."[23] Plato consistently, as he moves from level to level in the *Republic*, retains both the individual and the social in view, so as to permit, through adjusting them, the shift onto another level, as he had begun doing by the large-and-small letters analogy which first framed them. This, with all its inadequacies, is only the first among many sidesteps in the dialogue. Now, when he has settled the four virtues and the relations among them, the men who can maintain them permanently for themselves, turn out to be the philosophers, who as rulers can do the same for the state. Who these philosopher-rulers are, and what this Parmenides-like permanence is, now unfolds as a *perceptual* (Sun), *structural* (Line) and *genetic* (Cave) explanation. Having established one peak in his discourse, Socrates returns to the base question of justice, moving out into the theory of how mutations come about in the four (or five) types of government, a theoretical summary of the past. Questions about the fit of justice—always the ongoing subject—into such a temporal scheme lead to the millennial sequences of past, present, and future in the myth of Er at the conclusion.

"They will die as old men and hand on another such life to their offspring." This is said of an earlier stage in the hypothetical city (372d). It looks back thematically at Cephalus and ahead to Er. But it does not by itself provide the dynamic principle for historical sequence that Plato has Socrates move into after he has seemed to finish unfolding the principles the guardians are to honor and internalize.

At the end of Book Seven Socrates sums up, using the good itself (τὸ ἀγαθὸν αὐτό) as a pattern (παραδείγμα, 540a). He resumes over the whole center of the dialogue, picking up at the beginning of Book Eight where he had left off in Book Three (as he remarks, 543c) the homology between individual dispositions and types of social management or polities:

"Are you aware, then," said I, "that there must be as many types of character among men as there are [forms of] polities?"   (544d–e).

These polities mutate through series of psychological interaction, from which the organization of Kallipolis would immunize them. Thus released from diachrony, they would lose their subjection to the phases aristocracy, timocracy, oligarchy, democracy, tyranny (monarchy being curiously left out here, or included by implication in the first two). They would also, if managed as the discussion recommends, lose their vulnerability to the Hesiodic declination, and they would also lose the contrast of Hesiod's gold and silver to his bronze and iron ages (547a–b).[24] In this synchrony Socrates resembles a maker of statues (ἀνδροποιός, 540c). This new synchrony, in its immutability, once again (he does not remark) resembles in thought the closedness of Homeric society.

Already back in Book Two, discussing justice, he has introduced the puzzling case of the ring of Gyges, which removes the question to another society and another form of government, though one which accords more with the state of the *Republic* than does Athens, since it envisages a royalist authoritarian structure and not a democracy; in Plato's state, as in a kingdom, the subjects are obliged to be totally candid with the guardians. Glaucon's case will re-root the question in an actual Hellenic society, and therefore it will answer to the injunction not yet invoked of seeing the individual problems in the social. The monthly meeting of the shepherds is a season ritual on the "good king" model. The earthquake and the naked giant are proleptically analogous to the Cave, to Er, and to the *Timaeus*.

They relate that he was a shepherd in the service of the ruler at that time in Lydia, and that after a great deluge of ruin and an earthquake the ground opened and a chasm appeared in the place where he was pasturing; and they say that he saw and wondered and went down into the chasm; and the story goes that he beheld other marvels there and a hollow bronze horse with little doors, and that he peeped in and saw a corpse within, as it seemed, of more than mortal stature, and that there was nothing else but a gold ring on his hand, which he took off and went forth. And when the shepherds held their customary assembly to make their monthly report to the king about the flocks he attended wearing the ring. So as he sat there it chanced that he turned the collet of the ring towards himself, towards the inner part of his hand, and when this took place they say that he became invisible.   (359d–e, tr. Paul Shorey)

Now there is a problem about the ring of Gyges that Plato does not discuss. This is what one might conjecture to be the historical circumstance of someone invisible. Gyges could not, in fact, over the long run or even the short, escape detection because the process of inference would reveal his existence and his involvement. He would then, visible or invisible, be caught in the shame (*aidos*) that the lack of which, in the *Protagoras*, makes a man inhuman. He would also have problems of bare survival (when and how to eat) as well as of socialization (with whom?). But Plato, asking the question about how such a man might handle the imperatives of justice, lets it stand in its (suppositious) historicity. The event floats as a history tinged with legend in the slightly remote area discussed by Herodotus, Lydia, and of a king.[25]

The key structural analogy that small letters are to big as the individual to the state (368d) implies a) a graduated process, b) a distinct fitting together, c) a total correspondence (if the letter analogy holds), d) a composite reference to both when taken together, e) a lack of reference—empty sound—if the letters were to be taken singly.[26]

Two principles will have been combined here by the end. First is the principle explicitly adduced of an analogy between individual structure and social structure, a principle introduced as orienting the whole discussion of social structure in the first place. This occupies Plato through the whole center of the *Republic*, Books Two through Seven. The second principle, largely suspended until Book Eight, is the historicizing principle of a causally intricate mutation from one social structure to another, based on the same analogy of individual temper to social form. This principle goes beyond the developmental perspective of either Herodotus or Thucydides, since it provides through its long series for a recursion. Both these principles, if seen in the light of Greek traditions, do not entirely part company with a Homeric perspective. The first principle, the analogy between the individual and the social, is a corollary to the closed society, homogeneous enough so that its members conform in all respect to its universal codes. Even the second principle, that of historical mutation, in so far as the society works its way round to an initial position, dimensionalizes the time sequence represented in the *Iliad* by Nestor's memory of earlier battles and the heroes of an older generation. But while Plato's second principle also resembles Hesiod's five ages of man in offering a sequence of dominant psychologies, it differs from Hesiod's presentation by providing for a causality of interactions in the roles taken by members of the large social group, individually and collectively. In this, however, it resembles the causal pattern presented by Thucydides, who does not apply his causality, even in the Pentekonteteia or in the Archeology, to the large sequences of time envisaged by the myth of Er and the *Timaeus*.

In the *Republic* especially the course of Greek history stands at Plato's disposal, in a way beyond the resources of any of his predecessors except Herodotus and Thucydides. It stands ready to be drawn on for illustration in the detail and in the pattern. So the typology of states in Books Eight and Nine, along with the principles under which they mutate, underlies the discussion and can be drawn on at any time. In Book One Thrasymachus offers an oversimple and unhistoricized version of the later governmental typologies. "Some cities are governed by tyrants, in others democracy rules, in others aristocracy" (338c). He reduces them to mere power: "I affirm that the just is nothing else than the advantage of the stronger" (338d). This could be taken for a more aggressive summary of the underlying thesis of Thucydides in such nodes of tension as the Melian dialogue, and Plato's dimensionalizing historicization would be itself a revision thereof. As Thrasymachus goes on his view remains still not far from the gist of Thucydides.

Arguments and debates about tyranny, oligarchy, and monarchy are often mounted as a way of criticizing democracy, as Raaflaub has analyzed them. These debates get folded into tragedy, which therefore reflects them, as in Euripides *Suppliants*, and elsewhere.[27] Plato, however, dimensionalizes these types on a time line, while at the same time he abstracts them:

> Are you aware, then ... that there must be as many types of character among men as there are [forms of] polities? Or do you suppose that polities come "from the oak and the rock" and not from the characters of those in the cities?   (544d)

The comparativist particulars set the pattern at a remove of scrutiny, interposing a level of something approaching Max Weber's thought-types (*Gedankentypen*). Plato's phrase is "the schema of a polity in a rationale" (λόγωι σχῆμα πολιτείας): "if we may outline the schema of a polity in a rationale and not carry it out precisely, since even an outline may suffice for us to see the most just and the most unjust man" (548d). While not abandoning specific Greek states, Plato has not yet put himself at the synchronic remove of the abstraction in Aristotle's *Politics*. The model types are preponderantly Greek, but he does touch on other variants. Finally in the *Laws* (756e) he sets up an elaborate election scheme proposed by the Athenian, "the election come about this way would strike a mean between monarchy and democracy—a mean that a polity should always strike."[28]

The first type he discusses in the *Republic*, the timocratic, is already a historicized descent from his ideal among the five types, the aristocratic, to which the Kallipolis he has been outlining since Book Four would correspond. The timocratic is explicitly historicized to begin with as the "Cretan or the Spartan" (544c), anticipating the values of the *Laws*, which places an old Cretan and an old Spartan at the center of its demonstrations. Very soon a principle of change is required by inner dynamism in a state because "however small [a state] be, if it is of one mind, it is impossible to be moved" (545d–e).[29] He here also raises the possibility of a Homeric description of "revolution" (στάσις), then goes immediately to cycles of plants and bodily fertility.

"Revolution" begins through unseasonable births, in wrong ratio, so that gold and silver, inclining to virtue in his adaptation of Hesiod's ages of man, pull against bronze and iron. "At the same time a mixture of iron with silver and bronze with gold will generate an inequality and an inharmonious anomaly [ἀνομοιότης καὶ ἀνωμαλία], and from that war and hostility as the Muses say" (547d).

This equals a mix of aristocracy and oligarchy in a second phase that will have three qualities: an imitation of aristocracy, an imitation of oligarchy, and a third quality of its own. Plato then gives a list (547d) of the particular characteristics in this phase and an analysis of the dynamics of interaction, wherein men in this polity are avid for wealth like those in an oligarchy and for buying "private love nests" (548a). They will be miserly, will flee the law, and will prefer gymnastics to music. "With high spirits ruling [θυμοειδους κρατοῦντος] they will love strife and honor." In the character corresponding to this polity,[30] there will also be a specific problem at the time of hoarding gold and silver (548b–c).

At a next stage slaves will urge the son of a family (who loves wealth the more the older he grows, 549) to punish debtors; and listening to them on the one hand and to the father on the other, he will strike a balance in the soul between the rational (λογιστικόν) and the desiring (ἐπιθυμητικόν), becoming a lover of honor and of strife; the individual man will resemble the social polity he inhabits.

All this interaction leads to a further type, straight oligarchy, which is contrasted with plutocracy (550d), as always "by hypothesis" (κατὰ τὴν ὑπόθεσιν). In oligarchy respect for wealth gains over respect for *arete*, and this process generates a split city, the rich set against the poor (551c), "always plotting against one another."[31]

A law comes into being that enforces a wealth qualification for rule by arms and "terrorization" (φοβήσαντες). Under this rule men, neglecting virtue, acquire money just by selling their property, rather than undertaking productive activity (552a–c). They risk becoming drones, and do. The son of the timocratic man sees his father thus misgovern and lose his position, collects property himself, and has become oligarchic. He loses sight of honor and becomes governed wholly by greed, imposing this principle on others (553a–d). He would not be without conflicts in himself[32] but would be a double man (διπλοῦς), "his better desires gaining over his worse" (554c–d). As at every stage, there is an exact psychological correspondence between ruler and the oligarchical city (555b)—while there are also present the seeds of the dynamism that will cause the historical process to mutate into the third stage here, democracy: the impoverished who are not ill born (οὐκ ἀγεννεῖς, 555d) will plot against the rich, whose children are idlers (556c–d), and the strong poor man will see this when he stands beside the weak rich man in battle. So the poor rise up and form a democracy. In what is possibly a pointedly ironic description "this could be [κινδυνεύει] the most beautiful of all polities" but it offers too many choices, becoming "anarchic and variegated" (ἄναρχος καὶ ποικίλη, 558c4).

The individual develops in a drift towards ungovernable appetites (560c–61c), though he may recover some temperance, but will keep vacillating (561d–e), till then comes the fourth stage, described, with continued irony, as "most beautiful." This is tyranny. The city seeks liberty (ἐλευθερία), which brings it pliable leaders (562e). Parents court children for agreement, slaves become equal to masters and women to men (563b). The counterreaction changes it (μετα-βάλλειν, 564a) to excess of subjection (δουλεία). There are three kinds of persons in a democratic state: forceful leaders, an insistent populace, and the cultivators of their own farms (565a). The state comes under the attention of the last. Seeing the stagnation of the other groups, they become "unwilling oligarchs" (ὀλιγαρχικοὶ γίγνονται οὐχ ἑκόντες). A man of this sort becomes first a protector (προστάτης) and then a tyrant through a growing appetite for control. If he is exiled and returns (566a–b), he becomes more severe (566–69). But his changing private army will have to be maintained and will fight ever more fiercely against the protests of the people—given over to the "wild and lawless Form of desires in every person" (572c–d).[33]

Throughout all this account Plato's carefully managed slight distance of abstraction couples the types of government and their relation to human psychology in such a way that his comparison of large with small, social with individual, can uncoil in a presumed historical series without coming unraveled. The force is maintained and historicized of his common phrase "in private and publicly" (ἰδίαι καὶ δημοσίαι). This effectually allows for four simultaneous levels against which the Kallipolis is measured and fleshed out, a dialectical possibility quite beyond his predecessors and, in that complication, beyond even such successors as Aristotle. Throughout this series there are envisaged a private real historical life, a private ideal existence, a public real life based on and including the history of specific states, and finally a public ideal combining considerations of the other three, the Kallipolis.

Aristotle's *Politics*, by contrast, while it is a systematic advance upon Plato's scheme, has sacrificed the openness of this remarkable dimensionality. He condenses the analogy of individual to society into a simple assertion of congruity: "It is the same for a single man and for the state" (*Nicomachean Ethics*, 1094b).[34] Presenting his own polity from scratch in the *Politics*, Aristotle gives up Plato's temporal flexibility, merely drawing atemporally on illustrations throughout, and in his elaborate critique of the proposals in the *Republic* and the *Laws* (1261–265). (Of course Aristotle approaches these proposals systematically, which is the way they are presented, while I am taking them at the angle of their historical modulations.) In his occasional recourse throughout to geopolitical illustration, Aristotle criticizes individual states and drops the Platonic mix of levels and times. Yet he stays with Plato's types of government, comparing them atemporally rather than examining their mutations. Good are monarchy and aristocracy; bad are tyranny, oligarchy, and extreme democracy. Here, too, the presentation remains atemporal, and the historical illustrations are simply illustrative.

More flexible, indeed, than Aristotle's are the whole procedures of Herodotus and Thucydides, and bolder in a confrontation of ultimates is Aeschylus in the *Oresteia*, where an intensity of poetic statement and a radical paradox of dramatic situation are brought to bear on solving an Athenian judicial procedure in relation to Athenian society. The same is true for Sophocles in the *Antigone*. Yet the easy abandonment of all the tensions in such questions can be illustrated by Xenophon's passing remark in the *Hellenica* (B, iii, 32ff), where he discusses types of government in practical, present context and simply says that "the best government seems to be that of the Spartans."[35] This is, of course, close to Plato's own view, which is much aspectualized and modified as always—and historicized in a way beyond the historian Xenophon.

Plato moves on, and back, in Book Nine of the *Republic* once more to the just and happy man, measuring him by analogy to a type of government, and mathematicizing the difference between the king and the tyrant (587–88). But he shifts at the end, in the myth of Er, to the macrohistorical sequence with which he begins the *Timaeus*. The last clause of the *Republic* is macrohistorical: it refers in round numbers to a millennial journey, "both here and in the thousand-year journey which we have gone through, may we fare well." The summary offered at the beginning of the *Timaeus* refers to the main theme of the *Republic*, "the chief point is what sorts of things and out of what sorts of men [a polity] would become best." But then he soon goes on to delineate a still larger macrohistorical perspective, shifting from that history to its own comprehensive system comprising cosmology, physiology, and eschatology all together, setting the union of body and soul into an "eternal nature" (φύσις αἰώνιος, 37d). The stretch of time is personalized and historicized in the report from Critias, whose grandfather at ninety told the ten-year-old boy what the aged Solon told him of the history he had brought back from Egypt. Solon is deemed to span a still longer period in his grasp by being called the "freeest" of poets (ἐλευθερώτατος) so that not even Homer and Hesiod are to be "more esteemed" than he (20c).

Solon is said to have been told by the Egyptian priest that nine thousand years ago the Greeks and the Egyptians had the same social structure and customs, and the Greeks stood against the conquerors from Atlantis but were finally overcome. This long-range history offers abundant lessons: "you will find many patterns (παραδείγματα) of things for you now" (23e). The Egyptian priest also says that all Greeks are children (22a), implying a congenital incapacity to absorb the very wisdom he is offering them through Solon—who is then implicitly presumed to transmit that wisdom, along the lines of this fable, in the reforms that he did enact, not mentioned by Plato here. But contemplating the order of the universe will possibly restore these millennial Athenians to their former state (27a–b).[36] What the priest offers, in fact, turns to a remote and legendary past to provide what the systematic inquiry of the *Republic* claims to provide, a justice-centered and harmonious state—and always in a historical perspective, as though the long view of the *Timaeus* were a supplement and corollary to the *Republic*—to which, indeed, it refers. In the *Timaeus*, (25e) Critias remarks on how close to the Atlantis is Plato's version in the *Republic*, told "yesterday." And such a long-range perspective can come in at any time, as when in the *Laws* the Athenian refers to "the length of time ... and the changes in it" (676a7–8),[37] making it clear that he means a longer span than recoverable human history. In the *Critias*, which picks up Solon's account again, the Athenians are said through the cataclysm of nine thousand years previous, which also destroyed Atlantis, to have lost their previous "virtues and laws" (109e), and a measure is offered, in ten-thousand-year cycles, for still other natural cataclysms. States remotely past (Atlantis) and future (ideal Kallipolis) measure and replace the present, unnamed polity loosely identified with the Athens of 490, or of the period 430 to 350, roughly Plato's lifetime.

The past is idealized but Plato expands it in ways that keep legendary history continuous with real history. If the story about Atlantis is taken as a myth, it differs in its referential structure from all the others in Plato's work to which we give that name.[38] They are visionary, permanent or recursive, allegorical or easily allegorized, and harmonizable—to use the very terms of the *Critias*—with the *logoi* it fills in and opens out from. The *Critias* offers itself as an account of an actual, though remote past, validated in its very disappearance by earthquakes and other large-scale physical phenomena. This is repeatedly described as a *logos* (and so by inference not a *mythos*) even if a *logos* that carries with it an account also of the genesis of the gods. It refers to a drug but also to a knowledge of drugs (106b5). It offers a much further preliminary definition of discourse. "Mythologizing" (or "tale-telling," μυθολογία, 110a) is paired with inquiry into "matters of old" and actually applied to history, for which Solon is cited as a source. Some of this terminology, and the construction of a remote past, resembles, again, the terminology and procedure of the Thucydides of the Archaeology.

Harvey Scodel asserts in a different connection that for Plato "unity is epistemologically prior to diversity."[39] For Plato's writing this is just the question. With Plato, for reasons of the very dramatic structure of the dialogues, to which Scodel is quite sensitive, there is no way out of the quandary for *either* unity or diversity, except in arbitrary hermeneutic emphasis. In the *Charmides* there is a discussion about the knowledge of knowledge (ἐπιστήμης ἐπιστήμη), and this possibility comes about through the very conception of the dialogue form, as distinct from and beyond holding dialogue in the marketplace like Socrates. Plato's grasp of the comprehensive and flexible coupling of history with system through fluidity of presentation is inventive, well beyond Socrates in type, as in doctrine. The expansion of the consciousness he both exemplifies in his person and codifies in his writing is correlative to the expansion and intrication of questions of the Form and its relation to particular manifestations, including problems about the Third Man and the like. The particular consciousness of history that he engages into his work is a necessary accompaniment to the whole. Instead of a phenomenological reduction, so to speak, his angling of persons and times and types of times in the dialogues executes an amplification, an enormous one. This historical and historicizing dimension to Plato's dialogues is crucial to their philosophical bearing, which is not the case with most philosophical discourse before his time or afterwards.

Notes

1. This Number is so complicated and requires so many steps in its arithmetical and geometric calculation, that many scholarly studies are attached to solving it. See James Adam, *The Republic of Plato* (Cambridge: Cambridge University Press, 1965 [1902]), I, 264–318.

2. He discusses the semantic-phonetic basis of *historia* at *Cratylus* 437b. He uses it as "inquiry into nature" (*Phaedo* 96a8), and again as general inquiry coupled with *nous, (Phaedrus* 244c8). In *Sophist* 267e2 *historike* is the adjective for an informed mimesis. And that is all. Plato uses a more old-fashioned sense of the word than does his predecessor Herodotus, who uses the word in a sense that can be made to include the modern sense.

3. Anaximander, B1, διδόναι ... δίκην καὶ τίσιν ἀλλήλοις τῆς ἀδικίας κατὰ τὴν τοῦ χρόνου τάξιν. The Homeric term δίκη receives a comparably intense abstract workout at the hands of Heraclitus (B23, 28, 80, 94, 102).

4. These interactive discussions in historians and tragedians are well schematized by Kurt A. Raaflaub, notably in "Contemporary Perceptions of Democracy in Fifth Century Athens," *Classica et Medievalia*, [Copenhagen], Vol. 40., 1989, 33–69. Raaflaub gives the background for such discussions in the topical focus of literature, back to the Homeric poems, in "Die Anfänge des politischen Denkens bei den Griechen," *Historische Zeitschrift*, Vol 248 (1989), 1–31. As Bruno Gentili says, "In reality the problem of the techniques of cultural communication occupies a large space in Plato's thought and represents one of its nodal points, both on the plane of theoretical reflection and on that of his activity as a writer" ... As Giovanni Cerri affirms, "That which interests him is the psychology of reception, the dynamic of communication." Giovanni Cerri, *Platone sociologo della comunicazione*, Prefazione di Bruno Gentili (Milano: Arnoldo Mondadori Editore, 1991), vii, 31.

5. Compare 693d5 and 697c–698.

6. κατὰ φύσιν τὸν Πίνδαρον ἄγειν δικαιοῦντα βιαιότα-τον. A more usual quotation from Pindar, referred to by Plato elsewhere, is one that Herodotus also makes, and somewhat in contradiction with this one, that "Law [or custom] is king of all," (νόμος ὁ παντῶν βασιλεύς).

7. βουλόμενος ἰδεῖν τό τε ἀληθές ἅμα, καὶ τὸ βέλ-τιστον.

8. G. R. F. Ferrari (*Listening to the Cicadas*, 16–17) compares the opening and details of the setting in the *Phaedrus* to the opening of the Hippocratic *Airs, Waters, Places*.

9. τῶι λόγω ἐξ ἀρχῆς ποιῶμεν πόλιν.

10. Φιλόσοφος δὴ καὶ θυμοειδής καὶ ταχύς καὶ ἰσχυρός ἡμῖν τὴν φύσιν ἔσται ὁ μέλλων καλός κἀγαθός ἔσεσθαι φύλαξ πόλεως. This notion of toughness and gentleness in both warriors and guardians is resummarized in the *Timaeus*, 17c–18a.

11. ἄνθρωπος δέ, ὥς φαμεν, ἥμερον, ὁμῶς μὴν παιδείας μὲν ὀρθῆς τυχὸν καὶ φύσεως εὐτυχοῦς, θειότατον ἡμερώτατον τε ζῶιον γίγνεσθαι φιλεῖ, μὴ ἱκανῶς δὲ ἢ μὴ καλῶς τραφὲν ἀγριώτατόν, ὁπόσα φύει γῆ.

12. For necessity and luxury as fundamental categories in Greek thought, mythological and other, see Marcel Detienne, *Les Jardins d'Adonis* (Paris: Gallimard, 1972). The myth of the fast-growing luxury gardens of Adonis is touched on and inspected in the *Phaedrus*, 276b–c (though Detienne does not explicitly discuss Plato's handling of this myth in his book).

13. His range of approaches is outlined by Walter Burkert, *Greek Religion*, 321–37.

14. K. J. Dover, *Greek Popular Thought in the Time of Plato and Aristotle* (Oxford, Blackwell, 1974). Dover bases himself on inferences largely from comedy and from forensic practise, as well as on a careful inspection of the vocabulary that assigns moral values.

15. Marcel Detienne, *L'Invention de la mythologie*, 189.

16. Paul Veyne, *Les Grecs ont-ils cru à leurs mythes*? 151. "For mythical ages according to Plato (*Politicus*, 268e–69b; *Timaeus*, 21a-d; *Laws*, 677d–85e), who rectifies them and believes in them neither more nor less than Thucydides or Pausanias. See Raymond Weil, *L'Archéologie de Platon*, Paris: Klincksieck, 1959, p. 14, 30, 44." Veyne raises telling questions, but his vagueness about assessing Plato shows in his lumping together of Plato in this note with a Thucydides who broke rigorously with myth and a Pausanias who did a loose and relatively uncritical topographic survey hundreds of years later.

17. Marina Barabas, "The Strangeness of Socrates," *Philosophical Investigations*, 9:2 April 1986, 89–109. Barabas presses hard to show that the

portrait of Socrates, even in the *Symposium*, contains a radical imperviousness (her reading of Alcibiades' ascription of *sophrosune* to Socrates' resistance to seduction) against ordinary Greek expectations of social interaction and response. These questions are generalized and explored in depth by Gregory Vlastos, *Socrates: Ironist and Moral Philosopher*. For still further qualification and amplification of Socrates' role, see Alexander Nehamas's review of Vlastos, "Voices of Silence: On Gregory Vlastos' Socrates," *Arion*, Third Series, vol 2, No. 1 (Winter, 1992), 157–86.

18. *Works and Days*, 336, κὰδ δύναμιν δ'ἔρδειν ἱερ'ἀθανάτοισι θεοῖσι.

19. τὰ λοιπά μοι τῆς ἑστιάσεως ἀποπλήρωσον, 352b5.

20. G. C. Field, *Plato and His Contemporaries* (London: Methuen, 1930).

21. An analogy between Cephalus and Socrates is argued by C. D. C. Reeve in *Philosopher-Kings: The Argument of Plato's* Republic (Princeton: Princeton University Press, 1988), 6–7, "striking similarities between Cephalus ... and Socrates ... Both men have avoided injustice and impiety. Both face death with good hope ... Neither knows what justice is [*Apology* 21b4–5] ... Even for Plato, however, Cephalus will not count as completely virtuous: for complete virtue philosophical knowledge is required."

22. παιδεία μὲν οὖν φέρει καὶ νίκην, νίκη δ'ἐνίοτε ἀπαιδευσίαν.

23. χαλεπὸν εἶναι τὸ περὶ τὰς πολιτείας ἀναμφισβη-τήτως ὁμοίως ἔργωι καὶ λόγωι γίγνεσθαι.

24. The opposition between gold and iron is repeated in the *Laws* (645a–b): "so that the gold kind in us would conquer the other kinds, and thus really the myth of virtue about the marvels [equals puppets of the gods] we are would be saved."

25. Here history, once again, fuses into legend. Scholars have been given much trouble by the fact that Plato introduces this quasi-historical case as an instance of the capacity "to do whatever one wills, just or unjust" (359c). Adam (I, 126–27) is convinced that this story cannot refer to the historical Gyges whom Herodotus discusses, but all his evidence is *ex silentio*; Herodotus and other ancient sources do not specifically mention the ring story. Yet it is interesting that there is a thematic link with the story in Herodotus. The giant whom Plato's Gyges spies upon unseen (a foretaste of invisibility) is naked, as is the wife of Caundaules, on whom Herodotus' Gyges also spies unseen. In both cases the clandestine look leads to a change in fortune.

26. At 338–39 Socrates already anticipates the later shift from small to large letters by bringing up what begins as the question of the individual and justice and applies to it the tendency of tyranny, democracy, and aristocracy

"each to enact laws for its own advantage" (338e).

27. See Raaflaub, as cited above, Note 4.

28. Ἡ μὲν αἵρεσις οὕτώ γιγνομένη, μέσον ἂν ἔχοι μοναρχικῆς καὶ δημοκρατικῆς πολιτείας, ἧς ἀεὶ δεῖ μεσεύειν τὴν πολιτείαν.

29. ὁμονοοῦντες δὲ κἂν πάνυ ὀλίγον ἦι, ἀδύνατον κινηθῆναι.

30. Adam, ad loc, notes that these attributes may describe Spartan housing arrangements. In a timocracy the practice of common messes (ξυσσίτια), is also as in Sparta (547d).

31. ἀεὶ ἐπιβουλεύοντας ἀλλήλους.

32. οὐκ... ἀστασίαστος... ἐν ἑαυτῶι.

33. ἄγριον καὶ ἄνομον εἶδος ἑκάστωι ἔνεστι.

34. ταὐτόν ἐστιν ἑνὶ καὶ πόλει.

35. καλλίστη μὲν γὰρ δήπου δοκεῖ πολιτεία εἶναι ἡ Λακεδαιμονίων.

36. Pierre Vidal-Nacquet in *Le Chasseur Noir* (Paris: Maspero, 1981) compares the "things great and wonderful" (μεγάλα καὶ θαυμαστά) of the *Critias* with the same phrase at the beginning of Herodotus. He says Plato takes the Atlantes from Herodotus (4.184–85; *Timaeus* 24e) (343, "Athènes et l'Atlantide.") "But Plato shows us even in this that he presents his native city at two different angles: the city of Athena and the olive is identified with the primitive Athens; the city of Poseidon, master of the horse and of the sea, is incarnated in Atlantis" (345).

37. ἀπό χρόνου μήκους τε καὶ... τῶν μεταβολῶν εν τῶι τοιούτωι.

38. Harry Berger offers some trenchant speculation on this topic in *Second World and Green World* (Berkeley: University of California Press, 1988), 36. "Plato's position is diametrically opposed to that of Critias. By sharply outlining the backward-looking attitude which treats the story as literal while he himself presents it as myth or allegory, Plato conveys both the sense of loss and the act of recovery. This act consists in the dialogue itself: here the remembered image is valued not for its pseudo-historical accuracy but for its cognitive significance as an allegory of loss and recovery. The allegory implies that the soul can never simply return to the past or malinger in its green world but must go the long way around until the sense and image of loss have been transformed into the desire and vision of future fulfillment." [We may accept Berger's framing categories and his questioning without acceding to his conclusion.]

39. Harvey Ronald Scodel, *Diaeresis and Myth in Plato's* Statesman (Göttingen: Vandenhoeck and Ruprecht, 1987), 12. Scodel bases his view on *Philebus* 16b ff.

Chapter 11

Afterword: Philosophy and Poetry

Since Plato is the foundational philosopher par excellence, it is appropriate that much of the contemporary discussion about him is applied, often astutely, to the refinement of the positions he may be taken to have evolved, even though he often changed at least his emphasis and perhaps also his mind, as the chapters above have been partially aimed to show. But it is not my intention to offer any counterpart for Abelard's *Sic et Non*, a work setting up in confrontational passages from the church fathers abundant proof that they spoke on two sides (at least) of a question. It is not just that there is considerable variegation and slippage among Plato's doctrinal positions.

The doctrinal positions themselves, what has counted foundationally as philosophy since shortly after his time, are incommensurately but inextricably connected to another mode of thinking, or other modes, involving both "myth" and "poetry." Eric Havelock has shown how elaborately Plato has resisted the body of myths and procedures of which Homer is a chief transmitter.[1] Yet the component of myth does, of course, remain a large residuum in him. So, for example, he has Socrates declare at a key point of the *Republic* that the classes are to be kept distinct by a more extreme form of myth, the "noble lie" that man is born from the earth (414b–e). Beyond this, Plato has consistently melded traditional myths with his own invented myths, so that the traditional sirens, for example, in the myth of Er at the end of the *Republic* (617b), function in a new way as providing the music of the spheres, and in a new location, the heavens. The Fates are there too (617c–18a), performing their traditional function in a new location and in a context of afterlife judgment for which Plato has invented some elements while drawing still others from mythic tradition. While, of course, he does not use meter, his stylistic rhetorical turns do employ rhythms in a more structured way than, for example, Herodotus and Thucydides do. He allows himself recourse to figurative language freely, sometimes at great length and with great complexity.

Plato does not correspond to his predecessors like Empedocles and Parmenides who cast their thought in verse and also thought poetically, though Aristotle's remark about Empedocles in the *Poetics* has the effect of detaching that writer's thought from his poetry by just characterizing the poetry as added meter.[2] Nor does Plato correspond to Lucretius, who gives a lift through poetry to philosophical positions that mostly existed in Epicurean doctrine before he wrote.[3] Still less does he correspond to a poetic-constructive thinker like Blake, who fuses and combines mythological and allegorical entities in an integrally poetic expression.[4]

What is the propositional force not only of Plato's myths taken by themselves but of the relation between myth and argument in the dialogues? How does the persistence of Socrates' irony bear on this overall question, in addition to its bearing in the separable propositions?

The questions about Plato all belong globally together when they demand with equal force to be treated in isolation: so before we related the myths to the arguments—but also afterwards—we would want to ascertain the role and function of Socrates in the dialogues. How does that role relate to the positions and procedures of the historical Socrates, for which they are the major source (though not of course the only one)? What is the philosophical bearing of the positional backing-and-filling found in such dialogues as the *Meno*, the *Protagoras*, the *Gorgias,* and the *Cratylus* (among others)— especially with reference to the supplementations of myth offered therein? How does one dialogue fit with another, and what is the bearing of groups of dialogues like the *Statesman*, the *Sophist,* and the *Theaetetus* on the whole work? Does this kind of organization relate to the organization of tragedies into tetralogies? The question is germane even though Plato would ban tragedy in an ideal state (*Republic* 603c, 607a; *Laws*, 800–1; 817b), since the groupings of dialogues are in some ways congruous with the groupings of plays into tetralogies, when such groupings have no congruity, so far as we can tell, with the organization of any other treatises at his time or before.

Quite apart from his agreements or disagreements with Plato, Aristotle isolated and centered the propositional side of Plato that he had learned in the Academy and made it normative, or indeed all but wholly determining, for philosophical discourse. This situation makes it all the more difficult for us to recapture the interconnectedness of the kinds of statement in Plato and to find a way of accounting for the large overall statement, his work, into which they enter.

Prevailingly and variously, however, the philosophical propositions, as I have been urging, are set into indissociable conjunction with the metaphoric and the mythic. Both blend in the work but also preserve their distinctive character through the markings in the text that cue them to their interactive functions, so that they resist a resolution into some such final status as the "white mythology" of Derrida.[5] Already in Plato philosophy paradoxically resists full assimilation to metaphor and myth by employing and grounding metaphor and myth in a context of argument.[6] The *Republic* does not just employ a myth at the end and at the high point where the Sun, the Line, and the Cave are extensively presented. It also tends to have Socrates break into figurative language at crucial turning points. Most of the first two books of the *Republic* are so self-contained in their reasonings about the preferability of justice to injustice that they have been taken for a separate treatise. But the transition to the exposition of an ideal state, the Kallipolis, along with all the questions raised by such a conception, takes place not through argument but through analogy, the analogy

of reading large letters (equals the state) when you cannot see the
small (equals the individual):

> Since we are not terribly skillful (δεινοί) it seems to me, I said,
> that we should make the sort of inquiry here that we would if some-
> one had set the task of reading small letters from far off to people
> who do not see very sharply, and then someone got the thought that
> the same letters exist indeed elsewhere, larger and on a larger
> ground. It would appear a godsend, I think, to read the latter first
> and then to examine the smaller ones, if they happen to be the
> same.   (368d)

As the parenthetical qualifications of this last sentence indicate,
this analogy cannot at any point be divorced from the Socratic irony,
which the initial disclaimer of not being terribly skillful continues to
insist on, and yet this analogy is the hinge for a shift on a very large
scale. The analogy carries right on through much of the rest of the
Republic, with all the logical questions left unexamined about how far
and in what ways the structure of the individual in his bearing towards
justice does homologously correspond to the state. The analogous
conception itself is characterized not as any result from an *elenchos*
but as a godsend or windfall (ἕρμαιον). This term, attributing such a
find colloquially to Hermes, may or may not have a live metaphorical
force. But the term "skillful," δεινός, powerfully mounts the Socratic irony while delicately overrriding it. On the limiting side,
δεινός abjures lack of skillfulness as a standard maieutic ploy for
advancing the discourse: the only thing you know is that you do not
know. Often that ploy sets off the supposedly knowing against the
supposedly ignorant, but the latter, in the person of Socrates, turns out
to be an understater, an εἴρων, who is revealed as a sort of ringer in
the game of argument.

The plural here, however, δεινοί, downplays the side of the term
that would distinguish Socrates from the other speakers. All those present, who may stand for all human beings generally, are from that
vantage in the same boat. Their sight does not go very far, and so they
need such aids as the "large letters"—and the metaphoric analogy
that mounts the large letters. They are caught with the approximative
limitations of human, as opposed to divine, language as these limitations are expounded in the *Cratylus* and elsewhere. At the same time

sight is itself one of the chief metaphorical conceptions of the *Republic*. Sight governs the whole relation to the Sun in that elaborate analogy. And sight also is the key determinant in the later exposition of the ascent from the Cave. The root for sight, *vid*, is enclosed in the term for Form, εἶδος. All of these considerations bear on how we are to read "deinos" here, in its relation to sight, and all are somewhat suspended as the analogy they ambiguously introduce takes over.

After an expanded demonstration that has continued, along with other topics, for several books, the congruence between the individual and the state is called a dream and a god-led chance occurrence, "Completely, therefore, has this dream (ἐνύπνιον) been perfected for us we said we would surmise, that straightway as we begun to found the state by the help of some god we chanced to come upon a beginning and some type of justice" (443b–c). But added to this qualification and mediation—with the same set towards language as in the "windfall" from Hermes of the earlier characterization—the justice under examination is further qualified in the next sentence as a "sort of image of justice," εἴδωλόν τι τῆς δικαιοσύνης. Then later the congruence is spoken of as a pattern of a perfect fulfillment, a *paradeigma* (472c).

Shifting ground to ask what current Greek states would need to attain this ideal, Socrates states that the change would not be small or easy. The process is once more referred to a metaphor: "I proceed on the very point which we compare to the greatest wave; and it will be said, even if it will dash absolutely like a wave in cachinnations of laughter and in scorn" (473c). The ground of change is to have philosophers become kings or kings philosophers so that "legitimately and sufficiently political power and philosophy conjoin to the same thing" (473a). Reason alone can be given a chief role but it will not do the whole job. It is only at this relatively advanced point in Book Five that Socrates introduces the key Platonic conception of the Ideas or Forms (476). The step-by-step *elenchos*, taken by itself, leads, Adeimantus says, to an impasse, as in the closeout at the end of a game of draughts (487b–c). The full illustration of the conjunction between political power and philosophy, which will take two further books, is another large set of three metaphors, wherein each one has a complex and delicate substructure, the Sun, the Line, and the Cave.

First, however, the question of how philosophers can help a city when they are useless to it is answered by an image, that of a ship with a captain of limited capacity and mutinous sailors. This may help explain, Socrates says, even though no one image fully corresponds. So he urges that they conceive a composite image, "the way painters mix up images to depict goatstags" (488a). In the light of this image it comes clear that "the many are bad" (490e), corrupted by not being able to meet high demands. The notion of corruption itself, a sort of low-level analogy between the body and the mind, recurs throughout (as 588c in its discussion of the diseased soul; and injustice is compared to a disease, 444).

A guardian-philosopher must know how "the just and the beautiful relate to the good" (506a) and "whether knowledge (ἐπιστήμη) is the good or pleasure." Socrates then continues his ongoing analogy of understanding to the sense of sight through the agency of the sun:

> Τοῦτον τοίνυν, ἦν δ'ἐγώ, φάναι με λέγειν τὸν τοῦ ἀγαθοῦ ἔκγονον, ὃν τἀγαθὸν, ἐγέννησεν ἀνάλογον ἑαυτῶι, ὅτιπερ αὐτὸ ἐν τῶι νοητῶι τόπωι πρός τε νοῦν καὶ τὰ νοούμενα, τοῦτο τοῦτον ἐν τῶι ὁρατῶι πρός τε ὄψιν καὶ τὰ ὁρώμενα.

> This, therefore, I said, declare me to say is the offspring of the good, which the good has generated in analogy to itself, so that this itself stands in the region of thought to mind and to things thought as this very thing in what is seen does to sight and to things seen.

(508b–c)

This analogy (or proportion, one of the senses of ἀνάλογον) soon gets to the elaborations of the Sun, and then the Line, and then the Cave.

Then, after a survey of the homology between types of individual character and types of state, Socrates touches base still again on the question of justice with which he began. He moves still again to image instead of to argument, in answer to one who maintains that "injustice is profitable to the completely unjust person who is reputed to be just." "Now, I said, let us hold dialogue with him now that we have agreed, for acting unjustly and performing just acts, what proper force each has. How? he said. By fashioning an image of the soul with a rationale (λόγωι) so the man who says those things may see what he is saying" (588b).

The image of the soul offered is, once again, in another domain from reasoned arguments about the nature of man. Socrates begins by comparing man to the Chimera, Scylla, and Cerberus: "Fashion the single image of a variegated, many-headed beast, having heads in a circle of tame beasts and wild, and having the power of changing and growing from itself all sorts of these ... Then form another image, one of a lion, and one of a man, with the first much larger than the second ... Then join the three into one. Then confect the image of one thing on the outside, that of the man ... so it appears to be one creature, a man" (588c–e).

Now ordinarily the comparison of a man to a lion is positive rather than negative, and it connotes the very courage that Plato is at pains to praise throughout his work and at key moments earlier in the *Republic*. This positive figure of the lion rests on conventional assumptions of the animal's strength and courage, so much so that it is a standard example.[7] Plato heavily revises this in two ways, first of all by giving the lion a negative cast and then by enclosing it as a monstrosity under the skin of a composite man.

This "lion" of injustice is soon identified with all the tempestuous and self-seeking impulses in a person. If given its way it will starve the "man," the human head wrapped along with all the animal ones inside the composite man. Under justice, however, the "man" would control all the other "heads" in this composite image (589a–b).

The metaphor transposes again when Socrates declares that a person who stays in control will "watch after the constitution in himself" (ἀποβλέπων ... πρὸς τὴν ἐν αὐτῶι πολιτείαν, 591e). Here the term *politeia*, "polity," which is the regular word for the constitution of a government, is transposed metaphorically to the management of impulses within a single person. This management anticipates, as well as corresponds to, the management of the state, of that which gives its name to this whole treatise, the "Politeia" or "Republic." What is already implicit in these figurations is what is now declared, that the state is an ideal state, "the city that lies in words (λόγοις), since I think it exists nowhere on earth" (592a–b).

Having said this, Socrates makes an abrupt transition at the beginning of Book Ten to the poetry he had not discussed since Book Three. In addition to the doctrines there elaborated, as I have partially examined them above, the very sense of digression here has the air of revealing a pressure to explain the method that has been hovering over the exposition and repeatedly breaking into it. He undertakes at length, then, to clarify, legitimate, and to qualify the kind of poetry in meter that is *not* set into conjunction with reasoned discourse, the way the "poetic" and mythic components of Plato's dialogues are.

When he has finished with the long presentation of placing poetry in what is conceived as its proper role, Socrates has effectually rounded out his arguments. He turns from Homer back to the "great contest" (μέγας ἀγών, 608b) for the polity of the soul, and then to the immortality of the soul itself, seen as a "composite" (σύνθετον, 611b), which must be brought to a "pure" state from being covered with its incrustations like the sea god Glaucus by the detritus of the sea (611d–e).

The question of how the soul becomes diseased is referred, finally, to a mythic story for which many mediations are offered. This story, the myth of Er, is first of all compared to what it is not, a story told to Alcinoos, the king of a legendary land in the *Odyssey*. The juxtaposition of Alcinoos and Er has the effect of suggesting the time of the Trojan War, without adducing any of its specificities. Er's story is located at a vague past, rather than in modulated historical circumstances, by being placed in a remote Greek-inhabited colony of Asia minor, Pamphyllia, a name with an allegorical cast ("All-Tribe"). The story Er has told, then, stands at a remove in time, offering a midrange historical perspective toward the millennial cycles of which this myth offers an account. Thus it mimes in the mode of "history" the displacement from reality which poetry itself constitutes, in Plato's own account, and in the partial blend of disparate elements, philosophy and poetry, that are here combined. The myth of Er is still more removed from a constructed historical setting than the account in the *Timaeus* is, which is said to have been told to the grandfather of the narrating Critias by the aged Solon, and so given a link to the remembered history of the sixth century.

Er's tale is of a near-death experience. "The myth was saved ... and will save us if we believe it" (μῦθος ἐσώθη ... καὶ ἡμᾶς ἂν σώσειεν, ἂν πειθώμεθα αὐτῶι, 621b–c). The myth or story has been "saved" because Er has waked after his wounds in battle and remembered his vision. He has seen souls after death being judged, the unjust ones sent to Tartarus and the just reaching the heavenly spheres, eight of them set into a sort of machine with whorls and spindles, making music with a siren on the rim of each sphere. The three Fates sit on thrones there and deliver lots for each soul to choose. The whole of the *Republic* is then offered as bearing on the choice. So the entire demonstration at the end is absorbed in a myth, and the long argument of the work opens to a millennial vision of eschatology. Here at the end of the *Republic* the historical situation of Er is touched on, but in such an attenuated form as to be all but absent.

The *Republic* runs, indeed, in a straight line from the discussions in the first book about *arete* and self-interest to the celestial deployment of souls in the last book according to the level of virtue they have attained. There are many thematic ties throughout the *Republic*. One could connect the happiness in moderate justice of the aged Cephalus at the beginning of Book One with the apocalyptic happiness of the virtuous as envisioned by Er at the end of Book Ten. Cephalus' characterization of himself as he faces approaching death sets into motion the whole discussion about justice: as he worries about punishment in the afterlife his chief consolation is that he can be "conscious of having done no wrong" (μηδὲν ... ἄδικον ξυνειδότι, 331a). At the same time Plato coordinates throughout the *Republic* a vast multiple attention to questions about justice, virtue, knowledge, the person, the state, and the soul. These questions intertwine to such a degree that the most various accounts may be framed of how the parts of the dialogue fit together.

Plato's whole procedure, here and elsewhere, is an example and paradigm of the way philosophy and poetic thinking merge and border on each other, resisting assimilation to each other as they enrich each other. But the paradigm depends on factors and conditions that make the conjunction so far unique. Any conception of the interrelation between poetry and philosophy must account for Plato and face the limit of its incapacity to account for how these constituents could come into such equipoise in this rich domain of human language.

Notes

1. Eric Havelock, *Preface to Plato*. Havelock sees the argument against poetry as the main thrust of the whole *Republic*. "Once the *Republic* is viewed as an attack on the existing educational apparatus of Greece, the logic of its total organization becomes clear" (13). "Plato attacks the very form and substance of the poetised statement, its images, its rhythm, its choice of poetic language" (5). "Plato's target was indeed an educational procedure and a whole way of life" (45).

2. "Homer and Empedocles have nothing in common except meter," Aristotle, *Poetics*, 47b18–19. This statement also somewhat discounts the component of thought, and even of rudimentary philosophical thought, in Homer.

3. Albert Cook, "The Angling of Poetry to Philosophy: the Nature of Lucretius," *The Reach of Poetry* (Lafayette: Purdue University Press, 1995), Chapter Eight.

4. Albert Cook, "Blake: the Exaltation of Fluidity" in *Thresholds: Studies in the Romantic Experience* (Madison: University of Wisconsin Press, 1985), 29–62.

5. Jacques Derrida, "La Mythologie blanche, la métaphore dans le texte philosophique," *Marges de la philosophie* (Paris: Minuit, 1975), 247–324. As Derrida's title implies, he really confines himself mostly to the presence of nonce metaphors in philosophical writing, giving a fair share of his attention to Plato (as well as to Hegel). Nonce metaphors are subordinate to our larger problem, which is the coordination of poetic or mythic thinking with propositional thinking, rather than the presence of live or dead metaphors in propositions. As Derrida says (251), speaking of separate locutions and mainly individual words, "the primitive sense ... is a sort of transparent figure, equivalent to a proper sense. It becomes metaphor when the philosophical discourse puts it in circulation. Then is forgotten simultaneously with the first sense and the first displacement. The metaphor is no longer noticed, and it is taken for the proper sense. Double effacement." Later, here, he adduces Kant's hypotyposes, the schematic or direct ones, and the symbolic or indirect (267), expanding his explanation while still keeping it confined just to individual locutions or separate, if global, metaphors like the sun in the *Republic*. He cites, for Plato, the organizational categories of Victor Goldschmidt, *Le paradigme dans la dialectique platonicienne* (Paris: Presses Universitaires de France, 1947).

6. See, for example, Hans Joachim Krämer, "Die Platonische

Akademie," 198–230. See also the various discussions of the dialogue form in Charles L. Griswold, Jr., ed., *Platonic Writings, Platonic Readings.*

    7.   For man as lion, Aristotle, *Rhetoric* 1406b20–26.

Index

About the Author

Albert Cook's writings include twenty books of criticism, eight books of poetry, and translations of *The Odyssey* and *Oedipus Rex*. His theoretical criticism has been concerned for several decades with questions about the philosophical bases of the literary use of language.

Among his books that deal wholly or partly with classical antiquity are *The Dark Voyage and the Golden Mean: A Philosophy of Comedy*; *The Classic Line: A Study of Epic Poetry*; *Enactment: Greek Tragedy*; *Myth and Language*; *Figural Choice in Poetry and Art*; *History/Writing*; *Soundings*; and *The Reach of Poetry*. Professor Emeritus at Brown University, he lives and works in Providence.